ACES OVER THE OCEANS
THE GREAT PILOTS OF WORLD WAR II

EDWARD H. SIMS

AERO
A division of TAB BOOKS Inc.
Blue Ridge Summit, PA 17214

To Bente, Christian, and
Frederik,

and

the Fighter Pilots of
World War II

FIRST EDITION

FIRST PRINTING

Copyright © 1987 by Edward H. Sims

Printed and published in the United States of America by Aero, a division of
TAB BOOKS Inc.

Library of Congress Cataloging in Publication Data

Sims, Edward H., 1923-
    Aces over the oceans—the great pilots of World War II.

        Bibliography: p.
        Includes index.
        1. World War, 1939-1945-Aerial operations.
2. Fighter pilots—Biography. 3. World War, 1939-1945—
Naval operations. 4. Naval aviation—Biography.
5. World War, 1939-1945—Biography. I. Title.
D785.S498 1987   940.54′4′0922   86-23147
ISBN 0-8306-8392-5 (pbk.)

Contents

Foreword

By Colonel Francis Gabreski, USAF (Ret.)

Edward Sims, my friend of many years and also a fighter pilot in World War II, has written another superior book. It isn't about himself; he has never included in his books anything about his missions over Germany. As a newspaper editor dedicated to accuracy (he publishes a syndicate which distributes features and editorials nationally), he has always sought out the most successful fighter aces and very accurately reproduced, in their words, their most memorable missions.

Back in 1958, Ed was the first writer to recreate fighter missions in such detail and his first book, *American Aces*, was a bestseller. Following that book about USAAF aces, he wrote a sequel about the top-scoring U.S. Navy and Marine aces (*Greatest Fighter Missions*), and then living in Europe in the Foreign Service he wrote *The Greatest Aces* about German, British, and American pilots. That book was a best-seller in Germany. General Adolf Galland, the former commanding general of Luftwaffe fighters, wrote the foreword and thanked the author for his fairness and objectivity.

My good friend Johnnie Johnson, the top-scoring fighter ace in the Royal Air Force in World War II, wrote the foreword for the British edition, which enjoyed several printings also. Ed's fourth book, *Fighter Tactics*, has recently been reprinted by TAB BOOKS and covers four wars. Interviews with World War I, World War II, Korean, and Vietnamese aces are included in this classic account.

It has been some years since *Fighter Tactics* was published and I was glad to know that Ed had finally finished another, *Aces over the Oceans*. This is an account of 12 missions over water, many by famous fighter aces.

But this book is more than simply interviews with great fighter aces, some of whom unfortunately are now dead. It is also the personal reflections of some of these famous pilots, never before published, and the author's careful means of putting their postwar stories and their fates in perspective for the reader. Ed was fortunate to have been a fighter pilot, a writer, and then an American living in Germany and England after the war. He used these years to stay in touch with the most successful fighter aces, knowing they were historic copy and knowing he was one of the few ex-fighter pilots writing books about fighter battles.

In *Aces over the Oceans* you'll read such exclusives as the late Sir Douglas Bader's inner thoughts on the Battle of Britain, never before published. Ed spent long hours with Sir Douglas before he died and they became close. Bader and his wife visited Ed and his Danish wife, Bente, in America and Ed spent weekends at Bader's country home outside London. They collaborated on a book together just before Bader's death.

Ed sought out the more controversial Stuka ace, Hans Rüdel, and his view of Rüdel and his unreconstructed views are analyzed in enlightening reading. Both these great deceased pilots were interviewed about an interesting mission for this book before they died.

Ed writes about the late Gen. Gerhard Barkhorn, with 302 victories. Barkhorn and his wife and daughter visited Ed in America and they spent long hours discussing fighter tactics, campaigns, history, and the postwar world. Ed writes about Eric Hartmann, the world's top-scoring ace with 352 victories, whom he has often visited in Germany, and tells of one night he spent at the Hartmann home when the great German ace spoke candidly about the Russians and the West and the future.

The four missions by Americans in *Aces over the Oceans* were flown by four great U.S. Navy and Marine aces in the Pacific. We read about the grim days at Guadalcanal and a carrier mission flown by the Navy's second highest scoring fighter ace, Cecil Harris. We read about a British pilot attacking the *Bismarck*, about a fighter over Normandy on D-Day, and about a night torpedo attack off the coast of Norway.

These missions are recreated in detail, accurately, in the pilots' own words, as in all of Ed's books. They are nonfiction as exciting as any fiction. And as Ed knew the great aces personally—and wartime history thoroughly—the reader can depend on accounts in their proper perspective and accuracy down to the smallest detail. I commend *Aces over the Oceans* to all who admire courage and ability as exemplified in air combat.

Acknowledgments

I express appreciation to each of the pilots who are centerpieces in this book's chapters. All answered questions in writing and in person, and made the time needed available; it was a pleasant undertaking.

I am indebted to Herr Wolfgang Schilling, of Motorbuch Verlag, for his conception of the book, and to David Brown, Director of the Royal Navy Historical Branch in London. I owe thanks to John Lampl, of British Airways, and to Felix Becker of Lufthansa.

The late Werner Schroer, whom many believe to have been one of the very best of Luftwaffe fighter aces in World War II, in addition to answering questions about "his" chapter, helped in translations. Thanks are due to Franz Forster-Steinberg, to Air Vice Marshal J.E. Johnson, the top-scoring R.A.F. fighter ace and author, and to former Luftwaffe pilot P.W. Stahl, now a successful author.

My gratitude for help in many forms is expressed with love to my wife, Bente. Mrs. John (Pat) Smiley and Dorothy Guest "flew" all missions and won every encounter with the typewriter.

I express thanks to David Lindsay of Stuart, Florida, and Pebble Beach, a fellow pilot who joined in some of the travels and interviews in the making of this book.

The late Sir Douglas Bader and the late General Gerhard Barkhorn, before they died, both spent pleasant days with me as house guests, and were most helpful.

Herewith acknowledgment for permission to reprint excerpts from the following sources:

From *Bring Back My Stringbag* by Lord Kilbracken. Copyright 1979 by Lord Kilbracken. Reprinted by permission of Peter Davies Limited.

From *The Seafire* by David Brown. Copyright 1973 by David Brown. Reprinted by permission of Ian Allen Limited.

Introduction

Post-World War II literature about fighter pilots of that conflict—aerial warfare's most dramatic and colorful combat—has focused comparatively little attention on action over the world's oceans. There are good reasons. Combat by navy fighter pilots was usually not sustained. Combat scores achieved by the most successful navy aces therefore were not so high. And, early in the war, the aircraft flown were not as advanced.

From the German viewpoint, the segment of World War II aerial history is almost a void. In World War I the German Navy produced a number of fighter aces, but Herman Göring insisted on commanding everything in the air that engaged in combat in World War II. Reluctantly, Admiral Erich Raeder turned over this naval function to the Luftwaffe. Except for reconnaissance and similar types, the German Navy was almost totally grounded in World War II, not even operating torpedo bombers, the function of practically every other navy.

Also, because Hitler initially sought to avoid war with England and felt—at least until 1938—that it could be avoided, he built no aircraft carriers. The one belatedly underway when the war began was too little, too late, and never finished. There were no German Navy dive bomber pilots, fighter pilots, or torpedo bomber pilots.

One needs little imagination to realize what several German strike forces with carriers could have done early in the war in the Atlantic to often-vulnerable Allied shipping. That is one of two potentially decisive naval preparations Germany could have made to win the Battle of the Atlantic. Had the German Navy been instructed to go all-out in building submarines in 1936 or 1937, or had three or four aircraft carriers been built, it seems quite possible Germany would have won the Battle of the Atlantic by the end of 1941—before America entered the war.

Germany began the war with only 57 submarines, many training submarines. Had she possessed 250 (later in the war she possessed twice that number), Allied supply lines would likely have been strangled within 18 months. Carriers could have sailed into the Atlantic with excellent chances of success, for they would have carried a complement of ME 109s, which could easily have protected them against any aircraft the British Navy had in 1939, 1940, or 1941.

Had the *Bismarck*, about which we will read in this book, been accompanied by a carrier in 1941, its fighters would very likely have turned back the obsolete Royal Navy Swordfish that scored fatal torpedo hits on that formidable battleship in May of that year.

The Royal Navy's air arm was almost as neglected as the German Navy's. But it was given new life at the last minute; the Fleet Air Arm was reaccepted in principle in 1937, and regained physically by the Navy in 1939, on the eve of war. The Royal Air Force had prior to that assumed responsibility for Fleet Air Arm operations and fleet torpedo bombers and fighters had been relatively neglected. Thus the Royal Navy, unlike the navies of the United States and Japan, began the war with obsolete aircraft, and few of them.

Of these four powers, only the United States and Japan began the war with large, modern Fleet Air Arms. The British Navy, as David Brown in *Carrier Fighters* points out, began the war with only 232 front-line aircraft and 36 fighters. The German Navy began with practically nothing. Göring had promised to have in operation 14 various naval air groups by 1941, basing his plans on Hitler's assurance there would be no war with Britain until at least 1942. Of these, only two were operational at war's outbreak, and they were under Luftwaffe, not Navy, control.

Such historical facts have to be taken into consideration in writing a book about pilots flying over the seas. In the U.S. and Japanese navies, there were many fighter pilots engaged in long, fierce campaigns against the enemy's carrier and land-based fighters. They saw extended periods of aerial fighting, much of it carrier-against-carrier. That was not quite the situation with Royal Navy pilots, since they were not confronted with German carrier pilots, nor did the Italians rely on carriers in the Mediterranean. That is not to say the task of Royal Navy fighter pilots was easier. On the contrary, they were—at least in the beginning and until the Seafire became available—often opposing the best of the Luftwaffe (and the Italian Air Force) with relatively slow Fulmars, or other slow aircraft. Later in the war they operated with better aircraft in the Pacific.

The feats of the Royal Navy's torpedo bombers (at Taranto,

against the *Bismarck*, against shipping in the Mediterranean, etc.) caught the public's fancy as much or more than did the Royal Navy's fighter aces, so attention is given to these pilots in this book.

There was no German Navy Fleet Air Arm; thus missions describing German fighters over the sea necessarily involve Luftwaffe pilots.

In selecting twelve missions flown by pilots of the United States, Germany, and Great Britain over the water, therefore, not all the missions could be fighter operations. The U.S. Navy operated dozens of carriers and thousands of fighters, and the four missions in this volume about Americans all involve fighter aces. Three of the four over-the-sea missions of Luftwaffe pilots were also flown by fighter aces. One was flown by a Stuka pilot who became an ace. The four missions of Royal Navy pilots recreated in this volume include two by fighter pilots as well as two by torpedo bomber pilots. All missions reported in detail are those the pilots themselves consider to be highly memorable, or which involved an event of major significance in World War II. All were recreated in interviews with the pilots.

The missions were flown over seas as diversified as the tropical waters of the far Pacific Ocean and the cold, icy waters of the North Atlantic and the North and Norwegian Seas. They involved slow aircraft such as the Swordfish and Stuka, and the best, like the Seafire, Hellcat, and ME 109. All describe extremely dangerous flying and exceptional pilot ability.

The tone of some aviation literature glamorizes air heroes and their achievements as a thrilling time of near-sport. That legacy was created in World War I because of aviation's infancy and romance, and because, too, there was a certain chivalry attached to individual aerial combat in the 1914-18 war. But war is a form of mass death and destruction—and madness—and that should be kept in mind. Nevertheless, in this century, fighter pilots of all countries have, in general, been young men doing their duty for their country, as they have been encouraged and expected to do by their governments and fellow citizens.

It is fitting that those who accomplished the remarkable be remembered. Such bravery and spirit may still be needed if individual freedom is to survive in this world. The young generation in the western world today might therefore profitably reflect on the burdens, sacrifices, and heroism that were the lot of another generation in the air, now even more the decisive theater of military operations.

Chapter 1

Barkhorn in the Channel

In questioning the greatest fighter pilots of the Second World War for many years, one of my oversights among German aces was Gerhard Barkhorn. One of two men in aerial history to shoot down more than 300 aircraft, he was awarded the Oak Leaves with Swords to the Knight's Cross of the Iron Cross, an award that went to few German airmen. He was a remarkable flier and leader both during and after the war, and on into the mid-1970s.

Yet circumstances prevented me from meeting Barkhorn until the preparation of this book began in the late '70s. Circumstances had also conspired to rob him of Germany's highest award (the Swords and Diamonds) in 1944, and perhaps a victory total as high as that of history's highest-scoring ace, Erich Hartmann. On May 31st that year, Barkhorn had flown five missions and was over-tired. Another mission was scheduled. He volunteered to fly a sixth—escorting Germany's greatest Stuka pilot (whom we will meet in Chapter 4 of this book), Hans Ulrich Rüdel. On that sixth mission he was shot down and seriously wounded and spent four months in a hospital. Admirable though volunteering was, Barkhorn pushed his luck. In the five months prior to that, he had scored 70 victories. Had he maintained the pace, he would have accounted for another 56 in the months he was hospitalized—the good-weather months. That would have made him the war's leading ace, surpassing Hartmann.

Of course, in war there are a million *ifs*, and no one can be sure what would have happened. What can safely be said is that Barkhorn, second-highest-scoring fighter pilot of all time, would almost certainly have scored many more victories had he flown during the long-daylight days in the summer of 1944. When Barkhorn went down that 31st of May, 1944, he had 273 kills to his credit, 42 more than Hartmann. During the summer months, when Barkhorn was recovering and out of action, Hartmann shot down 70 aircraft. Barkhorn—and Germany—didn't have another summer of combat.

Hartmann saw Barkhorn as one of a kind. He told the author in 1981: "Gerd is the only leader I know for whom every man would gladly sacrifice himself. Father, brother, comrade, friend; he's the best." Lt. General Johannes Steinhoff, recent Inspecteur of the post-war Luftwaffe and one of the war's greatest fighter aces himself (176 kills), singles out Barkhorn among all World War II pilots, noting that he never made a victory claim that wasn't confirmed.

Hartmann flew many missions as a squadron commander in Barkhorn's Gruppe II, in legendary Jagdgeschwader 52. The third-highest-scoring ace of the war, Gunther Rall, was Kommandeur of Gruppe III in JG 52. These three aces among them shot down over 900 aircraft on the eastern front (and a few on the western)! Even today, their records carefully confirmed, this is almost unbelievable.

Like Hartmann, Barkhorn was a relatively slow starter. His first victory came after 119 missions (more missions than most U.S. fighter pilots and many British pilots flew in the entire war). That was in the summer of 1941. Like Hartmann, Barkhorn preferred the Messerschmitt 109, and flew it throughout the war. At the end, General Adolf Galland selected him to be one of the first to fly the world's first jet fighter, the ME 262. His wartime flying career ended, in fact, in the crash of his jet fighter at Munich's airport (the same one in use today). Just clearing the stadium-like stone steps on the side of the field, he crash-landed into an HE 111, immediately burning. Though injured, he was not badly burned. Only two days before, Steinhoff had been badly burned in a similar crash. These two irreplaceable pilot losses were a blow to Galland, the unit (JV 44) commander.

Barkhorn was luckier than Hartmann in that his American captors didn't turn him over to the Russians. Instead, he was sent to England. Taken into custody on May 5th, 1945, from his home near the Protestant Church in Tegernsee, he was returned in September. It was a very difficult time in Germany, especially for those with small children. Barkhorn and his wife had two daughters at this time, one almost two and the other six months old. He worked in the forest for a time to obtain heating wood for his family. Later he worked for 80 Pfennigs an hour in a photo factory and remembers that the ration in 1945 was 50 grams of meat per month.

Later he moved to Trier and went into the automobile business (VW). After that, as a new Luftwaffe began to organize, he rejoined the German Air Force. He rose in postwar years to the rank of general and commanded the first wing of the new Luftwaffe's jet fighters. In 1975 he retired. He lived near Munich until his death in a car accident in 1983. He was still youthful (and handsome) in appearance when I first interviewed him in the late '70s. He was still active, vigorous, and alert when he and his wife and daughter visited me in America in 1982.

About his slow start in achieving victories, he said: "I was a slow starter. You have to learn carefully. A good fighter pilot must have some spirit, experience, and then much luck." When I heard him refer to luck, I replied: "But one can't be lucky in combat three hundred and one times!" To which he said: "Yes, you can. You must have luck." And he added: "I was shot down six times, seriously wounded twice and hospitalized—my leg and knee. But I was lucky. I had good teachers and learned much from Heinz Schmidt, lost in August 1943 after 173 victories, and Waldemar Semelka, lost in 1942 over Stalingrad after 65 victories. I took over the squadron from Steinhoff, and had only 10 victories at the time. These two taught me how it was done. Of course, the Russians were easier to shoot down than the British or the Americans. Russians were not trained as individuals. Some were very good but the average Russian pilot was not. I encountered a very good one near Kharkov in 1942 and we engaged in the toughest kind of acrobatics for 20 minutes. He was flying a YAK. Toward the end of the war the YAK 9 and some of their other aircraft were comparable to ours. And they always had so many! I remember when we were on the Crimea, our one Gruppe was opposed by about 1500 Russian aircraft. I think I shot down more than 50 enemy aircraft in one month.

"The key to victories in the air is getting behind your opponent, getting close, and shooting straight. All fighter pilots are the same, in this sense. How you get behind, of course, is your business—from low or high, etc."

Barkhorn's final score might have been higher had he not been recalled from combat in 1940, while serving in France. His first mission was in January that year. In March, however, before the major air battles began, he was unexpectedly removed from flying duty. His brother had been killed and his mother wrote to Luftwaffe chief Herman Göring, asking that he be recalled. It wasn't until July that he managed to get back to his squadron. By then France had fallen. To many then, it looked as if the war was over.

Barkhorn sheds an interesting light on the still-lingering controversy over which aircraft, the Spitfire or the ME 109, could outturn the other: "In 1940 we 109 pilots didn't think the 109 could outturn the Spitfire. Maybe later, when we got the F models, we could; I'm not sure. I shot down Spitfire Vs in Russia."

On the subject of the 109 versus the FW 190, Barkhorn is partial to the 109. "I flew the 190 too. I couldn't do much with it. One needs a few hundred hours with a new aircraft so that you and the fighter are one. At the end of January 1945, I was made Kommodore of Jagdgeschwader 6, operating in Silesia, equipped with FW 190D-9s. While there we acquired two ME 109s and went up and compared them with the 190s in simulated combat. I could outturn the 190D in our practices with the 109s. I'm a 109 man. Note that the top Luftwaffe pilots flew 109s.

"And that was the best way to get a victory: Outturn your foe. In most of my kills, I outturned the enemy. Only the RATA—we couldn't outturn it. We would wait above—altitude is half a life— and dive down when we could get a good shot at it. In turning, we'd say the enemy had to fly through out bullets! Some pilots could score victories from the side, in deflection shooting. I once saw Rall shoot down an opponent from 90 degrees. But for most of us, it was a case of outturning him and getting behind, in close. In the turn you pull until you grey-out to get behind. Keep in mind that you really don't fight against another aircraft. You fight the man in it."

With much admiration for the late Professor Dr. Willy Messerschmitt, Barkhorn had never met the builder of the ME 109 until the designer's 80th birthday in the late 1970s. That occasion in Augsburg was the only time the two met. Soon thereafter, in 1978, he and other Luftwaffe pilots attended Messerschmitt's funeral. By then he had retired from the postwar Luftwaffe after serving a tour as Chief of Staff of NATO's 4th Allied Tactical Air Force and then Chief of Staff of the 2nd Allied Tactical Air Force.

When I contacted Barkhorn, I asked him to recall an especially interesting mission over the sea for this book. He promised to go back through his records. The day I arrived in Munich to question him at last—November 28th, 1978—snow blanketed Bayern. I was greatly relieved to reach Munich, having started that day from Jidda, in Saudi Arabia, on Syrian Airlines, before daylight.

A Lufthansa flight from Damascus reached München-Rheim (where Barkhorn had crashed his ME 262 in 1945) at 5:00 P.M. When I got to the Bayerischerhof Hotel after some really wearing days in the Middle East, I wanted first a bath and a family-type meal at the nearby Franziskanner, plus a night's sleep. I bring all this up only because I felt I could understand that day, in a small sense, the feeling German pilots serving in the east experienced when they got back to "civilization" from Russia, on leave. It had been a long time since I had enjoyed such a good night's sleep and quiet meal. In Saudi Arabia I had stayed in the embassy with the United States Ambassador John West. Yet it was a distinct relief to reach Germany. And it was at this hotel 10 years earlier that I had interviewed other legendary German fighter pilots, including the late, unforgettable Josef Jacobs of World War I.

Barkhorn was on time next day at noon, though it was still snowing outside. He looked every inch a flying officer—trim, neat, in grey-checked business suit with red, flowered tie and yellow scarf. His hair was slightly greying but full and his eyes grey-blue. He was 59 years old, but he looked about 45. On his right cheek he carried a small scar and although only five feet nine inches, he looked taller, being fit and trim. He had been out of the Luftwaffe three years but carried himself with military bearing. Like Hartmann and so many of the greatest aces of the war, he was utterly relaxed, easygoing, and unaffected. I thought to myself after only minutes (and I instinctively liked him) that here was a wholesome human being as well as a legendary flying immortal with nothing of the pompous. He remarked at once that few people today are interested in his flying record! I soon began to realize how much I had missed in not having sought out Barkhorn earlier.

On this snowy morning Barkhorn had driven his wife into Munich before our meeting. Though well disciplined, he smoked cigarettes (Lords; Hartmann smokes Peer Exports)—only a few a day. During lunch, though he enjoyed several glasses of white wine, he didn't touch bread or sweets.

"I get only a few letters these days from Germans, mostly young, wanting to know about the war. Most of the letters come from America and England." We laughed about the criticism of the modern-day Luftwaffe by Germans in recent years, about the Lockheed F-104 Starfighter especially, which the newspapers often criticized as a pilot-killer. "I was five years a Geschwader Kommodore, often flying 104s," he said. "We had some crashes, of course, but the U.S. Navy had more losses in the same period and

5

little fuss was made about it. Now we're getting MRCAs, so maybe things will quiet down. Aside from that, there's not much interest about the Luftwaffe or its past. No one in Germany is much interested in that.''

I told him that, to the contrary, air historians were still much interested in his remarkable record, that aviation buffs all over the world were showing interest in the great aces of World War II. One reason is that the last aces of World War I are dying, and that a World War II nostalgia, similar to that which so long surrounded Richthofen and other legends of the 1914-18 war, was evolving. Yet to my suggestion that he record his experiences in book form, Barkhorn only laughed and said there wasn't much interest. But he was not to disappoint me. He had gone back through his log and picked out a mission over the water which had been exciting and dangerous—at the very beginning of his combat career. He had written down his impressions and details on several sheets of paper to help in my reconstruction.

"It took place in October of 1940, in the West,'' he said, and he then began to describe events that day.

He was a lieutenant in Gruppe II, JG 52, on the Channel coast, near Calais. By that time all serious thought of a German invasion of England in 1940 was over. On October 20th, in fact, daylight bombing in strength against England had been terminated by the Luftwaffe. Small-scale raids, using fighters carrying bombs, and night bombing were to constitute the future form of the Luftwaffe's aerial offensive in the West. On October 29th, 1940, the day with which we are concerned, Hitler's mind was far from the aerial campaign in the West. He had just completed a 4,000 mile train trip that took him to France, and to a meeting with the late Dictator Francisco Franco of Spain. The day before he had met Mussolini in Florence. Mussolini had, to Hitler's dismay, invaded Greece. Franco had declined to join the war against the West, or to allow German passage through Spain for an attack on Gibraltar. Hitler must have had second thoughts about having helped him to power, and in fact never uttered kind words about him again.

Vichy French leaders, including Marshall Petain, had met with Hitler and were willing to cooperate on the continent, but not to join in the war. From France, Hitler had rushed to Italy, hoping to forestall the Italian attack on Greece (Italy was already at war with Britain and Hitler thought Egypt was the more appropriate Italian goal). But he arrived too late and had to make the best of a bad situation—a situation that would require him to conduct a spring offensive through the Balkans and delay his attack on Russia. So on the 29th, when Hitler returned to Munich, the air campaign in the West was a secondary German consideration, at best. But to Barkhorn, one of the Third Reich's young and eager fighter pilots yet to score an aerial victory, and one whom Hitler would one day admire greatly, it was to be a momentous day—which almost ended what was to be a unique flying career.

Tuesday morning, October 29th, the French Channel coast dawned clear except for a slight haze. A fall chill was in the air—normal for this season. In a white masonry French house on the edge of the fighter base at Peuplingue (near Calais), Gerhard Barkhorn and his roommate were awakened shortly after sunup by an orderly. They washed and shaved and walked a short distance over three-inch browning grass to the officers' mess. Like their ME 109Es, camouflaged and parked among nearby trees around the field, the officers' mess was within walking distance. Barkhorn already knew there would be no morning mission, so the pace was leisurely and only after he had eaten did he walk to a field-grey tent on the side of the field and ask about orders. Barkhorn's Squadron Commander, 1st Lt. Rudolf Resch, a Saxon (killed as a Gruppenkommandeur in 1943 in Russia after 93 kills), confirmed that 6th Squadron pilots would fly no mission that morning. Pilots sat at tables in grey canvas chairs and smoked, played cards or chess, or listened to the radio. They listened either to a German or English station on a Luftwaffe-grey field radio, whichever had the best music. A brown field telephone was on one of the tables.

Shortly before noon it rang and pilots were ordered to fly an escort mission. Fellow 109 pilots from nearby Calais-Marck were to carry 250-kilo bombs beneath their fighters and bomb the London docks. Pilots later to become famous—among them Johannes Steinhoff, then a Squadron Commander, Major Trubenbach, Barkhorn's commanding officer, Lt. Schuman, and others—were briefed by Hauptman Ensslin, the Gruppe commanding officer, who promised good weather. Bombing and escort altitude over London would be 7,000 meters. The escort would rendezvous with the fighter-bombers over the Channel. Takeoff time was 1346.

Pilots hurried to lunch, and checked with ground crews. This was to be one of the new-tactic raids on London.

The ME 109s from Calais-Marck carrying bombs were under command of Hauptman Herbert Ihlefeld, who would eventually score 130 victories. Barkhorn's 6th Squadron was the escort. But unknown to Barkhorn and other German pilots at this time and vitally important—and revealed only 30 years after the war in 1975—the British were intercepting and decoding Luftwaffe orders. Therefore, British fighters were usually found by incoming Luftwaffe attackers to be waiting ahead, above, in position to effect an advantageous bounce. The secret code-breaking intelligence was known as Ultra; it had begun decoding German battle orders in the summer of 1940, just in time to help in the Battle of Britain. The Luftwaffe was, in effect, fighting that crucial battle blindfolded, while the Royal Air Force's Fighter Command often knew not only Luftwaffe targets but the strength of attacking forces.

All of this, of course, the confident German pilots didn't know in 1940. They were perplexed that the Luftwaffe's bombers, destroyers, and Stukas had been so badly treated in the Battle of Britain (its fighters had done well). They knew they were up against formidable fighters in the Spitfire and Hurricane. Yet morale among German fighter pilots was high. They were confident they could fight on at least even terms, and always dive away from Spits or Hurricanes because of their fuel injection advantage. They felt the 109 was, overall, superior. (Recent claims by a British writer that the 109 could actually outturn both are as much a surprise to them as to RAF fighter pilots, and are not accepted. General Adolf Galland is among former German aces who fought in the battle to restate his conviction that the Spit was superior in a turn—in July, 1985.)

Barkhorn pulled lambskin boots over blue Luftwaffe trousers. He wore gloves and a heavy flying jacket since it was late October—very cold at altitude. Squadron 6 pilots drove to their aircraft in a grey Kübelwagon at 1:30 P.M. They inspected the green-black on top, sky-blue on bottom, fighters. Barkhorn questioned Corporal Albert Kusterer, who maintained his fighter (and who would be with him until 1945) about the aircraft's condition. They waited briefly for the signal to start engines. The Squadron Leader's Daimler Benz 601A inline coughed smoke from ten stacks. The three-blade prop whirled, blowing smoke faster back over the Geschwader emblem, a black and red shield with white sword.

Barkhorn, waiting among some trees on the edge of the newly harvested French field, climbed into the cockpit and Kusterer took his place at the crank. Barkhorn recalled: "He was a Schwabe and seldom forgot a detail. I never aborted a mission as long as he was caring for my fighter." When the first props began turning, Kusterer was already cranking. The engine was soon roaring and

Kusterer jumped off the wing.

Wind swirled dust back from the now-turning props of the low-winged fighters as they taxied into takeoff position, Barkhorn on the wing of a more experienced pilot. At 21, he was relatively inexperienced. Already his parents had lost one son. His older brother had driven over a French mine on the West Wall shortly after the Polish campaign. His younger brother, Dietrich, would later be killed over this same channel that Gerhard was flying over today. They had all been born in Konigsberg, their father a building engineer, in happier days. Their father—called into the Volkssturm as the Russians approached East Germany in the last months of the war—is still missing in the East. Only Barkhorn and his mother, of a family of six in picturesque Konigsberg, survived the war.

The green and blue fighters swept over the grass and up, and began climbing into a hazy blue sky on a northwest course. As they left the field at Peuplingue behind, bomb-laden 109s from Calais-Marck to the east were also climbing on a converging course, all spinners now pointed toward London. Barkhorn could already see the coast of England ahead when Ihlefeld's 109 "bombers" came into view on the right, converging. Both groups of 109s were at 5,000 meters. They joined, escort on the sides, and continued to climb into the northwest as the Dover coast approached ahead below.

The sky was almost cloudless and visibility for bombing London's docks would be good. The fast formation crossed the coast at 6,000 meters, continued climbing, and soon had big, sprawling London in view straight ahead. No interceptions yet! But every German pilot expected to encounter RAF defenders. And within seconds, contrails high above were called in over the radio. Barkhorn saw them at 8,000 meters, ahead, and guessed Spitfires. As always, the English defenders were ready and waiting!

Huge London now came closer and closer and the JG 52 fighters reached 7,000 meters just a few miles from the great city, bisected by the Thames winding its way through the metropolis. Antiaircraft bursts began to dot the sky around them—black puffs, smoke and shrapnel. But the 109s were small targets and very high. Barkhorn's airspeed indicator showed 420 kilometers.

The docks appear below. Escort pilots are required to hold formation, not allowed to break off and go after the Spitfires, ahead, above, moving left. This is to cost them. All the air forces would learn, before the war was over, that escorting fighters should be free to intercept interceptors, or would be almost as vulnerable as the bombers flying on their fixed, slower course. On this October afternoon Barkhorn held position, the 109s crossing the city's outskirts and nearing the docks. It was approximately 2:30. The sun was in the west, to the left. The haze and sun didn't completely hide enemy contrails but made it difficult to discern individual aircraft.

The "bombers" are dropping the 250 kilo bombs, now streaking toward the docks below, where visibility is much better than looking into the western sky. As the first bombs hit, 6 Squadron is executing a 180-degree left turn, into the sun, escort still in formation.

The bomb-carriers can now fly faster, and all fighters dip their noses downward to accelerate in the turn. Barkhorn hasn't fired cannon or machine guns. The flak hasn't hit anyone. Warning shouts on the radio: Spitfires—three groups streaking down out of the sun and haze. Barkhorn rubbernecks to sight his foe but doesn't see the enemy. Fellow pilots push throttles full forward and begin to maneuver. The sky becomes a churning, scrambling scene of Spits and 109s, the Spits firing eight Brownings as they attack at great speed, from above. Barkhorn hears *thump! thump! thump!* Still, he can't see his tormentor, who has hit him before he had broken formation. He banks to one side and the other—still can't find his enemy, who apparently has pulled up above again, with his great speed. He sees something worse: He's trailing a white "flag" and black smoke is also streaming out behind. Oil coolant! The engine is losing coolant (the white stream) and heating up. Speed falling. He finds himself all alone. His attacker has flown on elsewhere. He has lost sight of all his comrades. The Daimler Benz runs rough and smoke and vapor stretch out behind for miles. Altimeter still registers 6,000 meters but Barkhorn is steadily descending. Can he get back—if other Spits don't find him? He scans the sky ahead in vain for a cloud layer. None to be found this late-fall afternoon. Yet his prop is spinning, if slower, and he's trading altitude for speed. The clean design of the Messerschmitt gives him good speed in only a slight descent. This makes him cautiously hopeful. Ahead he can see the coast of England between Dover and Folkestone. Altitude 5,000 meters. Still no enemy. But his comrades, up above at high throttle, are now crossing out over the channel, almost home free.

Black smoke continues to billow out behind and mark his descent as the altimeter winds down, now nearing 4,000 meters. The engine now sounds very rough and his temperature gauge reveals a very hot engine. If he can just keep going . . . the channel is only 50 kilometers wide . . . if he can get within sight of the French coast . . . maybe friends will see him. His hopes are interrupted. Behind, a speck in the sky! He banks slightly right, then left. Spitfire! An enemy pilot, coming down from above and behind to finish off the cripple. But this time he has, at least, seen him.

What to do? He can't fight—no power. That would also doom his slim chance of getting back to France. He watches the silhouette behind get larger and larger. He's almost to the coast and needs his altitude but knows there's only one chance—dive! Just as the closing Spit's first shells streak by on the side, Barkhorn pushes the stick forward hard. The 109 goes over into a steep forward dive just as the silhouette behind is within range. Gaining initially in the dive, the 109 hurtles straight downward, accelerating rapidly, still pouring vapor and black smoke. The altimeter needle turns faster and faster as Barkhorn drops 1500 meters almost straight down. He must now pull out and eases back on the stick, blood draining from his head as the force of gravity pulls most of his body's supply into the lower part of his body, dimming his vision. The 109 holds together; it obviously hasn't been structurally damaged.

Barkhorn watches the nose of his fighter cross the last English fields and landscape out front and, finally, the coastline as he levels off. The altimeter reads 2,000 meters. He anxiously searches the sky behind, below, and above on both sides. He's lost the Spitfire, which must have overflown him, not realizing he was flying so slowly with a damaged engine.

He crosses the coast to the right of Dover and gets only a few bursts of flak. But smoke is leaking into the cockpit. Ahead, is that the French coast at Cap Gris-Nez? Will he make it? At that moment his engine seizes. Now he knows he won't get back, can't cross the water separating him from JG 52 comrades now approaching Calais. He's losing altitude steadily and although he needs to fly only about 30 kilometers, his altimeter reads only 1,000 meters. The question, then, is whether to belly the fighter in on the English coast or bail out—either over the coast or the Channel. He has only a few seconds to decide. Water or the coast? If it's land, if he bellies in on shore, he'll be taken prisoner; yet to go into the water so far from France? He just can't accept becoming a prisoner of war. On he glides, another kilometer in increasing smoke. Now he must get out of the badly smoking fighter. The engine is finished, could catch fire; if he descends lower, he might not be able to bail out safely. Jump, now! Barkhorn remembers the ordeal:

"When I crossed the coast I asked myself what I should do. Make a turn and a belly landing on the shore? Prisoner of war? The Squadron would write my parents and report Lt. Barkhorn missing. Although when you belly into the sea, we've been told, the fighter floats 30 seconds, bailing out seemed safer. Get the plane on its back and drop out of it! We've often discussed this technique. I am still high enough, and—strangely—not frightened. They'll find me, I think to myself."

So Barkhorn opens the canopy, moves the stick sharply left and with his right foot pushes right rudder. The 109 turns over, but also noses down. He doesn't drop out. He recalls: "Why do I not fall out? Damn! I've forgotten to trim the plane for inverted flight. And I'm falling almost straight down. Now I push the stick forward—my seat belt is already unfastened—and the nose goes up. I'm upside down and falling, and falling. On my left chest is the silver-covered handle of the parachute and I must reach and grab it with my right hand and pull. I'm tumbling through the air, but grab it and yank. Three seconds—they seem like hours to me—and then a jerk, and I see the white silk dome spread out above me. I've lost my right boot in the fall, and now the water comes rushing up and I am quickly in it—still thinking about my lost boot!

"The wind catches the half-open chute and begins to drag me along over the water, and under it, and I quickly open the lock and the parachute collapses. The water is pretty cold and I must get into my dinghy, still attached to my back. By now I've lost my other boot, the left one. It makes swimming much easier. Not far off I see a black buoy. I'll swim to it and then inflate the dinghy. It's not far and I begin to swim. But the current is strong. It's running northeast, sweeping me up the English coastline, not toward France. Now for the little cylinder, to turn the handle, so air pressure will fill the dinghy and provide me a little rubber boat, I'm already tired and cold. I manage to turn the air pressure handle and there's a hissing. The dinghy inflates. It's hard climbing into it, soaking wet and heavy, but I get over the side and fall in. I can't see land, just the white crests of waves and windswept spray. Can anyone see me in these waves? I could have made a belly landing on the seashore and wouldn't be so cold now. Why didn't I do it? Why did I try so hard to escape the Tommies? Channel swimmers, I remember reading, get a thick grease coat and do their swimming when the sea is calm—escorted by a boat. Can I reach the French coast in my little rubber boat? Hardly. I have neither a sail nor a paddle and the current isn't taking me to Gris-Nez or Calais.

"I'm drifting parallel to the English coast. The dinghy contains too much water, very cold. Also, it needs more air. I must use the tube, which enables one to blow it up by mouth. The tube is on the outside near my left foot. I lean forward and try to reach over the side and all of a sudden—maybe it was a wave—I'm in the sea again. But now I can reach the tube more easily and I blow to fill my little boat with enough air. I then turn it upright and am ready to get back in. But it's not so easy this time. My body is very stiff from the cold, especially my hands, and they fail to obey the command of the brain. I struggle desperately to lift myself over the side amid the waves, without overturning the little boat. Finally I get in. The water that drips from my uniform settles into the bottom—a few centimeters.

"No noise except the waves and wind. No living being can be seen, only seagulls, which glide over the waves without flapping their wings. On my left the anchor, a canvas sack trailing behind, keeps my boat in a steady position—and I can now see the English coast. Behind me—that must be Dungeness, and in the far distance, the cliffs of Dover. Nothing moving on the coasts, or above, to indicate anyone saw me fall into the sea. Minutes pass like hours and the cold creeps from my feet upward and covers the whole body. The little yellow dyebag which all pilots have in their dinghies I throw into the water. It produces a yellow streak to make it easy for rescue pilots to see us from above. When I first got into the dinghy, I had seen a Dornier air-sea rescue plane and hoped it had seen me. But he had been six kilometers away and didn't. I see 109s fly over, heading home, with other German aircraft—no British.

"I don't have my pistol to fire flares; it had been in my right boot. Half an hour, then an hour pass. The wind—which I cannot escape, as the sides of my boat are only hip-high—has cooled my body. In the wet uniform, I'm shivering. My hands are becoming yellow. I can still move them, to bail water out of the dinghy with a small canvas cup, fastened to the inside by a string. But I know I can't go on like this overnight, at this time of year. I keep working, bailing water, to stay as warm as I can.

"After an hour and a half, to the southeast, I see an aircraft. I can't hear it. It must be ten or fifteen kilometers away, flying low, midway out in the channel. It could be a FW 58 Weihe. Is it searching for me? I have no pistol to fire flares and in a couple of minutes it disappears to the southeast. Such a light plane can't come close

13

to the English coast; it's too vulnerable, of light frame and canvas. And it may not even have a gun. I don't know.

"I see a formation of planes, at high altitude, flying toward England. Another attack on London's docks? I can hear the engines very clearly. Those pilots are so much better off, in dry planes! They disappear from view and it's silent again. And then, as I ride up on a wave, I see a boat. It disappears when I go down. Is it my imagination? I think I must shout and also wave my arms. I shout until there's no voice left and my arms are heavy and dead tired. Is the boat searching for me? It's headed away. I must now turn almost all the way around to my right to catch a glimpse of it.

Now the disappointment and cold depress me and I conclude it's nonsense to think that I can get back to France from my position just off the English coast.

"In my despair, the sound of a motor catches my attention. I look toward France, up in the sky. It sounds like a 109. Louder and louder. More than one? I look and look. A beautiful sight, two Messerschmitts! They're flying directly toward me. I stand, as best I can, and wave, even wave my yellow dye bag. Will they see me? Can they spot the yellow dye in the waves below? They come on straight, then one dips and they roar over me and bank into turns. They must have seen me. They come back over my dinghy and dip low and one of the pilots waves. It's Lt. Gunter Witt, from my base. Now one flies off and I wonder what's happening. The other stays above, circling, dangerously near the English coast and very vulnerable so low over the water. Then I realize what's happening. The other 109 has gone to direct the boat to me. In a few minutes I can see the boat again, heading straight for the circling rescuer above—and me!

"The minutes drag by but the boat—I have no idea what type it is—comes closer and closer. It's fast, and that's good for it's now late afternoon and there isn't much daylight left. Soon the 32-knot rescue boat is near. I see sailors standing at the rail. They throw a rope over to me as the 109s above set course southeast for the safety of France. I manage to grasp the rope but haven't the strength to pull my body up. My hands won't close, won't grip it properly . . . too cold. The boat circles and another rope is thrown me. But again, though I catch it, I can't pull myself up on the other side either. Finally a sailor comes over the rail and hangs down to reach out for me. He gets his arm down to me and grasps my right hand with a firm grip. He gets me up within reach of other helping hands. They pull me aboard. Safe at last, in the now-fading light! The captain orders full speed toward France. As he does, a few spouts of water shoot up nearby. Coastal guns have finally discovered our boat and are firing on us. But we are increasing the distance, headed straight for Calais. I am immediately taken below deck and my wet clothes removed. Sailors rub me down smartly with a rough towel to stimulate circulation. It helps tremendously. They offer me cognac and many sips warm me and new energy rises up in me. In a few minutes I'm strong enough to walk back up on deck. We are about to enter Calais harbor!

"I had gotten away. The decision to bail out over the sea so close to England turned out to be a pivotal one in my combat flying career. I could have been taken prisoner and would have survived, and would have learned to speak English well. But it would have been a dull and empty time. I would not have scored an aerial victory. My first was not to come until July of the next year. I would have been sent to Canada. But I wouldn't have really been a fighter pilot, wouldn't have been married, to become a father when I did. And my strongest desire at that time was to get back to my squadron. Luckily, I made it back.

"As we debarked at the pier in Calais, Major Woldenga was there to greet me and take me back to the base. I was dressed only in grey socks, a corporal's uniform and full of cognac, so, in all, the effect on my superior officer was more negative than positive.

"When we reached Peuplingue, I found they had given me up for lost. I was the only pilot in the squadron who had been shot down. My orderly had already begun to pack my things. It was after six P.M. and I was given a great welcome, a wet welcome. We all enjoyed my birthday party that night."

Barkhorn, whose career almost ended that October day, was a slow starter. He was to fly more than a hundred missions before scoring a victory. He remained in France for a time after parachuting into the Channel, then his unit was posted to Belgium, then Holland. It was ordered east when the invasion of Russia was about to begin and there—later wearing glasses, which greatly helped his vision—he began to compile the record that was to make him one of history's two highest-scoring fighter aces.

In June 1943, still on the eastern front, he became Kommandeur of Gruppe II, JG 52, and then Kommodore of JG 6, in January of 1945. At the end of the war he was flying ME 262s under General Adolf Galland. In all, he flew a total of 1104 missions, and reached the magic number of 300 victories on May 1st, 1945—the second German fighter pilot, and the last, to do so. After his crash at Munich, caused by engine failure in one of the ME 262s jet engines, he was hospitalized at Tegernsee.

From the hospital Barkhorn went home, across the lake, and there, his head still in white bandages, he was waiting on May 5th, 1945, when U.S. soldiers entered his home. One came into his room and Barkhorn gave up his pistol in surrender. Nervously, the American took the pistol and gripped it too hard. It fired—into the table in the room. The American soldier, white-faced, then accompanied him out of his house and on the drive to Starnberg. After a time there, he went on to Heidelberg and from there was flown to London, where he was held as a prisoner with Galland and other distinguished pilots. In June they were freed. On their way back to Germany they found hostile crowds. At Cherbourg, where they debarked from a ship that had brought them from Southampton, they were stoned by angry Frenchmen. Barkhorn remembers that Walter Krupinski, another famous fighter ace, wore his Knight's Cross that day and was hard hit.

Barkhorn was back home on his mother's birthday, September 9th. It was not a happy time. His father was still missing. The last they had heard of him was from a card sent by a friend, which had come in July. His father, 60, had been put into the home army in February of that last year in the hopeless effort to stem the Russian-Asian flood sweeping westward. When Konigsberg fell, his home, he was captured. After the card in July, the family never heard from him again. So on that September day, Barkhorn, his wife and two small daughters, and his mother were the new, displaced Barkhorn family from Konigsberg. Helmut, as related, had fallen in France in October 1939, and Detrich was shot down on The Western Front in August 1943, flying with the Richthofen Geschwader.

A constant theme in all of Barkhorn's reminiscing is that in fighter warfare, it's not the aircraft as much as the man flying it that makes the difference—especially when both are piloting good fighters. He disagrees with many British and American fliers in their analysis of the ME 109 and the FW 190. Allied pilots tend to rate the 190 the better of the two.

"Note that all the top Luftwaffe aces flew 109s," Barkhorn pointed out. And although he didn't think, in 1940, that in his "Emil" he could outturn the Spitfire, one wonders if he could have, had he been willing or able to pull it around tight enough in a curve. Len Deighton, in his provocative *Fighter* (Jonathan Cape, 1977), claims the 109 could theoretically outturn the Spit and the Hurricane, with a comparative turning radius of 750 to the Spit's 880 and the Hurricane's 800. Deighton claims arguments about which aircraft could outturn the other usually hinge on the recklessness and daring of the pilots—which one would push his fighter closest to its limits. (We'll hear more, from other aces, about this in later chapters.)

Other great 109 aces have insisted they never felt outclassed in their 109s right up to the last day of the war. Erich Hartmann is one of them. Yet it's true that practically all Spitfire pilots and most Luftwaffe pilots believed in 1940—and probably still believe— the Spitfire could outturn the 109 at the time of the Battle of Britain. Thus it's fascinating to pose the question whether, after all these years, it's really possible that the late Dr. Willy Messerschmitt's famous little fighter was better, in the hands of the best pilots, than most experts, pilots, and historians have realized in postwar years.

Admittedly, most pilots were reluctant to stress their aircraft to the limit, at which point it might break up under the strain. Yet when the FW 190 appeared in 1941, RAF pilots almost immediately concluded it could outturn their Spitfires, whereas they were confident they had been outturning the 109s for a year. Barkhorn, as Kommodore of JG 6 in Silesia in early 1945, flying 190s, brought two 109s to his field. He and his pilots engaged in simulated combat. According to Barkhorn, the 109s invariably got the best of the 190s in the dogfighting. Perhaps the question will never be completely resolved. Barkhorn always thought the Spitfire, in 1940, was better at turning than the ME 109E! Was that because he wasn't the competent pilot he later became? But then, who can compare such judgments with the greatest fighter aces of the war?

The last time I saw Gerd Barkhorn was in 1982. He, with his wife Christl and daughter Ursula, paid us a visit in the mountains near Asheville, North Carolina, in early spring. Nights we sat on the balcony, at 3,500 feet, looking over Cane Creek Valley's lights below. It was almost like sitting on a balcony at Stimmer See, looking out at the Kaiser Mountains and over the valley near Kufstein.

Barkhorn was still lighthearted and easygoing, liked by all who met him. He enjoyed good company and discussion and still enjoyed a cigarette and white wine. At almost any time of day his automatic answer to the question, "Would you care for a glass of wine?" was "Of course."

Chapter 2

Attacking the *Bismarck*

In May 1941, Germany's greatest battleship—the best battleship in the world at that time—was hunted from the air in the Atlantic Ocean, found, and destroyed. It was an operation that shouldn't have taken place. Both Hitler and the admiral commanding the foray into the Atlantic, Vice Admiral Gunter Lutjens, opposed it. But Grand Admiral Erich Raeder, whom Hitler deferred to up to this time, but not afterward, refused to cancel this long-planned, bold strike at British shipping. The head of the German Navy had his way.

An irony of the resulting German disaster was that the world's most modern battleship was, in the end, doomed by the most obsolete aircraft still on operation in the war—the Royal Navy's slow, open-cockpit, biwinged Swordfish. That was all the Royal Navy had to deliver torpedoes with in 1941. The Navy had only regained control of its own Fleet Air Arm in 1938. The Royal Air Force, created in World War One, had taken over naval aviation. And in the prewar years the RAF neglected development of naval aircraft, especially torpedo bombers.

The *Bismarck*, a 53,000-ton supership of its day, was so constructed with compartmentation that it was most difficult to sink. It was equipped with the most modern radar-assisted fire direction and gun control. It could steam at close to 30 knots, which could move it 800 miles in a day. (When finally cornered and sunk, it went down only about 400 miles from Brest, the French haven Admiral Lutjens was desperately trying to reach, and would have reached in another 16 hours.)

The British Swordfish aircraft that prevented *Bismarck* from reaching Brest scored a lucky hit on *Bismarck's* rudder. Fatefully, that hit occurred at the last likely moment of twilight the big ship could have been stopped short of its own air cover. Had that torpedo not struck the rudder—and it hadn't been aimed at it—at day's end on the 26th, *Bismarck* would have had all night to steam eastward safe from air attack. The next day, ME 109 fighters would have been overhead. This attack by Swordfish from the carrier *Ark Royal* on the 26th stemmed from a sighting by a Coastal Command, U.S.-built Catalina flying boat. It spotted *Bismarck* that morning between 600 and 700 miles from Brest. The mission was a "hunch" mission, ordered at the last minute by Coastal Command's air commander, Sir Frederick Bowhill.

There were other ironies and might-have-beens. *Bismarck* had slipped away from her pursuers at 3 A.M. on the morning of May 25th (after having sunk the battle cruiser *Hood*, a 48,000-ton ship, in a few minutes on the 24th). But Admiral Lutjens was unaware he had escaped from British cruisers that had been clinging relentlessly to his heels. Fearful an action at first light might prevent transmission of the details of his success on the 24th, he radioed Berlin two long reports of that action. In London and elsewhere, British listening stations intercepted these signals, from which radio direction chart plots were made to relocate *Bismarck*. Incredibly, even after this, inaccurate plotting on Royal Navy charts resulted, and *Bismarck* was given another chance to escape. Because of the faulty plots, the great ship pulled several hours away from her pursuers. Only when halted by a hard-jammed rudder at the last minute on her last day without fighter cover was her fate sealed.

The intensity and drama of the *Bismarck* tragedy is hard to overestimate, and the many circumstances that combined to do her in mock the logical probabilities of naval warfare. *Bismarck* was initially to have been accompanied by sister ship *Tirpitz*. But *Tirpitz* was not ready in time. Then the plan was that battle cruisers *Scharnhorst* and *Gneisenau* would sail from Brest to join her. They were damaged just before the planned operation and couldn't participate. Lutjens himself gallantly sent *Prinz Eugen*, his only escort, off on her own after sinking *Hood* and damaging the new battleship *Prince of Wales* on the 24th. Could she have helped *Bismarck* fight off the vulnerable Swordfish on the 26th with her anti-aircraft fire?

Another might-have-been involved U-556, commanded by Lt. Commander Herbert Wohlfahrt. He found himself in a position to attack *Ark Royal* early on the day that carrier's Swordfish torpedoed *Bismarck*. U-556, however, had expended all its torpedoes!

Of the more than 2,000 officers and men aboard *Bismarck*, many of the pick of German Navy, only 110 were rescued. Admiral Lutjens was not among them. But *Bismarck* had exacted a toll. Of *Hood's* crew of 1419 officers and men, only three survived and there were additional fatalities on *Prince of Wales*, which had taken four 15-inch hits from *Bismarck's* guns and three 8-inch hits from *Prinz Eugen's* guns. (*Bismarck* had taken two 14-inch shell hits from *Prince of Wales*.) *Prinz Eugen* successfully reached Brest. So the two navies both lost major ships and the Royal Navy also suffered damage to one of its newest battleships.

Bismarck's sinking was nevertheless a turning point in the history of the German Navy in World War II. Hitler, appalled at *Bismarck's* loss, never again allowed a battleship sortie of this kind. The tragedy was also the beginning of the end for Admiral Raeder, who never completely regained Hitler's confidence and was to be replaced by Admiral Karl Doenitz in 1943. Yet the gamble seemed a reasonable one and had not *Bismarck's* rudder been jammed by a chance torpedo hit, Raeder's plan might have brilliantly succeeded. In both Raeder's and Doenitz's memoirs, they recall the *Bismarck* episode as a near-run thing. Doenitz notes that he had placed a screen of seven U-boats in the southwesterly path of *Bismarck* and her pursuers on the 24th, as requested by Lutjens that day, with the hope of torpedoing *Bismarck's* trackers. But again, fate intervened. Because of leaking oil and the resulting need to make for port, Lutjens was forced to turn south and then southeast, thus bypassing his U-boat allies.

Fifteen years after *Bismarck* went down, a popular account in Germany attributed *Bismarck's* final sinking to scuttling charges (neither Raeder nor Doenitz mentioned this in their postwar memoirs). It seems scuttling charges were set, but also that the awful pounding absorbed by *Bismarck* was probably more responsible for her sinking than scuttling charges. If they were the primary cause of *Bismarck's* demise, then surely more of *Bismarck's* crew should have been disembarked and the big ship given the coup de graĉe before 10:36 A.M. on the 26th, at which time she was a battered hulk littered with dead. In this connection, some postwar German naval accounts seem to overly stress the scuttling of German vessels, especially U-boats. This was seen as an honorable fate. *Bismarck* never surrendered. Her flag was flying as she went under.

But so much for fate and destiny and might-have-beens, and on to the story of the ancient Swordfish against the *Bismarck*, in May 1941, with which we are concerned in this chapter.

In London in 1978 I attempted to locate a Royal Navy pilot who had taken part in the attack on *Bismarck*. Royal Navy historian David Brown knew one who lived on England's south coast but our first efforts were unsuccessful. British researchers explained that most *Ark Royal* pilots who had taken part in the decisive attack on *Bismarck* had been lost during the war, for Germany had had her revenge on *Ark Royal* in November 1941, only six months after *Bismarck* went down. U-81 torpedoed her amidships 30 miles from Gibraltar, and she sank before she could be towed to port, with heavy loss of life. Those pilots who survived later suffered heavy losses in Far East operations. In 1980, however, I finally located a Swordfish pilot who took part in the torpedo attack on *Bismarck*. Near Portsmouth, I had the long-awaited opportunity to interview him.

Before relating his memorable experiences in this action— aboard carrier *Victorious*—the reader should be told something about the remarkable aircraft he and eight other *Victorious* pilots were flying. British pilots called their Swordfish the "Stringbag," because it was the Fairey Aviation Company's response to a request for a fleet of aircraft that could fulfill almost every Navy requirement. The six essential functions originally specified were reconnaissance, shadowing, spotting, convoy escort, torpedo and dive bombing, minelaying, and the carrying of other very heavy loads. To provide all these functions in one aircraft with a low landing speed for carrier landings, a satisfactory speed for dive-bombing, stability and endurance for torpedo bombing and convoy duty, etc., was quite an accomplishment. Designer Marcel Lobelle had produced a prototype to meet these requirements in 1934. It was immediately successful and named the Swordfish. But because someone remarked that no housewife could cram a wider variety of goods into her string bag, that name caught on. Ever afterward, the biwinged torpedo bomber was known by its pilots and crews as the Stringbag.

Little further development had occurred by 1939, when World

War II began, and thus the Royal Navy began the war with a slow, now-obsolete, biwing torpedo bomber. Because demands for RAF aircraft became so quickly critical and had priority, the Navy had to wait, and ended the war in 1945 still flying Stringbags—the only British aircraft operational at the war's beginning still operational at its close.

The Stringbag carried a 1610-pound torpedo, cruised at 90 knots, and dive-bombed—almost straight down—at 190 knots. She could pull out of a near-vertical dive in 500 feet and was capable of flying at very slow speeds in various attitudes without stalling. She was, in reality, and in many ways, a hangover from the First World War—with open cockpit, a Vickers gun firing through the propeller (which veteran Stringbag pilot Charles Lamb described as only one stage advanced from the bow and arrow), and a rear-firing Lewis gun. She carried a crew of three—pilot in front, observer next, and gunner in rear. They dressed in goggles, helmets, and other gear reminiscent of World War I air combat.

This, then, was what British pilots flew above the oceans of the world for six years in World War II. Though the United States provided Britain more modern aircraft in the later years of the war, the Stringbags were still irreplaceable in the view of many and were even sent on strikes off the Norwegian coast and on Murmansk convoy runs as late as the spring of 1945 (which we will hear more about in Chapter 12). A good claim can be made that pilots who braved the cold in these obsolete, open-cockpit aircraft and flew long missions over the icy northern oceans, year after year, were the bravest of the brave. If they went down in the sea, they were probably without hope. Often their mother ships couldn't stop long to search for them, or knew not where to search, or found it impossible to conduct a search in foul weather or at night.

One intrepid soul who flew the Swordfish in 1941 was Lieutenant Philip David Gick, born in 1913 in Portland (Dorset), son of the late Sir William John Gick and educated at Ramsgate College. "Percy" Gick joined the Royal Navy in 1930 after failing both the Navy's executive and engineering examinations. He persevered and after entering in engineering after all ("someone fell off a motorbike and I got my chance"), he managed to transfer to "executive" and then into aviation. He became a pilot and after two and a half years as a midshipman won his wings. That was in 1936—the year Hitler reoccupied the Rhineland and signed a reasonable naval limitation treaty with England. In 1939 he was stationed at Leuchars in Scotland, and the outbreak of the war found him on his back in a hospital, unhappy over his physical state, with no opportunity to participate. But he was to see much combat in time, and would end his service as Rear Admiral Gick, C.B., O.B.E, DSC and Bar. He retired in 1964 to go into the boatbuilding business near Portsmouth. It was to his hometown and boatbuilding company that I traveled on a biting cold, rainy winter day (in 1980) to hear the story of his effort against the *Bismarck* in 1941.

The train from Waterloo Station was on time at Havant at 12:26. In a red Rover parked in front of the station sat the pilot whose eyesight enabled him to be among the first to sight the massive form of *Bismarck* and its 2,000-man crew steaming south on May 24th, 1941. Gick wore blue slacks, blue sweater, red scarf, and blue canvas deck shoes. His hair was grey and thinning; he was 67. But he is still alert, quick of movement, clear (green) eyed, and trim. An easy smile and welcome explained his local popularity. He has been happily married for 40 years, is the local hero, affectionately called "The Admiral" by young and old. We drove to the Crown Hotel Pub in Emsworth, the admiral's favorite watering hole, and began looking back. I asked him to tell me in detail of stirring days in May 1941. He began:

"From a hospital, where I found myself in 1939 at the beginning of the war, I was assigned the task of training torpedo pilots. I carried on this training until April 1941. Then I became senior pilot of 825 Squadron, under the command of Lt. Commander Eugene Esmonde. We were working up at Machrinhanish, in Swordfish. Ours were built by Blackburn and so we actually called them Blackfish at the time. Our tactics included dropping torpedoes about a thousand or so yards away from a target at low altitude—dummy torpedoes. We were using cameras in the wings and trying hard to perfect our technique. There was a rumor we would be going into action soon, but no one knew that it would be as soon as it was.

"Training continued well into May and by then I had designed a machine to develop pictures taken by the wing cameras within two hours, so that we could know almost immediately after a simulated attack how well we had done. Before that, it had taken two days to get the pictures developed. We were making progress, but most of the young pilots were only just beginning to perfect their technique. None had ever landed on a carrier. Suddenly, on May 21st, there was a cable from the Admiralty. We were to prepare to board *Victorious* at once!"

What had produced that telegram was the sailing of *Bismarck*, from Gdynia, May 18th. *Bismarck* had passed through Denmark's Great Belt and put into Bergen on the 21st. She had been spotted there from the air (for the second time). That news spurred the admiralty to order still-green pilots training with Gick to board *Victorious* at once. *Victorious* was already loaded with Hurricane aircraft to be delivered to Malta and had no time to discharge this cargo. She could therefore carry only nine Swordfish and six Fulmars for air defense.

Sir John Tovey, the fleet's commander in chief, knew well that Captain Bovell of *Victorious* wasn't yet ready for operations, that his pilots were untrained in deck landings. But Bovell, when queried, said *Victorious* should sail (after consulting his air officer commanding, Commander H.C. Ranald, and his senior squadron commander, Lt. Commander Esmonde). On the 21st Tovey ordered *Hood, Prince of Wales*, and attending ships to sail for patrol of the Denmark Straits. On the next day, late on the 22nd, after a Coastal Command pilot had defied bad weather to reach Bergen and reported *Bismarck* and *Prinz Eugen* departed, he sailed with the rest of the fleet, including *Victorious* and her nine Swordfish and Swordfish pilots, including Gick. Their mission was to intercept the two German warships.

From the German side, the now-underway sortie of *Bismarck* culminated long and careful efforts and constituted the climax of the German Navy's Atlantic operations in World War II. The projected three-month cruise of *Bismarck* was intended to strike a blow against British shipping which would disrupt vital supply lines. And had not air power (RAF attacks on *Scharnhorst* and *Gneisenau* at Brest) disrupted German Admiralty plans by preventing these two formidable ships joining *Bismarck* and *Prinz Eugen*, that might well have occurred. It's doubtful if *Ark Royal's* slow Swordfish would have been able to bring *Bismarck* to bay had she enjoyed the outer-screen protection of other powerful warships.

Bismarck and *Prinz Eugen* had begun training for this mission at the end of February (as soon as the ice in the Baltic had melted) and there had been careful attention to every detail. A repositioning of tankers and supply ships in the Atlantic had been required. A large number of U-boats had also been assigned to assist in the operation, code-named "Rheinuebung."

It was unfortunate *Bismarck* had to operate without *Tirpitz* or the two battle cruisers at Brest, and unfortunate that she was spotted by reconnaissance so early in her departure. It was also unfortunate (from the German point of view) that German naval opinion at the time favored passage into the Atlantic through the Denmark Straits rather than between Scotland and Iceland. This was probably because of considerable publicity given the British project of mining the passage between Scotland and Iceland. But as of May 1941, the minefield between Iceland and Scotland was still ineffective. The British began that mining effort late in 1940 as an anti-submarine measure. In such stormy and deep water, however, mines don't last long, and in any event, surface ships protected by paravanes and crossing at right angles on a steady course were in little danger.

The soon-to-come surface action in the Denmark Straits was not immediately fatal to the German ships. Indeed they won the day. But they were tracked almost continuously ever afterward, and without surface or air support to come to his aid, Admiral Lutjens was at a disadvantage, though he came very close to escaping the dragnet and reaching a French port. It should be kept in mind that at this time not a ship in the British or U.S. navies was equal to *Bismarck* or *Tirpitz. Hood,* soon to be destroyed by *Bismarck,* packed quite an offensive punch, and was the biggest ship in the British Navy. But she was in some respects under-armored, even though a 42,000-ton ship, the product of British naval thinking just after the Battle of Jutland. She was over 20 years old.

Bismarck and *Prinz Eugen* had a rather uneventful passage above Scotland and by late on May 23rd were approaching the Straits. There, at 7 P.M., two British cruisers (*Suffolk* and *Norfolk*) flashed the electrifying news that they had picked up the German ships on radar and had begun shadowing, after a close escape in an uneven gunfire exchange. The hope was that at dawn on the 24th an engagement could be initiated by capital ships of the Royal Navy. Vice Admiral L.E. Holland, commanding the approaching squadron of *Hood* and *Prince of Wales* and six destroyers, detached his destroyers at about 2 A.M., allowing them to continue northward. His two capital ships turned southward to steer a parallel course with the German ships. Meanwhile, Sir John Tovey, in command of a considerable fleet including *Victorious,* battleships, cruisers and destroyers, was steering a westerly course southeast of the Germans, hoping to intercept if *Bismarck* and *Priz Eugen* escaped *Hood* and *Prince of Wales* and emerged on a southward course from the Denmark Strait.

On the morning of the 24th, at 5:49 A.M., Admiral Holland in *Hood,* guided by reports from the shadowing cruisers, caught first sight of the German ships. He ordered fire opened on *Prinz Eugen* by mistake. Three minutes later he corrected his mistake and within seconds both ships opened fire on *Bismarck*, which had also spotted the British ships. The German ships opened fire on *Hood*. The dramatic battle between these four powerful ships was surprisingly brief. *Hood* appears not to have hit *Bismarck*, but a fire began almost immediately on her own middle deck, in the first minute of action. After three or four minutes of firing, observers on *Prince of Wales*, trailing *Hood*, which had just made a turn 20 degrees to port, were stupefied to see two huge splashes beside the biggest British ship and an almost instantaneous explosion. Sheets of flame leap high into the air where *Hood* had been. Her magazines had exploded! *Prince of Wales*, following in the turn, had to reverse rudder to miss the wreckage and debris, and all her crewmen saw of *Hood* after the explosion—and that only briefly—were the bow and stern, upturned and sinking.

The German fire was more rapid than the British and on *Prince of Wales* the splashes and near-misses became frequent as both the German ships now turned their attention on her. The British ships had also converged at an unfavorable angle, at which all guns could not fire. *Prince of Wales* was soon chased out of the action. A shell had smashed her bridge and caused considerable fatalities. A new ship, with gun company reps still aboard to help fire the guns, and a crew not yet fully trained, *Prince of Wales'* Captain J.C. Leach realized that if he remained engaged, he would likely follow *Hood* to the bottom. Thus, he turned away after having taken seven hits, four 14-inch (from *Bismarck*) and three eight-inch (from *Prinz Eugen*). Interestingly, neither *Suffolk* nor *Norfolk* came within range of *Bismarck* in this engagement, though they had joined up with the two bigger British ships at dawn. *Suffolk* fired about six salvoes from 14 or 15 miles off, but they fell far short. The two cruisers remained shadowers of the German ships, which now didn't choose to follow and finish off *Prince of Wales*, which they might have done. That, of course, wasn't Lutjens' mission. But the only surviving German officer of the action, Baron von Müllenheim-Rechberg, has written that many German crewmen were disappointed this was not done.

Most of the rest of that day was an anticlimax. But for Gick and all British seamen and aviators, the news that the Royal Navy's biggest ship had been destroyed in a few minutes, and *Prince of Wales* damaged and forced out of action, was a shock. Tovey's squadron, including *Victorious*, set course to intercept—hopefully late that day. They now became the British hope. Other British ships including Force H, from Gibraltar, were ordered to converge toward the German ships.

Now Admiral Lutjens was faced with hard decisions. Unfortunately, an important technical fact about radar aboard *Suffolk* and *Norfolk* was not appreciated by him. It would later affect his decisions with ominous consequences. *Bismarck's* immediate problem, however, was an oil leak caused by one of two solid hits scored by *Prince of Wales*. (Another had pierced a boat on deck.) The hit that mattered had penetrated the port oil bunker. Oil was pouring into the sea and also onto the deck. Salt water was seeping into the bunkers. The damage was mostly underwater and couldn't be seen. *Bismarck* took on a slight list to port, her speed was slowed, and the forecastle sank slightly. Lutjens sent divers down into the ship to place pipes to pump the oil aft and a collision mat was placed over the shell hole. In about two hours, speed was resumed. But pumping went on for many hours and it wasn't until the next morning that the forecastle was back up again.

Being shadowed constantly by the two British cruisers, Lutjens also had to decide what to do about *Prinz Eugen*. He assumed he would inevitably be caught by a major British squadron. Should he allow his sister cruiser to escape on her own while there was still time? Making the gallant choice, he decided, at the proper moment, to set his cruiser free. He had defeated one squadron with only eight 15-inch guns to his opponents' 17. He couldn't be sure he would repeat that in a second or third engagement, now damaged.

As that day waned, Sir John Tovey's mixed fleet steadily neared from the east, guided by radio reports. *Victorious* pilots were put on the alert for a torpedo strike as soon as the carrier closed within 100 miles of *Bismarck*. Gick and fellow Swordfish pilots were now to have their chance. They still had daylight left. British ships were on double daylight time and it wouldn't be dark until almost midnight at this longitude and time of year. On board *Victorious*, Gick was wondering not only when he and his eight comrades would be ordered into the air, but how those pilots who had never landed on a carrier would perform. He, his observer, V.K. "Duke" Norfolk, and gunner L.D. Sayer, knew the fleet was steaming at full speed to intercept *Bismarck*.

All were thirsting for revenge. Their position was 300 miles east of *Bismarck*. Admiral Tovey was following a course to allow him to intercept even if *Bismarck* turned north, but which might let *Bismarck* get away if she continued to the southwest. Just after midday, in fact, with *Norfolk* and *Suffolk* still shadowing, *Bismarck* took advantage of fog and turned back on her tormentors. Curiously, *Norfolk's* captain had had an uneasy feeling that *Bismarck* might do just that, and although apparently not warned in time by radar, he also turned backward in the fog. When visibility suddenly improved, *Bismarck* loomed up on the horizon only eight miles away. *Norfolk* beat a hasty retreat.

Bismarck wasn't trying only to attack the cruisers. She was maneuvering to prepare *Prinz Eugen's* escape. And the cruiser later got away, not to be seen again by British eyes until safely back at Brest some days later. *Bismarck* resumed her course southwest. On board the *Victorious* as the day waned, pilots were concerned about the weather. It was cloudy and rainy. *Victorious* was rolling noticeably at 27 knots. Aboard, some were uncomfortable because battleship *Repulse*, behind, was fully extended at 27 knots and, not wanting to reduce revolutions, was periodically riding up quite close on the quarter in poor visibility.

During the afternoon, two aircraft flying from Iceland had tracked the *Bismarck*. But by 4:40 P.M., the last of the two had flown back to base. Aboard *Bismarck*, Lutjens decided to turn more southward because of his loss of oil and the need to return to Brest. This, unfortunately for the Germans, took *Bismarck* (and her pursuers) out of the path of a pack of waiting U-boats further to the southwest. During the afternoon, too, Admiral Tovey decided to send *Victorious* and four light cruisers on ahead of his slower ships to get *Victorious'* aircraft in position to attack. But *Bismarck* made things more difficult by a turn to the west, after circling back and opening fire on one of her trackers, *Suffolk*. In this brief engagement, *Prince of Wales* also opened fire at *Bismarck*, scoring no hits. *Bismarck's* temporary sally to the west took the great ship farther away from the oncoming carrier. *Prinz Eugen* had escaped to the southwest, and was now steaming alone, free of tracking enemy ships.

Thus the tense hours of that critical day, May 24th, dragged on. Aboard *Victorious* the nine crews of the readied Swordfish were on standby. It was now almost 9:00 P.M. and there was still good light. Captain Bovell of *Victorious* had expected to be within 100 miles of *Bismarck* by now but was not. He continued to steam a closing course, still guided by *Suffolk* and *Norfolk's* position reports. Another hour passed and charts showed *Bismarck* 120 miles distant. It was now or never, 10:00 P.M., still light. Despite the fact that a strong northwest wind was increasing and that there were intermittent and heavy rain squalls, Captain Bovell ordered the nine Swordfish to take off. This was the moment Gick, Esmonde, and other air crewmen had been waiting for.

Gick had long been in flying clothes—bogus leather jacket, fur-lined, brown helmet with Gosport tube, socks, and heavy flying boots. He and other pilots had been briefed as to route in *Victorious'* small briefing room. They were waiting on deck, in their cabins, and in the briefing room, for word to take off. Their aircraft had been run up and were standing, wings extended but three-blade props still, ready to be started at the signal.

At the word go, the nine pilots hurried to the biplanes, with observers and gunners, and the three crewmen quickly buckled belts in each of the nine Stringbags. Fitters were ready with the crank to start the 760-horsepower engine. They cranked until the whine was just right, then pilots pulled a small nickel-colored metal ring on the port side of the cockpit attached by a piece of wire. This engaged the Pegasus and the engines belched smoke and fired. They soon smoothed into a steady roar which could be heard above the gusting wind.

Victorious normally launched aircraft at close to maximum speed, 30 knots or better. The biwing silver-grey Stringbags rose and fell slowly on the moving deck as wind and rain splashed down from dead ahead. Aircraft No. 5A, piloted by Esmonde, was the first given the flag, and roared slowly off the end. *Victorious* was now making 30 knots, and it was just after 10 P.M. Slowly the others joined formation and all headed west. The fixed landing gear, blunt nose, and numerous wing struts—plus two big wings—limited speed to 90 knots or less. The Mark-II-N torpedoes slung beneath the fuselage weighed over 1600 pounds. Two horizontal rods in front of the pilot contained rows of lights and pilots had been trained to aim at enemy ships by measuring lead with these lights, starting at 2,000 yards. The speed represented between one light and the next was five knots. Thus, if a ship was making 20 knots, a pilot should have the fourth light from the end on the intended victim's bow, which pointed the aircraft and torpedo in the right direction to lead the victim sufficiently.

The nine Swordfish from *Victorious* separated into flights of three, led by Esmonde, Gick, and Lt. H.C.P. Ballard. Flying on each side of Gick, to the rear, were pilots W.F.C. Garthwaite and Sub-Lt. D.P.B. Jackson. All the Swordfish stayed low over the water. Visibility below the clouds was best, and all eyes remained fixed on the heaving sea to the west. The first ships expected to come into view were *Norfolk, Suffolk,* and *Prince of Wales,* now all steaming on to the port side of *Bismarck,* where they had taken station after the last *Bismarck* turnabout, just after 6:00 P.M.

It wasn't until about 11:20 P.M. that the Swordfish pilots—now flying just up into the clouds to protect themselves against expected antiaircraft fire—at last saw a ship through an opening below. Some assumed this might be *Bismarck.* Esmonde prepared to attack. When the Swordfish came out of the clouds, however, it was seen to be *Norfolk,* which realized the Swordfish were pointed in the wrong direction and so signaled the fliers. Esmonde, Gick, and the others read the signals and followed *Norfolk's* suggested course— toward *Bismarck,* further to port. Once again another ship appeared as if from nowhere. This time it was the U.S. Coast Guard cutter *Modoc,* which fate had placed in the midst of the unfolding drama. The nine Swordfish again reoriented themselves and flew onward on the heading provided by *Norfolk.*

Ten minutes later, near the base of the cloud and rain, Gick's observer, Norfolk, was the first to make out the outline of the great German ship ahead of his small radar set. "I've got the *Bismarck!*" he fairly shouted. "On the port bow. I've got *Norfolk* behind. There's something odd in between!" (This was *Modoc.*)

Esmonde's observer was having trouble with his radar and could only pick up *Norfolk.* The Swordfish were below 1,000 feet. Esmonde ordered them to prepare to attack. The usual tactics were to dive from 1,500 feet at a good angle and release torpedoes at exactly 60 feet, after a short low-speed run-in. When the Stringbags were lumbering in straight and level at only 80 or 90 knots, they became highly vulnerable. Each pilot's left thumb was now ready on the stick for the moment to release torpedo. Suddenly, through a gap in the clouds as they were climbing to 1,500 feet, *Bismarck*—they were heading straight for her—came into clear view. She opened fire at once with many guns on the slow bombers. Gick and the others quickly spread out. The antiaircraft fire had separated the Swordfish and Gick could not only see but smell the black smoke and cordite.

"Esmonde chose to go straight in," Gick recalls. "We were on the port quarter. "Speed" Pollard took his three Stringbags off on another course, to come in from the other side. I decided to continue climbing to get in the best possible position for a torpedo run. Then *Bismarck* seemed to concentrate fire on the three of us. We were suddenly flying through very heavy black puffs of smoke. Nor-we were too low to see much anyhow."

On the other side of the enemy ship, Pollard and his two fellow pilots had brought their bombers down low and made a run from the starboard side. They too had dropped their "fish" and were now seeking to avoid antiaircraft fire and get back to *Victorious*. It was after 11:30 P.M. and darkness would arrive just after 12:30 A.M. (the 25th). That was because they were on double summer time, as explained, and also because they were also far to the west—about two hours behind Greenwich time by the sun. Ships' clocks were therefore more than four hours ahead of the sun. The real time of sunset—Greenwich time—that night was 8:52 P.M.

The nine Swordfish had all survived! All were winging their way to the east and oncoming *Victorious*. Captain Bovell and officers and men on every ship in the converging forces were tensely waiting for news from the torpedo attack. Though the pilots themselves didn't know it, one of the nine's torpedoes had struck *Bismarck* amidship, killing one and injuring another six crewmen, and Admiral Lutjens was forced to lower speed again. Every new blow hurt, and affected morale. To the three hits registered that morning by *Prince of Wales*, then, pilots from *Victorious* had added a torpedo hit.

The flight back to *Victorious* was an anticlimax, but one of considerable tension. The Swordfish had to find *Victorious* or crash into the sea. There would have been little time for *Victorious* or other ships to give up the chase and search for downed pilots.

Aboard *Bismarck*, crewmen thought they had downed several of the slow, silvery-grey bombers; in fact, all had escaped and were now winging their way through a darkening and rainy sky back to where *Victorious* was supposed to be.

The return flight, thankfully, proved to be shorter than the flight outbound; *Victorious* was on a following course, and had closed the distance by more than 50 miles since the nine had taken off.

Gick was concerned for his fellow pilots, most of whom he had trained since mid-April. Though they had learned their tactics and learned to fly the Stringbag, they had not had any practice landing aboard a carrier. With a heavy sea running, finding the carrier was but the first task. A tougher one might be getting all nine aircraft back aboard safely.

The Stringbags stayed low over the water, and were scattered widely. But general formation was kept and Esmonde was still in folk shouted: 'Don't worry. It's all bursting ahead.' We didn't know it at the time but not long ago I saw and heard the German gunnery officer on BBC television. He explained that *Bismarck's* gunnery tables stopped at a speed of 100 knots. In other words, her tracking didn't compute below that speed! That's why, probably, all the bursts were in front of us. We were doing only about 80 knots!"

"Esmonde meanwhile pointed his nose toward the big battleship and his three Swordfish prepared to drop torpedoes. Just as they did—and they missed—the *Bismarck* turned toward me. By that time, I was slanting in to the attack myself but this turn in my direction threw our aim off and I decided to discontinue the run. I broke off the attack and turned to port and got down just over the top of the waves. There was quite a sea running and when we completed our turn, we headed back in *Bismarck's* direction. It was obvious she had lost sight of us down so low. We continued to come in on her again, slightly on the port bow. I had "Pat" Jackson on my left and William Garthwaite on my right. Pat and I stayed low but Bill then got up higher and they saw him, and opened fire on us again. Pat and I were literally going over the waves. This time the secondary armament was firing at us and it was heavy fire—four or five inch and .303s. I could see the big ship's silhouette ahead over the waves and we now prepared to drop. Coming on a little while longer, we were about 2,000 yards out when I lined her up in the sights.

We were using a control gear—there was a reel of wire to hold the torpedo steady—and I held the wire and counted three and then pressed the grey button on top of the stick with my thumb. All three of us dropped at the same time and three 18 foot-long torpedoes sped toward the big battleship. I turned hard to port and stayed right on top of the water. Then Norfolk suggested we get some pictures of the great warship. So I pulled up a bit higher and we began to take some. The 15-inch guns of *Bismarck* opened up on us again. We were still in front of her and could clearly see them firing, and the shells were very close. One suddenly hit in the water just beneath us. We hadn't gained much height yet and that huge splash of water shot up and hit the Stringbag hard. It took the fabric off the bottom of the fuselage and knocked us about a bit. Sayer cracked: 'Some rotten sods have knocked the bottom out of our house!' That relieved the tension. But we stopped taking pictures and got away as fast as we could. We didn't stay around longer to see whether our torpedoes struck *Bismarck* or not an the lead, as he had been since takeoff. It was now 12:30 A.M. on the 25th—and barely 20 minutes of daylight remained. Just then several crews called out ships to the east, steaming in their direction.

Esmonde signaled he would land first and got aboard safely. Gick circled *Victorious* once and was directed to land second. Constantly watching the heaving deck and the Deck Landing Officer with his yellow bats as he descended, he had to be sure he put the Stringbag down close to the end, where the hook would engage the arresting gear. He gauged speed and distance accurately and they thumped to a jerking halt as the wire caught. As soon as he had switched off the engine, Gick climbed out and hurried to the bridge to encourage the green pilots in their landings. His heart was often in his mouth. But each pilot, encouraged on the radio, and having seen Esmonde and Gick land successfully, made a successful landing on the always-moving flight deck. Gick was relieved and proud. The closest call had been his when a wave rolled over the carrier's deck as Gick landed. Water splashed into the Swordfish. Once again, Sayer relieved the tension. "I've got a bloody drain in this house," he said, referring to the torn-open bottom of their aircraft.

Lutjens carried on. But he must have been getting tired from the strain of being for days constantly on alert. He had been shadowed now for 30 hours. Three hours later his chance came, and he cleverly took it. The three shadowing vessels to his left were zig-zagging, as was *Bismarck*. For brief periods, they would lose *Bismarck* on radar, then pick her up again. On one of his zags to the right, which must have been carefully planned and executed, Lutjens took *Bismarck* out of radar range to the starboard. But now, instead of zigging back to port, he increased speed and set course westward. This succeeded in giving the three British ships the slip, at about 3 A.M. on the morning of the 25th. They continued on their normal tracking course, but *Bismarck* didn't come back on their radar screens. This was soon reported and caused dismay in London and aboard all British ships. *Bismarck* was once again free of the hounds that had been dogging her heels since the evening of the 23rd. Lutjens had circled to starboard and cut across and behind the path of his trackers and headed east for Brest. If he could have two days of uninterrupted steaming, he could reach air cover and safety.

But a short time after his "escape," Lutjens made an understandable but fatal mistake—one that would cost him ship and life. He gave his position away to listening Allied radio operators. Thinking wrongly he was still being tracked on British radar screens (because *Bismarck's* radar search receiver was still receiving the enemy's high-frequency pulses), Lutjens transmitted a long signal to Berlin describing his position and relating events of the day, then another. What he didn't know was that *Bismarck's* search receiver received high-frequency enemy pulses from a great distance, and that radar sets on British ships weren't regaining these impulses from that far away. British sets would have needed double the energy they had to receive the signal back that *Bismarck's* set was picking up after only a one-way journey.

In the Admiralty in London, the German transmissions caused a stir. The British were dumbfounded that *Bismarck* would give its position away in this manner, just when it appeared they had escaped the net. Likewise, Berlin and Paris (Gruppe West) were stunned. Paris sent an urgent signal to Lutjens to keep quiet. There, by monitoring the reports of English ships, it was known the British had lost *Bismarck* at 3 A.M. Alas, for *Bismarck*, the signal from Paris was not in time. British listening stations picked up the *Bismarck* transmission. Once again they located their quarry. But it would now take some time to once again catch the great ship.

Dawn on Sunday, the 25th, came and the German crew knew there were no British ships in sight or trailing directly behind (even though their position had been given away). *Bismarck* had, during its night escape, gained several hours on her foes—and now had to be headed off, or intercepted, by someone other than Sir John Tovey's force. To complicate the British predicament, Tovey's fleet had steamed northward because of mistaken plotting. Pilots aboard *Victorious*, of course, didn't know Tovey was steaming an errant course. At dawn they were looking forward to another chance to finish off *Bismarck*. And Captain Bovell prepared another strike. Basing their calculations on where they thought *Bismarck* should be, the Swordfish crews took off early and searched and searched. Six Fulmar fighters were also flown off. But search as they might, not a pilot, observer, or gunner sighted *Bismarck*. Although the aircraft stayed airborne until fuel was dangerously low, all returned empty-handed, including Gick, who recalled:

"We stayed out so long we were critically low on fuel. I was down to my last 12 gallons in reserve. Finally, we made it back to the carrier but when my tail went down aboard ship, the engine stopped. Pat Jackson was so low on fuel he couldn't make it back and was forced to ditch in the sea. We couldn't find him and he spent 12 days in a dinghy before a fishing trawler luckily picked him up." For Gick and others who landed back aboard *Victorious* that Sunday, May 25th, it was a frustrating day. Tovey's force was now too far north and behind *Bismarck* to catch up. Its only chance was that other units would slow or stop the German battleship, allowing it time to catch up.

Sunday was peaceful for the 2,000 Germans aboard *Bismarck* as they drew closer to a friendly port. The quiet was deceiving, however, for the Admiralty in London knew *Bismarck's* course. *Bismarck* had continued to transmit signals, and Force H was hastening north to intercept. Also, Coastal Command was sending out search aircraft. It was, in fact, on the next morning—Monday the 26th—that crewmen on *Bismarck* again began to feel they were being watched and surrounded. Aircraft appeared in the morning and the shadowing continued during the day. Yet spirits were raised when word was received that Hitler had sent many congratulatory telegrams, and had awarded the senior Gunnery Officer the Knight's Cross of the Iron Cross. Lutjens—it was his birthday—had won the same award. Further, 81 protective aircraft were promised for the next day, Tuesday, among them long-range bombers. So near and yet so far . . . .

Bismarck needed only to get through the 26th; on Tuesday it would reach air cover. Admiral Tovey, with the main force, had decided to abandon pursuit if *Bismarck* got within air cover range—200 miles from Brest or St. Nazaire. All Germany watched and waited. And as that Monday, the 26th, came to a close, it looked as if Lutjens had made it. But Force H, including carrier *Ark Royal*, was nearing from the south. And *Ark Royal's* long-distance reconnaissance aircraft had been tracking *Bismarck* for much of the day. Earlier, a Coastal Command Catalina had found *Bismarck* at 10:30 A.M., 690 miles west of Brest. But it wasn't until well into the afternoon that *Ark Royal* was close enough to launch an air strike. Just before 3:00 P.M., 14 Swordfish were launched. But—*Bismarck's* luck was good again—they attacked one of their own ships, the British cruiser *Sheffield*, which desperately dodged all the torpedoes, with appropriate comment.

Undaunted, *Ark Royal* readied another strike. At 7:10 P.M., 15 Swordfish took off in a second effort to find their German target. Now, at the very last hour, they approached. Shortly after 9:00, the 15 Swordfish sighted *Bismarck*. Like those from *Victorious*, they climbed into an attacking position and 10 minutes later began their runs. Of 15 torpedoes launched, two this time struck *Bismarck*.

The first struck the ship's armor belt and did little damage—as had been the case with the torpedo from *Victorious'* Swordfish. But one Swordfish pilot had been lucky. His torpedo chanced to strike the rudder on *Bismarck's* starboard side. The rudder jammed. This hit doomed *Bismarck*, still far enough in front of the chase to get home if she could continue steaming on course. (*Bismarck* would have been able during the night to cover about half the distance to Cape Finisterre, to which she was headed.) It was not to be. In spite of desperate efforts, Lutjens couldn't get the big ship to steam straight ahead. She kept turning into the wind. That night, for almost 1900 German officers and men, was to be their last. Destroyers arrived on the scene some hours later that night. *Bismarck*, circling, nevertheless fought them off. But the great ship's position was hopeless, since she could no longer make way.

Nor could U-556 help. She had watched in her periscope from a good firing position *Ark Royal* and *Renown* of Force H, steaming north to finish off *Bismarck*. U-556 was without torpedoes!

May 27th then was the fateful day for *Bismarck*. The great ship went under after British capital ships, which had come up within range, and aircraft pounded and torpedoed her mercilessly. *Bismarck* never surrendered and went down with flag flying, detonation charges having been set and exploding at the last.

What about Gick and *Victorious*, whose pilots had put the first torpedo into *Bismarck* late on the evening of the 24th? After the fruitless early morning search next day, the 25th, *Victorious* and the cruiser division under Admiral Tovey, short on fuel, were ordered to Iceland. Tovey's fleet had lost many hours steaming northward in error. Now Sir John headed southeast at maximum speed for *Bismarck* with *King George V* and *Rodney*, his destroyers, and a few other ships. The destroyers reached *Bismarck* during the night of the 26th and attacked with torpedoes; next day the big ships arrived on the death scene and joined in the kill.

The news of *Bismarck's* demise was not gleefully celebrated among Swordfish pilots aboard *Victorious*. They realized that almost an entire navy had been searching for the German battleship and, as fellow sailors, felt a twinge of sympathy for the Germans who had put up a gallant fight. But they also remembered the British seamen who died in *Hood* and appreciated the change in the naval balance in the Atlantic effected by destruction of *Bismarck*. Gick was soon to see a measure of Germany's revenge—and not long afterward. He and fellow pilots of 825 Squadron soon found themselves aboard *Ark Royal*, then operating in the Mediterranean. When *Ark Royal* steamed past a German U-boat, the German submarine was ready. U-81, as related, sent her to the bottom 30 miles from Gibraltar.

We were still seated in the Crown Hotel in Emsworth. Gick recalled that sinking:

"I flew off the *Ark Royal* for the next six months. We were doing anti-submarine work in the Med. I had, in fact, just landed. It was November 13th. Just after I landed there was a heavy explosion—an awful sound. U-81 had torpedoed us." (Lt. Friedrich Guggenberger, commanding, also torpedoed *Malaya* the next month.)

"The ship was obviously badly hurt and I soon had to board a cutter to escape to a nearby destroyer. Yet *Ark Royal* didn't sink immediately. After a while, we went back on board and I retrieved some personal belongings. We also tried to get the ship moving again and actually did have her underway. But the list became too great. Finally, her stack went under. At the very end I dashed about trying to be sure everyone would get off in time. Down below I found a lone stoker. I asked him what he was doing. He said he was staying at his post until ordered to leave. I gave him that order fast. As soon as I got him out, she went over."

And so it was that the carrier that did in *Bismarck* was herself done in, the same year, six months later.

Gick survived that and flying from other carriers, some in the Far East. In 1980, he was still quick, alert, and energetic. He showed me his boatbuilding sheds, and where he had dug a channel so that—at high tide—boats using his docks could navigate into the bay and beyond. "I had to borrow the money to start this business," he said. "And at one time when the creditors tried to foreclose a mortgage, it was a near-run thing. But I've managed to hold on and get enough orders to keep going. I don't think I'll ever do anything else. But I don't fly anymore. I fly commercially, yes, but I think I've finished piloting my own aircraft. After all, that was a long time ago . . . ."

Chapter 3

Bader Falls in France

In travels in postwar years, living in Germany, Britain, and America, I found more interest in the flying career and life of the late Sir Douglas Bader than in any other Allied fighter ace. Not only was Bader a Richthofen-type legend in Allied countries, he was well known in Germany and other countries. That's because his life contains all the ingredients of great, inspirational stories.

Until 1979, when he attended a German fighter pilots' reunion near Munich, Bader had not been much to Germany since 1945, when liberated as a prisoner of war after almost four years of captivity. He was not the quickest to forgive—or perhaps one should say forget—that Germany had started Word War II. And he intensely loathed Hitler and the Nazis. Yet he immensely enjoyed the 1979 reunion, and had always been willing to admire the accomplishments and admit the courage and ability of military adversaries. Not many years after the war, for example, he wrote a foreword for Hans Ulrich Rüdel's book, *Stuka Pilot*, though his and Rüdel's political philosophies could hardly be further apart. He became well acquainted with General Adolf Galland, who in 1941 entertained him at a Luftwaffe fighter pilots' headquarters just after Bader's capture in France in 1941. Then and after the war he has always liked the former German fighter commander and admired his combat record. They collaborated on films about the Battle of Britain (which, incidentally, usually perpetuate wartime myths).

In recent years Bader came to accept Luftwaffe victory claims, which for a long time he had found highly suspect. At the end of a visit to Bader's country place outside London in 1978, when driving me to the airport to catch a flight to New York, Bader finally offered this explanation of the higher victory totals of Luftwaffe fighter pilots:

"We pulled our chaps out of combat, promoted them up, and they weren't left in the active fighting for five or six years. But there were many in the Luftwaffe who were left in the active fighter war for so long they really became experts—with all that experience. And they ran up almost unbelievable scores."

Ten years earlier, on the night I introduced Eric Hartmann to Bader at a London dinner party I hosted, Bader was not all that comfortable in accepting confirmations awarded Luftwaffe *experten*, or even in being photographed in the company of top German aces.

Bader's fame was partly due to a film made about his life. It was, in turn, partly attributable to a prewar flying accident in which he lost both legs. It is also attributable to his spirited and fierce personality and his dogged determination in the face of adversity. But whatever the contributing causes, Bader remained until his death in 1982 the best-known and most-talked-about fighter ace of the Allied air forces in World War II. That is striking because he saw no action after late summer 1941, when he fell in France and was captured. To his last day, he refused to write anything about fighter combat in World War II that took place after August 1941. "I, of course, did all my fighting up to August of 1941 and I don't write about air combat comparisons after that," he told me.

He was a serious student of aerial tactics up to that time and had definite and interesting views on the Battle of Britain, in which he participated. In 1972, at the RAF Club in London, he outlined them to me in detail for the first time:

"Commander-in-Chief Hugh Dowding fought the Battle of Britain as if General Bernard Montgomery had said to one of his corps commanders, 'You fight the battle and call on other corps commanders if you need help.' He should have directed the battle. The tactics were wrong. There were three basic stages of the battle—shipping, airfields, and cities. Certainly in the last stage, when the Luftwaffe formations were building up almost always to about 17,000 feet or so and then coming in from their assembly area, headed northwest, we knew just about where they were coming—to London. Other RAF squadrons, at Tangmere and elsewhere, could handle them if they turned left and if they turned right they would be over the sea. Fighter Commander Keith Park was sending up squadrons from 11 Group and pilots were often getting caught climbing.

"Time and again I asked that we of 12 Group (to the north) be directed to intercept these incoming formations before they got to London. I was refused. We easily could have. The point is that the other side of the argument has often been told and I am telling 12 Group Commander Trafford Leigh-Mallory's side. 11 Group fighters could have attacked the enemy on his way home. Finally, Leigh-Mallory stopped the dispatch of our fighter units to 11 Group for this reason.

"The rules of fighter combat are: height, sun, and close-in shooting. I had read the accounts of the great World War One aces. The rules were the same. In 1940, directors would vector us into the fight. I wanted to be up-sun and I would turn away from the vector heading to get into the desired position. All a leader can do is take his formation to an advantageous position and then let them go in and do their best. That's all he can do. Formation is only to enable a group of aircraft to arrive at one place together."

At this time—1972—the Official Secrets Act had not expired in Britain, and few appreciated the enormous advantage RAF Fighter Command thus enjoyed in the Battle of Britain. RAF commanders often knew through decoding (Ultra) where and when—and in what strength—the German formations were attacking. Thus the quick and accurate vectoring of interceptors to the enemy was made possible. Bader's belief is that Park wasn't utilizing two of the three cardinal rules of fighter combat, height and sun. He thinks tactics could have been improved and that losses could have been far fewer. Whether true or not, it's true that Bader, advising Leigh-Mallory, suffered considerable resentment for his suggestions that the battle was not being fought on the best terms by the RAF. No doubt that was due in part to the gallant defense being waged, mostly by fighter pilots of 11 Group. These hard-put RAF pilots performed courageously in defense.

But it's also true that the Battle of Britain—perhaps because it was a strategic, historical, turning-point victory—has been enveloped in certain myths. Distortions about numbers and losses, which some reiterate despite solid evidence to the contrary, continue to sustain popular misconceptions. A reliable, concise summary of the two air forces in that struggle, founded on facts rather than myths, can be found in the chapter about the Battle of Britain in *The Greatest Aces*, published in 1968. It should be noted that when this was written, the extent of the RAF's advantage derived from decrypting and decoding Luftwaffe orders was not yet fully known. This revelation in 1975 reinforced and confirmed the conclusions of that chapter, and of similar sentiments expressed in *Fighter Tactics,* published four years later.

Dowding disproved the bomber-will-get-through theory of Göring, several British air marshals, Giulio Douhet, and Billy Mitchell in defeating the German bomber onslaught. He was then shabbily rewarded. That injustice helped create an unreceptive postwar atmosphere for Battle of Britain criticism. That, however, doesn't prove RAF tactics in the Battle of Britain were the best possible. They were, of course, good enough. What can be said with a heavy degree of probability is that while RAF tactics might have been improved, Luftwaffe tactics were even further off the mark. Of course, the Luftwaffe was up against the impossible, fighting a critical battle when the adversary knew its moves in advance.

In the planning of this book I felt the reader would like to hear something of Bader, who, after all, flew over the sea on every mission in 1941 (English Channel or the North Sea). And the mission that most intrigued me was the one on which he was lost, because there has been so much speculation about it and the events following Bader's capture of Adolf Galland's JG 26 pilots on the Channel coast. Galland and Bader have somewhat different recollections of these events, which is not surprising, much as two newspaper reporters come up with slightly different versions of the same news event. We touch on these differences in the following pages.

Another reason for presenting Bader's views in this volume is that he, in effect, was something of a spokesman for RAF fighter pilots who took part in the Battle of Britain. In this connection, he took issue with certain intriguing claims made in Len Deighton's provocative book, *Fighter* (Jonathan Cape, 1977). A most controversial claim in the Deighton book is that the ME 109E in the Battle of Britain could outturn both the Hurricane and Spitfire. I suspect that in theory and on the drawing boards it possibly could, and I suspect, with less confidence, that the very best Luftwaffe fighter pilots might have on some occasions been able to do so—and daring enough to. They thus extracted the maximum turning radius from the 109 without losing a wing. But it's true that both British and German pilots flying their competing fighters at that time thought the Spitfire could outturn the 109. Could it, then, be possible that the pilots themselves were wrong? The probability is that, considering the question from the *practical application* standpoint, it was an extremely difficult and daring proposition to pull the 109 into its maximum turn. As late as June 1985, General Adolf Galland told me he is convinced the Spitfire could outturn the 109E. And he said German 109 pilots had little trouble with structural failure. Some insist the 109's tail assembly and wings could be separated from the fuselage in extreme and violent maneuvers. The case outlined in *Fighter* is fascinating—in print, and further interrogation on this point might be productive. Galland, who shot down 104 aircraft in the West (and, as noted, was to become the Luftwaffe's General of Fighters later in the war), often flew against Spits. He minimizes the importance of the turning circle and believes the 109 was the better fighter of the two in 1940. Air Vice Marshal Johnnie Johnson, top RAF fighter ace, agrees the Spit could outturn the 109. I asked the late Werner Schroer about the turning radius controversy in 1980. He thought the best pilots (such as Hans Marseilles, with whom he flew in Africa) profited from the fact that wing slots came out automatically on the 109 when stalling speed was reached to prevent a stall. Good pilots sometimes also used flaps, so that the 109 could have utilized both flaps and the wing slots. A question is at what speeds could both be utilized? Galland says that the 109's wing loading was too high to permit it to turn at speed with the Spitfire.

Bader agreed. He explained:

"I don't care for the theory. In 1940 we could always outturn the 109s. What is important is the actual practice. I heard they had wing slots and that they sometimes came out. But we could invariably outturn the blokes and did. The 109s could always use their fuel injection, stick their nose down, and probably get away. But we of the Fighter Pilots Association don't accept a lot about the new theory that the 109's turning radius was better, and we drafted a letter recently making our points.

"What *could* outturn us when it first made its appearance in 1941 was the FW 190; until we got Spitfire IXs, it could outturn both the Spitfire and the Hurricane. Ask Johnnie Johnson. He'll confirm that."

Bader was flying a Spitfire the day he went down in France, on August 9th. To this day, how it all happened remains controversial. Galland, in his classic book *Die Ersten and die Letzten*, gives one account and Bader another. Galland's account has been, generally speaking, accepted. That's because he had witnesses to support his account, while Bader's recollection was his alone. No RAF pilot, not even his wingman, saw Bader go down. He was singly attacking six 109s when his Spitfire was hit.

And so, in an effort to somewhat clear the facts about this incident, I raised the question of August 9th once again in the preparation of this book with Sir Douglas. He gave me his version, which we will soon come to!

When the Luftwaffe in May 1941 withdrew much of its strength from the West to the East for the attack on Russia, the RAF went over to the attack on the western front. It was a costly decision and campaign and in the next two years the Luftwaffe won the struggle, measured in losses, on this front. As in World War I, the British strategy of constant attack gave the Germans the advantage. This time the Germans could utilize radar and radio and were forewarned of air strikes at French targets; when pilots bailed out, the British became prisoners. The Germans usually returned to operations. When fighters were forced to crash-land because of a malfunction, it was the Germans who recovered them, not the British. In other words, the shoe was on the other foot, as compared to circumstances in the Battle of Britain in 1940.

This continuous offensive, nevertheless, fitted in with Bader's temperament and he made the most of it. Fellow pilots sensed he was tiring by August of 1941. He was now a wing commander, leading three squadrons (145, 610, and 616) of Spit IIs against Galland's 109s of JG 26 across the channel. Dogfights were regular occurrences. As a reflection of the trend, the Luftwaffe getting the best of it, Galland that summer and fall shot down 25 aircraft, 21 of them Spitfires.

On August 9th, 1941, a sunny summer day with drifting white clouds at 4,000 feet, Bader took off at midday leading the Tangmere wing. They were stationed due south of London. He was leading the wing's three squadrons on a fighter sweep over France. While climbing out over the channel, his airspeed indicator packed up. He also lost sight of his top cover squadron—not a good start. But the two lower squadrons (24 fighters) and the invisible top squadron (12) were on course. Radio silence was observed so as not to alert the German radio listening service. The three squadrons (Tangmere Wing) of brown and green Spits climbed steadily over the 75 miles of the English channel on a southeasterly course.

By the time they reached 28,000 feet and prepared to cross in near Le Touquet, 20 miles south of Boulogne, Bader had the top cover squadron in sight again. About 20 miles due east of Boulogne,

Luftwaffe 109s from the vicinity of St. Omer and Abbeville scrambled to intercept. (Little did these pilots suspect that that night Bader would be lying in a hospital at St. Omer, where his father, a victim of the First World War, lay buried.) Bader was flying without his usual wingman, Alan Smith, away in London. He headed for the Bethune area. Jeff West, a New Zealander, was his temporary wingman.

"Dogsbody" was the radio code name for Bader. He had painted a DB on the side of his aircraft and a friend had suggested it stood for Dogsbody rather than Douglas Bader. From that time on, Dogsbody it was.

Shortly after crossing in over the French coast, Bader's top squadron sighted 12 109s ahead, 2000 feet below, also climbing—in a vulnerable position. The Spits had the advantage of height. The 109s had been sighted by Ken Holden, above, and Bader needed only seconds to find them; he then called in the bandits, ordered a bounce, and cautioned his comrades to take their time, saying there were plenty of them. Bader always flew with 616, least experienced of the three squadrons. He ordered 12 fighters to remain top cover, and prepared to dive on his victims ahead and below. In the finger-four flight with him were West, Hugh Dundas, and Johnnie Johnson—destined to become England's top fighter ace. Above, Holden led the top cover squadron of 12 Spits. Bader asked him to protect the lower 24, which now began their diving pass on the unsuspecting Germans. Since the Spitfires were painted light blue underneath (as were the 109s), they were difficult to detect from below. The Germans looking up saw little contrast. RAF pilots had the earth below their adversaries, a better contrast.

But while the 109s had been slower to see their adversaries, they caught sight of the diving Spits just in time. Bader had begun a steep, plunging dive, aiming at the center section of four 109s. West, Dundas, and Johnson spread out on each side and went screaming down with him. Their pass was not the best. Bader realized he was going too fast for a good firing pass. Just then, 109s on both sides of the Luftwaffe formation banked into turns, reacting to the other eight Spitfires of 616 Squadron now diving on them, off to the right and left of Bader's four-fighter flight. Bader's intended victim, the second 109 from the left in the center four-fighter flight, turned and seemed to slow its speed. With a feeling of horror, Bader saw he was about to collide and wildly dived downward alone to avoid a collision. Johnson also realized he was overshooting but managed to slow his speed and opened a hot fire on his victim, then saw pieces of the 109's right wing fly off.

The sky is suddenly a scene of individual dogfights. Galland is in the melee and shoots down two Spitfires. Bader plunges down to 24,000 feet and finds himself alone. Checking his rear and finding no enemy behind, he begins to climb to regain altitude. He's extremely vulnerable, alone over enemy territory among many enemy fighters. Holden, above, suddenly catches sight of more than 20 additional 109s, at height, about to bounce the lower two squadrons of Spitfires. He calls out excitedly, "For Christ's sake, break!"—forgetting to give the call sign. All the Spits below break and a wild action ensues. The Spits had initially caught some of the 109s below them at a disadvantage. The Spits themselves have now been bounced from above.

Below, climbing back up, Bader sights, out front, six 109s, in three pairs, abreast. He can't resist, though the odds are poor. His own admonition to Tangmere Wing pilots has always been never to attack such an enemy formation alone over France. Still, if they don't see him, he might pull it off. Pushing throttle forward and checking gunsight and gun switches, Bader noses down slightly for speed and begins to close behind the center pair. He comes on rapidly and soon finds the trailing wingman filling his yellow sight ring. He presses the button, eight .303s roar and ignite a trail of yellow flame streaming back from the victim. It suddenly explodes and wings over earthward.

Bader moves his stick slightly right to bring the center pair leader into his sight. None of the five has seen him yet and he opens fire on his second victim. The eight guns pour five into this 109 at 100 yards range and white smoke begins to stream backward. Just as Bader feels his luck is holding, the enemy pair to the left turns toward him. As his second victim's nose drops and the 109 starts down, bader banks hard right, toward the two 109s on that flank. In the vertical-wing turn something strikes his fighter. Was it a collision? Was it a good burst of 20mm or something larger, or what? To the end, Bader didn't know what it was—or never admitted it if he knew. Did one of the 109s shear off his tail in a collision?

"I don't know. I think it was a collision. I suspect it might have been another Spitfire and that the collision was fatal to that pilot. The Germans didn't credit anyone with a victory in my loss. Of course, it's possible it could have been a perfect hit from a shell. What I remember is that the stick got mushy right away. It wobbled every way, and when I glanced back, falling vertically, I could see there was no tail, none at all. The engine just nosed down, heavy as it was, and I was helpless to do anything about it," he recalled.

Bader was spiraling almost vertically down, out of control. The Spitfire—the front part, that is—was rapidly accelerating in its wild fall. Whatever had happened, it was time to get out of the doomed aircraft. But how high was he? Was there sufficient oxygen to breathe at this height? No matter, he must get out. He yanks off rubber oxygen mask and pulls the rubber ball above his head, which releases the cockpit hood. The wind suddenly screams and hits him hard in the face instantaneously. He releases the seat harness pin so he can lift himself up and out of the cockpit. He raises torso and two metal legs slightly with his powerful arms, having little push in his artificial limbs. The fierce wind catches him and jerks him halfway out of the cockpit. But his right boot catches on something by the seat. He can't get back down inside the cockpit, or get further out of it! The wild, spiraling motion of the vertically plunging fighter buffets his body repeatedly against the fuselage.

Desperately trying to keep his hand on the D-ring of his parachute—because he might not be able to grasp it again if thrown wildly out of the plane tumbling—he fights to free his foot. It's stuck fast. He's taking such a brutal beating he could soon be unconscious from the buffeting. If his hand jerks enough to pull the D-ring of his parachute, it will stream out and open—and probably tear to pieces. The struggle goes on for what seems hours, speed reaching perhaps 500 miles an hour.

At last, the right metal leg's leather straps snap. Minus that limb, ribs bruised, body battered, Bader is blown free of the doomed fighter and at once pulls the ripcord. When the parachute billows open with a hard jerk, he feels as if he were standing still in mid-air. It's so peaceful he almost wants to sleep and he has the sensation of floating upward in space.

He sees a cloud layer below, about 4,000 feet; he drifts down into it and out of the bottom, now seeing green fields and country-side below moving up toward him. He prepares to land as best he can with one leg, and just manages to avoid hitting a fence by spilling some air out of his chute with both hands at the last second, then hits hard. The fall knocks him unconscious.

The first thing he remembers after hitting the ground is looking up into the eyes of three grey-uniformed German soldiers. They lift him into a waiting car and drive to the hospital in St. Omer. There a doctor and nurse examine him. The doctor is surprised

to find what he assumes to be a one-legged pilot. Bader's pants still cover his other artificial (left) leg. The doctor removes Bader's pants and sees the second artificial leg. Expressing astonishment, he remarks that he has heard about Bader from German pilots, and knows exactly who he is.

When the doctor had finished his examination, Bader was given soup by a nurse and left to sleep, though each time he moved his head there was a sharp pain under his heart—broken ribs. As the hours wore on and it became dark, Bader realized with agony that tonight he was to have taken Thelma, his wife, dancing. Now she might not know he's still alive. His worry was quite logical; none of his comrades saw him go down. Back at Tangmere, they could only guess whether he had survived to become a prisoner or fallen in the battle.

Next morning Bader asked a visiting Luftwaffe officer to get word, somehow, to his wife that he was alive. The officer promised to do what he could. Bader was also bold enough to ask that a message be sent to the RAF asking his comrades to drop another artificial leg so that he could walk again. The German, taken aback by the novelty of such an original request, said he would also see if anything could be done about that. He promised to send someone to the scene of the crash of Bader's Spitfire to retrieve his right leg. That, in fact, was done and Galland's carpenters managed to straighten it out. The RAF, as requested, was messaged on the international Red Cross band, saying if a new leg was dropped for Bader, the delivery aircraft would not be fired on.

There are two versions of how that worked out. Galland, who had something to do with several gestures of chivalry to Bader, believes the RAF dropped the leg in a box under a parachute during a bomber attack. But Bader disputed this. He told me:

"The RAF didn't bomb the field when they dropped the new leg. Air Vice Marshal Sholto-Douglas mentions that in his book. It's an honest mistake."

When Bader had somewhat recovered, but was still at the hospital, Galland sent a staff car and three officers to bring him to JG 26 headquarters to a tea in his honor. Bader was, according to Galland, obviously surprised and impressed with the lavishness of the reception. Galland offered to show him around the headquarters and field. Bader accepted with pleasure. They visited various installations and drove out to one of the 109s camouflaged on the edge of the field. The whole field was extremely well camouflaged.

Bader was allowed to climb up into the cockpit. While inside, he asked Galland, with a smile, if he could take the fighter up for just one circle of the field! Galland says he was tempted but told Bader if he decided not to come back, he would have to take off after him. He thought it best they didn't shoot at each other any more.

Bader thought for many years one of the Germans standing on the wing of the 109 that day had a pistol in his hand. He once pointed out to me what he took to be a pistol in a photograph of the incident taken by a German photographer. On the other hand, Galland assured me there was no pistol in the officer's hand. Galland's account of Bader at JG 26 headquarters that day differs from Bader's in other details. Galland recalls that Bader was extremely interested in meeting the pilot who had shot him down, and Galland recalls Bader having said that pieces of his aircraft were flying off at one point. He says further that Bader didn't like the thought that perhaps one of the Luftwaffe's noncom pilots might have been his successful adversary. Because they didn't know who had shot Bader down (if someone had), Galland and fellow pilots selected a fine-looking, fair-haired officer and presented him to Bader as the man who had bested him. He says Bader was delighted to meet him and warmly shook his hand.

On this point also, Bader's memory is different.

"I didn't say that about an under-officer, feeling one shouldn't have shot me down. That's not me. It's an honest mistake. Also, I didn't ever say, as has been attributed to me [by Galland] that war is a game of cricket. That's also an honest mistake. Maybe they thought I did."

What is certain is that Bader was given special attention and special consideration by the Luftwaffe, and when Galland told Marshal Göring about Bader's visit, even the Reichmarshal spoke an admiring word for the fallen pilot's spirit. When, at the end of the war, Bader confronted Galland as a captive, he didn't reciprocate on an equal basis, though he did offer Galland a box of cigars! Galland felt, however, that since Germany had surrendered unconditionally and the war was over, it was time, perhaps, for more reciprocative consideration.

I recall these differing memories of two great aces who became friends not for purposes of proving one version or the other. These two legendary fighter pilots and mutual admirers simply had different memories. Their different stories of their meeting in France in 1941 might partly reflect Bader's resentment of Hitler and Nazi Germany. Hitler had been responsible for the war, in which Bader

had spent hard years in Colditz and other prisoner-of-war camps. This left its mark. Yet when I last visited Bader, in the 1980s, he had just attended a Colditz reunion and the ex-prisoners had invited one of the German officers who ran the camp to attend. I asked him why. "Because he was a first-rate chap," Bader answered, "and we all liked him."

Bader retained an unyielding determination throughout the war, even in prison camps. Before being sent east from France, after his capture, he managed his first escape from the hospital at St. Omer by tying several sheets together and going out the window. He had made contact with a friendly Frenchman through a nurse, and actually managed to elude his pursuers for several days, being captured only at the last minute because of an informer. Several more times he attempted escape from various camps, until German authorities sent him to a maximum security prison, Colditz. Even there he planned escapes and fueled protest movements.

When brought back to England in 1945, Bader was welcomed as a hero and that year was invited to lead the fly-past of fighters on Battle of Britain Day before the King and an assembly of distinguished officials. In 1956—he had resigned his commission and gone back to work for Shell Oil, whom he had begun working for in the 1930s after being discharged, legless, from the RAF—he was awarded a C.B.E. In 1976 he was knighted. His first wife, Thelma, whom he married shortly after being discharged in the early 1930s, died in 1972. He and his second wife, Joan, lived west of London in a comfortable country house with four dogs, two cats, and a few geese until his death in 1982. Until 1979, Bader drove the same impressive convertible, a black Alvis, which he had completely restored in 1977. It was, in a sense, his trademark, and it seemed to help hold back time, for in it Bader could easily be visualized in the 1940s, 1950s, or 1960s.

In it he carried his golf clubs and until his death he shot in the eighties or below. However, in 1979, he was involved in a wreck, in which the Alvis was damaged beyond repair. The cost of rebuilding it was too great. Somehow, it didn't seem right in his last three years that Bader, with short pipe and Foursquare tobacco aroma, wasn't driving that venerable Alvis. He drove it until the last as if he were in a dogfight. He drove me only once to his country place flashing through afternoon traffic—in and out at a fearful, grim, determined pace. I asked why he was pushing so. He didn't admit the pace was anything but the normal approach to the road.

Another time when he was visiting me in Sarasota, Florida, in the 1970s, he accepted my offer of a Mark X Jaguar. The first day he "piloted" it, my wife accompanied the Baders. She arrived home genuinely frightened, reporting that they had been zipping in and out of lanes at a terrifying pace, coming within inches of "adversaries." And so he lived life to the end with enthusiasm and vigor. In recent years he was a member of the Civil Aeronautics Commission and was until his death in wide demand as a speaker and writer.

He was accepted among pilots and the British population as the personification of the World War II fighter pilot, exhibiting that defiant spirit of the pilots who saved Britain from defeat in 1940. Bader, more than any other man, was a nostalgic individual memorial of those legendary days in the eyes of millions of Englishmen.

In my travels through various countries I have regularly asked various citizens about their country's most successful wartime fighter aces. In Germany the average citizen now knows the names Galland, Molders, Rudel, and, in more recent years, Erich Hartmann, Gunther Rall, Gerd Barkhorn, etc. In England, the common man knows the story of Douglas Bader. No matter where one is— in a cab, on an elevator, or in a department store—if the listener is asked about Douglas Bader, invariably the answer will be, "Oh yes, what a wonderful man," or words to that effect. Millions genuinely grieved when a heart attack took him from them suddenly in 1982.

The English, of course, are a people who remember, who are loyal to traditions and heroic leaders. So too are the Germans, but World War II in Germany is beclouded by the memory of Naziism there; that works to repress the admiration that otherwise would enshroud the great aces of the Luftwaffe in the Second World War. In the United States, a melting pot community, there's relatively less knowledge, pride, and memory about the great pilots of the Army and Navy fighter forces in World War II. Ask the average taxi driver, store clerk, or fellow citizen if he or she knows who the nation's leading ace of that war was, and the answer might be: "What's an ace?"

Bader is remembered in England partly, of course, because he was a handicapped maverick, an activist always fighting vigorously and with great charm for his view or his tactics. He marveled at the obsolete RAF instructions for fighter pilots in the opening days of the war. "It's amazing, really, how we RAF fighter pilots were told to conduct an attack on enemy aircraft at the beginning of the war. There were all these studies and the most absurd, involved plans for making a firing pass. Why hadn't they read Ball, Bishop, and McCudden of the First War? They told just how it was done. Why not ask the people who've done it, in other words?"

He was pessimistic in his last days about the trend in the western democracies to appease terrorists and terrorism, saying:

"We're appeasing again. The politicians don't learn the lesson. We're appeasing terrorists and terrorist nations, and sometimes refusing to help our friends who would fight with us if there's another war. The Communists and left-of-center nations today often dominate the United Nations. We've got to stop appeasing and be willing to take a firm position in our own interest and hold it, to support our friends."

At his death, Bader, at 72, was older than most World War II fighter pilots. But he had kept himself in good physical condition and acted and looked much younger than many who were years his junior. He drank no alcohol, ate sensibly, and exercised regularly. Thus his death was a shock.

There's little doubt that as a popular national hero, he ranks with Baron von Richthofen of World War I as a legend. The world is a less interesting place since his passing because of the power and charisma of his personality. His memory is hard to forget.

Chapter 4

Rüdel's Greatest Day

One of history's great individual efforts in military combat was that of Hans Ulrich Rüdel, the German JU87 Stuka pilot of World War II. Many experts and air historians believe Rüdel's record unequalled by anyother pilot in any war. He flew the slow Stuka dive-bomber throughout the 1939-45 war. Yet he became an ace (the only Stuka ace), having downed seven opponents in the air, some of them in fighters which enjoyed decided performance advantages over Rüdel and his rear gunner in their Stuka. By all odds, they should have shot him down. This feat was, however, a minor byproduct of stupendous achievements by the "Eagle of the East Front" in 2530 missions during World War II! Rüdel destroyed 519 tanks, sank three warships and 90 lesser craft, and demolished flak guns, armored cars, and other mobile equipment by the thousands.

Those incredible accomplishments were recognized; Rüdel was the most highly decorated German combatant in World War II. After he had received all his country's highest decorations, a special one was designed solely for him, as the first soldier of Germany's armed forces. He received it on January 1st, 1945, in the West, during Hitler's last, brief trip to that front during the Ardennes offensive. Hitler invited Rüdel to his headquarters for the presentation. If one studies the pictures of that event, at a time when all knowledgable military men knew Germany's armies were doomed (and long after Hitler's health had begun to fail), the dictator's eyes and expression still reflect admiration and intensity. Herman Göring, chief of the Luftwaffe, looks on with a beaten, benevolent stare of adulation. In these pictures also are Colonel General Jodl, Field Marshal Keitel, and Grand Admiral Doenitz—in other words, the top command of the German armed forces. Of the five high-ranking Germans admiring Rüdel that New Year's Day 1945, two were to be hung. Göring committed suicide. Hitler shot himself as Berlin fell to oncoming Russian hordes. Doenitz was sentenced (about which there was considerable controversy) to 10 years as a war criminal—to live on until the late 1970s. Rüdel continued flying against Hitler's wishes and was badly wounded near the end by Russian antiaircraft fire, losing a leg. He again resumed combat flying and fought to the end.

To some degree, Rüdel is the counterpart to the late legend of the RAF, Sir Douglas Bader, of the preceding chapter. Bader lost both legs before the war and managed to reenter the RAF and become one of his country's great fighter pilots, though his career was short. Rüdel also refused to let a physical handicap end an active physical life.

Like Bader, he was the son of a clergyman, and like Bader, he abstained from alcoholic drink. Like Bader, he was stocky and powerfully built, though not tall. Both were determined and certain in their views (which often landed both in trouble). Many think Rüdel was insufficiently repentant. But we are not analyzing political views. Rüdel was only 23 at the outbreak of the war, an age at which he had no political responsibility or participation. (He was never a member of the Nazi party). That's one of the niceties for air historians writing about fighter pilots—they were invariably youngsters who did their duty for their country when ordered to or drafted. No atrocity connotation attaches to them.

Judging Rüdel as a pilot by his record in the air, one is much impressed. To really comprehend the magnitude of his effort, however, is difficult. If one keeps in mind that the world's all-time top-scoring fighter pilot, Erich Hartmann, flew more than 1400 missions during the war, achieving 352 victories in air combat, and compares this with Rüdel's 2530 missions, the picture begins. This in no way demeans the Hartmann accomplishment, nor that of other fighter pilots who flew a very large number of missions. It merely shows what Rüdel, by comparison, did. When one compares the number of missions flown by Rüdel with the number flown by the most successful British and American pilots, the difference is even more striking. British and American pilots who flew several hundred missions were looked upon as veteran-veterans, and official policy was to withdraw such pilots from combat after a fixed number of missions, or so many combat hours.

The Luftwaffe didn't have the manpower for such a policy. That produced surprising results. It helped create a pilot elite in the Luftwaffe unmatched throughout the world in any other air force. Those experts who survived combat duty year after year became better and better until they were the unique air professionals of the Second World War. Pilots like Rüdel, Hartmann, Galland, Barkhorn, Rall, Steinhoff, Schroer, etc., attained a degree of flying skill, potency, and survivability in the air few attained. They worked harder and longer at it. They gained more experience and practice, and benefited from it. That helps explain the high scores and astounding accomplishments of German pilots in World War II.

Until his death in 1983, Rüdel never changed his original view that if Germany had not attacked Russia, Russia would, by 1943, have attacked Germany. He believed Hitler knew this and appreciated the danger of Communism as a world threat better than western statesmen. When he agreed with this strategic concept of Hitler, he often came under fire from those repulsed at any suggestion Hitler was right in *anything*—in view of atrocities committed by the Nazi regime. On the other hand, it requires courage today to defend Hitler's 1941 military strategy and, in effect, Hitler's decision to attack Russia—at a time when the popular tone is to suggest Hitler was invariably an amateur bungler in military affairs. Rüdel was consistent in his belief, which reflects his character, bulldog determination, and self-confidence, right or wrong.

In his own book, published in 1952 by Euphorion and later by Corgi in England, Rüdel asked his mother and father to write forewords. Retired Minister of Christ Johannes Rüdel wrote about his famous son that the old soldierly virtues of loyalty and obedience determined his whole life. His mother wrote, for the comfort of other mothers, that Hans-Ulrich had been a delicate and nervous child, weighing only five and three-quarter pounds at birth. Until he was 12 years old, she said, she had to hold Uli's hand during a thunderstorm. She was happy he had been granted a carefree youth. Rüdel utilized as the theme of his book, from his father's foreword, the maxim: "Only he is lost who gives himself up for lost." A third foreword for the English book was written by Douglas Bader, who until his death played 80-stroke golf on two artificial legs. Bader met Rüdel only briefly after the war, when he tried, with others, to obtain an artificial limb for him. He found in Rüdel's life much that he admired. While he disagreed with Rüdel's political thoughts, he rated him a "gallant chap."

Rüdel was born in 1916 in Konradswaldau, in Silesia. At age 20, in 1936, after a normal youth during which he excelled in sports, he made the decision to join the new Luftwaffe. The next year he began air training and in 1938 joined Gruppe I of Stuka Geschwader 168 near Graz. On January 1st, 1939, the year war was to begin, he was commissioned a lieutenant, and went into action in Poland that fall. From then until the end of the war, with but few periods of rest and inactivity, he was on active service. Not until the last months of the war was he to be seriously wounded, losing a leg and partial use of his right arm. He was back in action before he was completely healed.

Like no other German soldier or aviator, Rüdel was of special interest to all top Nazis, even as their world collapsed in 1945. Shot down and badly wounded in February 1945, Hitler ordered him brought to his bunker in Berlin. There not only Hitler but Göring, Goebbels, and many others paid him visits. Hitler, on several occasions before and after, ordered him to stop flying. Rüdel disobeyed. Hitler called him back to Berlin, soon after he rejoined his command at the front, to offer him a non-flying position as head of all German jet fighters. He refused the offer. Göring called him back a few days later to repeat the order. Rüdel again declined. Hitler called him back from the front once again, in another effort to get him to take the new post. Rüdel explained that the military situation (April 1945) was such that even if they assembled the 180 ME 262s said to be available, the Allies would quickly bomb the few major airfields still left in German hands from which the jets could fly. Hitler acquiesced again.

This was the last time Rüdel saw Hitler alive, although on the 25th Hitler summoned him to the Chancellery for the last time. Rüdel, leaving at 1:00 A.M. in the early morning of April 28th (his commanding officer had delayed his departure), attempted to land near the Brandenburg Gate on a wide Berlin street, but Russian shellfire was already falling on the thoroughfare. He was instructed to fly to Rechlin. From there (having actually landed at Wittstock and been driven to Rechlin by car), he reached Berlin by telephone, but was told it was too late. Rüdel wanted to attempt a landing in Berlin during the morning in a Stuka, but was ordered to fly back to the Sudetenland and continue to support Field Marshal Schoerner's army, which Hitler was hoping would launch an attack to relieve Berlin. Two days later Hitler was dead.

Rüdel attacked tanks to the end, though the stump of his right leg had not properly healed and flying reopened the wound. In those last months he served for a time near his home town, and he and fellow German pilots saw what happened to the German population as the Red Army overran town after town. They all felt that Germany was the central European bulwark against Communism, as it had been against Asiatics for centuries. They wondered how the democracies of the West could allow the Communists to penetrate into central Europe. It was a naive view by these young German airmen, who didn't realize the extent to which the rest of the world loathed the Nazis, nor did they know of the many atrocities that had been committed. Rather, they recoiled at the rape and pillage of a civilized western people by a brutish, slavish horde flooding westward, and felt they were fighting Europe's battle, the battle of western civilization. Rüdel believed the threat of Russian aggression today shows that the West should wonder, after all, if a German victory over Russia might have been less disastrous in the long run (except to unfortunate Jews until Hitler passed on) than the surge of Communist expansion that followed Russia's victory—and still threatens so much of the world today.

Although I had written four books about aerial combat in the Second World War, they had all been about fighter aces. I didn't realize Rüdel was an ace, but decided to pay him a visit. In September 1978, I journeyed to Rüdel's home near Kufstein. It's a Bavarian-style, balconied, white-brown, mortar-and-wood, compact two-story house. Ursula, his wife, 31, was born near Hanover two years after the war ended. She opened the door downstairs and led me up to a living room above. It looked out over the valley, behind which ranged the Kaiser Mountains. A red oriental rug set the tone; on it is a sofa behind a coffee table, enabling one to look out and down over the valley, toward Wörgl. Among the walnut chairs and furniture is a cabinet filled with models of the various Stukas—three shelves of them, 15 or 20 models in all. Rüdel had stood in front of his chair to greet me with left hand. His right, partly immobile, he held at his waist. His hair was whitish, at 62, but still full, as it was when blond during the war years. His eyes were brown-amber and he sported a deep tan. He was still a determined, forceful, confident personality. Ursula—and they had then been married only a short time—is trim and attractive, with brown hair and happy eyes. She wears a single gold band on the ring finger of her right hand. Obviously they were very much in love, the old eagle and his young wife, 33 years after the end of World War II.

While the autobahn out beyond in the valley below bustled with traffic, sailplanes lazily banked in a blue sky over the Kaiser Mountains. We turned back the pages of memories until day turned to night and the lights of the airport in the valley from the vehicular parade on the Innsbruck-Munich autobahn sparkled brightly. A full moon then rose over the Kaiser Mountains—truly a nostalgic setting for historic reminiscing.

Shortly after we began, I asked Rüdel if he could pinpoint a single mission—of his more than 2500—during which enemy aircraft fire was at its most intense. He thought for a moment. He answered positively; one mission above all others stood out in his mind. As he told me about it, my thoughts periodically flashed back to the glory years of the man in front of me, looking back to that fateful time for Germany. Rüdel thought that time was the world's last opportunity to kill Communism. And his military career was to be in the East, trying his best to do just that.

Hitler, of course, confidently believed he could crush Russia in one great campaign. The late highly-regarded Field Marshal Erich von Manstein laments in *Verlorene Siege* (Athenaeum-Verlag, Bonn, 1955) this fateful underestimation of Russian military strength and the tenacity of Russian soldiers. So too did Reinhard Gehlen warn Hitler that he was underestimating Russian military strength. Hitler, that summer of 1941, tried in vain to persuade the Japanese to attack Russia simultaneously in the Far East—as if he might have begun to harbor a doubt or felt a need for insurance. The Japanese refused his suggested strategy and instead attacked southward five months later.

Another factor that figured in the outcome of the greatest land campaign in history is often overlooked, even in brilliant studies such as Von Manstein's because the facts were not revealed until the mid 1970's. It was the critical help Russian leaders received from Ultra in Britain. Hitler's secret military orders were often decoded from the summer of 1940 onward, and while the Russians weren't let in on the specifics of the greatest intelligence coup of the war, they were periodically warned and informed of German military intentions. From the German point of view, the climax of the awful cost of this handicap came in the East in July 1943. The last great German offensive (Citadel) bled itself white against masses of forewarned Russian antitank armor, artillery, and tanks carefully placed in the path of this expected two-pronged offensive. Western intelligence had warned the Russians exactly where and when Germany's newly assembled and improved panzer forces would strike.

But all this was not anticipated on that summer day of June 22nd, 1941, when 200 German and allied divisions began an attack on Russia with great initial success. The onslaught was carried out by three army groups. The northern army group, with which Rüdel was soon to be involved, aimed to destroy Russian forces in the Baltic countries and advance against Leningrad. It was under command of Field Marshal Ritter von Leeb. Striking advances and great victories were won, one after another. The critical initial advance was probably that by Manstein's 56th Panzer Corps, which raced 185 miles into enemy territory in four days to capture the bridges at Dvinsk, in Latvia, opening the road to Leningrad, 300 miles northward.

The advance in the north slowed after that, beset by different views on priorities between Hitler and the Army High Command (OKW) because of different strategic goals. The OKW sought a decision on the central front, and the capture of Moscow. Hitler initially favored a strategy of victories first on the two wings, by the northern and southern army groups, and then attention to Moscow. The 56th Panzer Corps was halted on the 26th of June, while the rest of the advancing army caught up. After this pause, which allowed the Russians time to organize defenses, the advance was never again as rapid. In addition, northern panzer forces were not concentrated in an all-out drive on Leningrad. Nevertheless, by the middle of August, Luga, an important city and military training area 200 miles further northward, had been taken—the Northern Army Group was only 100 miles from Leningrad. (During this period, interestingly, von Manstein, when visited by General Freidrich von Paulus from OKW, of later Stalingrad fame, suggested that northern panzer forces there be withdrawn and allocated to the offensive against Moscow. Hitler thereupon decided to starve Leningrad into submission. Early in September, strong panzer and motorized forces were transferred to the central front.)

The fighting to capture Luga had been intense; it lies directly on the road to Leningrad, with airfields and other vital military facilities in its vicinity. One of the airfields adjoins Tyrkowo, to the south.

In September, Lieutenant Rüdel's 3rd Stuka Squadron of the Immelman Geschwader was posted there to operate against Leningrad and the Moscow-Leningrad supply route. Rüdel had gotten into combat only recently by flying a Stuka to his squadron, unordered to do so, after having refused combat duty in Greece and Crete. Commanders had found him overeager. Upon arrival at Tyrkowo, he gained limited combat experience, some of it on the Smolensk-Moscow central front. But he and other 3rd Squadron Stuka pilots were soon flying several sorties daily. By September 9th, round-the-clock bombing of Leningrad had begun.

On the 16th, pilots were informed that Russian naval units in the Gulf of Finland, to the north, were hampering German land forces with intense naval gunfire. The Russian fleet was based at Kronstadt, 12 miles west of Leningrad in the gulf; it included at the time two battleships, four or five cruisers, and a large number of destroyers. The Stukas were to prepare to attack the fleet, but meanwhile were to wait for the arrival of delayed-action 1,000-kilo bombs, which could penetrate the deck armor of the big ships.

Several days later, before the special bombs have arrived, an attack is ordered because of especially favorable circumstances. Rüdel takes part. Thirty aircraft in all attack (normal wing strength is 80 but losses have been very heavy). When they arrive over the fleet, Rüdel is the first to sight the battleship "Marat." He and his flight leader (Lt. Ernst-Siegfried Steen) dive-bomb the big ship amidst intense flak. Steen misses. Rüdel puts a 500-kilo bomb on the afterdeck. He observes fires raging on deck but can't accurately estimate the extent of the damage. But he knows a 500-kilo bomb won't sink such a ship.

On a sortie some days later, Rüdel again demonstrates the flying skill that will eventually make him Germany's most highly decorated officer. A hit with a 500-kilo bomb from Rüdel's Stuka sinks a Russian cruiser in minutes! These attacks are met with such concentrated flak that the nerves of the reduced number of pilots at Tyrkowo became strained. September brings blue-sky days, when Stukas have little cloud cover from which to dive on—and surprise—heavily-gunned naval targets. Daily, however, they fly to Kronstadt or Oranienbaum or Peterhof, or to all three. Daily, they are subjected to the heaviest concentrations of Russian antiaircraft fire.

Unknown to Rüdel and other Stuka pilots, Hitler is now turning his attention to Moscow (after much delay). Though from middle September, German tank crews have been able to see the gold spires of the Russian admiralty building in Leningrad, from the south, northern tank forces are now needed on the central front for the long-delayed drive on Moscow. Leningrad, with the capture of Petrokrepost, has been cut off and is being bombarded by 240-millimeter guns. The city and the four million people crowded into it are to be starved into submission. The Russian Baltic fleet is to be destroyed by the Luftwaffe's Stukas.

The sky on the morning of September 23rd, 1941, for a change is cloudy and cold over the flat, grass airfield at Tyrkowo. There is morning fog.

On this day the first hoar frost of the fall occurred in northern Russia, and farther south rain, and cold chilled German troops. At Tyrkowo, Rüdel emerges from a two-man tent and dresses, in darkness, in Luftwaffe blue pants and blouse. He eats quickly and prepares to fly, spirit soaring. The much-awaited 1,000-kilo bombs have arrived two days before. The day before, Luftwaffe reconnaissance aircraft sighted battleships *Marat* and *October Revolution* in Kronstadt harbor, along with other Russian warships. Rüdel surmises that *Marat* is being repaired after the bomb damage he had inflicted a week earlier. This is the day, he and his flight commander Steen agree, they will complete the job and finish her off.

Only 18 Stukas are ready for operations—many more would be available if the Geschwader were at full strength. With helmet, earphones and flying glasses, Rüdel is soon standing beside his big green-brown-tan Ju 87 Stuka, looking up into a sky of low cloud and fog. The 45-foot wingspan of the dive bomber—developed from a concept pioneered in the U.S. Navy—dwarfs Rüdel and his gunner, Scharnovski. It's 8:00 A.M. and because of the fog, they're told not to fly the first scheduled mission of the day. An hour passes before the weather improves enough for 3rd Squadron to take off. Rüdel is to fly Commander Steen's wing. Big three-blade props now start spinning as the 1400-horsepower Jumo 211 D engines thunder into life. Ground crews scatter and wave and the Stukas taxi carefully to takeoff position, the big bombs between landing gear struts, directly below the pilot.

Dust gusts backward, the countryside reverberates for miles around, and the tan straw-grass lies flat as the Stukas roar downfield at full throttle and lift off from Tyrkowo. They soon climb into low cloud, speed 200 km per hour, in close formation. Soon 3rd Squadron is over a layer of white cumulus, still climbing, compass heading due north. The ship-targets are 100 miles away. The Stuka was designed to carry 750-kilo heavy bombs. But today's heavier bombs are for the battleships. Range today is no problem;

the Stuka can reach targets more distant than Russia's Baltic fleet, which should be sighted in less than an hour.

Tension and excitement increase as the sea ahead draws closer. Clouds thin out as 3rd Squadron reaches 7,000 feet, 8,000, then 9,000. Steen now assumes level flight, the bombers flying a straight northward course. The blue-green Gulf of Finland, eastern tip of the Baltic Sea, appears. Fighters—ME 109s—converge on the target. Then enemy fighters are called in and some begin passes on the slow bombers. Steen and Rüdel manage to hold course; enemy fighters don't single them out for attack. The Stukas cross the shoreline below. Heavy flak rises and fills the sky all around with black and white puffs—shore and naval guns! Kronstadt harbor comes in view 10 miles ahead, the largest naval base of Russia's Baltic Fleet (built up over many years on this formerly Finnish island guarding the entrance to Leningrad).

Rüdel has never seen such heavy flak. The clouds that would protect the attackers have disappeared. The roar of engines and flak bursts is constant. The four minutes of the run-in are thus the most nerve-wracking. Finally, Steen and Rüdel both catch sight of the *Marat*, below and ahead. She's at the end of a twin pier, two smaller vessels at her side, near the stern.

"Konig One" breaks radio silence to order the dive—that's Steen. Rüdel, "Konig Two," acknowledges and prepares to follow his leader down, just behind him. The Stukas spread out over the sky at varying altitudes to complicate the aiming of gunners below. Guns of the 23,000-ton *Marat* haven't yet opened fire on these aerial harbingers of death closing from above, though flak remains heavy.

Rüdel sees a heavy cruiser behind *Marat*, the *Kirov*, just before they dive. He can read Steen's stern expression as the leader concentrates on the bigger target below and wings over down toward the battleship. Rüdel follows just behind. They soon accelerate to 450 km and the wind howls by the canopy as the Stukas remain pointed downward at 80 degrees, an extreme diving angle.

Steen's aircraft is diving faster, pulling away! Rüdel can't understand why. He began the dive only five meters astern, but is now far behind and dropping back. To gain speed, he quickly retracts flaps, assuming Steen must have done this. Rüdel's speed builds . . . 500 km, 550 km, 600 km! Too much! He finds himself closing Steen and pushes his stick forward to steepen his dive to avoid chewing off the tail of his commander's Stuka. Keeping an eye on the *Marat* below and Steen's Stuka, Rüdel is totally and almost desperately occupied . . . he's dangerously close . . . can see just ahead the terrified expression on the face of Steen's gunner, W. O. Lehmann. He'll smash into Steen's tail and rudder if he doesn't act. A hard push forward on the stick, then right past and below, he dives almost straight down, near 90 degrees, behind and below his leader. (Unknown to Rüdel, Steen had not retracted flaps; he had used throttle to increase speed.)

The *Marat* now begins to fill his sight, growing bigger and bigger as he hurtles straight at her at 600 km. He can see sailors below racing back and forth on deck with ammunition . . . the ship grows even bigger . . . dangerously near. He must quickly release his bomb and pull out. Already he's too low, and he quickly presses the bomb release, then just as quickly hauls the stick back with all his strength. The pullout started at only 300 meters. Blood drains from his head and he fights desperately to prevent the mushing Stuka from crashing into the sea. Slowly, it seems, the nose pulls up across the water toward the horizon. Rüdel and Scharnovski reach the bottom of their diving arc only about five meters above the surface, blacked out. Scharnovski, behind, had had the ride of his life—wondering if they could pull out in time.

Rüdel thunders over the harbor's surface and a few lesser ships and heads for the Russian shoreline 10 miles to the south. Scharnovski shouts: "She's blowing up, sir!" Facing rearward behind him, his gunner can see the explosion that wracks *Marat*. A column of smoke rises hundreds of meters into the air. Rüdel banks slightly to have a look. The big ship appears mortally wounded . . . Rüdel's bomb hit the magazine, producing a tremendous explosion. Over the radio congratulations come from all sides; even the Geschwader Commander congratulates him. Excitement and exhilaration swell up within, and just then a voice comes from behind—Scharnovski: "Two Russian fighters closing!"

Rüdel drops to the surface, flying only a few meters over the water, so low he's on the same level as Russian gunners on concrete antiaircraft gun platforms just above the water. Other Stukas are still attacking the Russian ships. He's jinking constantly to avoid the fire of Russian gunners who swing antiaircraft guns on target frantically as he roars by on their level. They reach shore after an ordeal skimming the waves and cross inland. Are they safe? Have they escaped the enemy fighters? Scharnovski answers over the intercom: "Rata behind us!" Rüdel looks back . . . there he is . . . close. He wildly stomps on one rudder pedal and then the other to throw the Russian fighter's aim off, meanwhile shouting frantically to Scharnovski to open fire with his 7.9mm machine gun. Scharnovski doesn't fire. Rüdel repeats his order, furious. Still Scharnovski doesn't open fire. Rüdel threatens to put him under arrest, still jinking and staying just over the treetops, desperate, for the Russian fighter is much faster and more heavily armed. He fears it's only a matter of time. Rüdel now sees tracers passing to the side. Scharnovski's voice: "ME109 behind the Rata!" Hope! Until the German fighter finally sends the Rata flaming it seems an eternity. But then the Rata crashes; they watch the triumphant German fighter pilot fly past in a victory salute.

Slowly, after that, Rüdel gains altitude. He flies all the way back to Tyrkowo, however, at low altitude, elated but constantly scanning the sky behind. He's home before most of the others, aglow with the pride of victory. After he lands it's still mid-day. Other Stukas land. A parade is ordered to celebrate the successful attack. The Wing Commander telephones and asks who dropped the bomb that blew up the *Marat*. But the celebration is cut short. A call from wing—the Stukas are to attack again, immediately. The target this time is *Kirov*, behind doomed *Marat*.

Pilots, instantly grim again, once more hurriedly prepare to take off. Rüdel and Scharnovski are among them, after refueling and rearming with the heavy bomb. But fate now prevents Rüdel from flying this second mission. Steen, who had struck a hole while landing, damaging his aircraft, had borrowed another from another flight. He damages the landing gear of that one, too. He climbs out, runs over, and jumps up on Rüdel's wing, apologizing but ordering him out. He commandeers Rüdel's aircraft, and will take Scharanovski with him. Rüdel, keenly disappointed, watches the others take off, grounded, so to speak, after his greatest day in the air.

Less than two hours later 3rd Squadron begins to return. Rüdel waits for his gunner and commander to land. He asks returning pilots, one by one, what happened. They tell him Steen was hit diving on *Kirov*, at 2000 meters. Mortally wounded, he dived straight at the target to the end, his bomb exploding so close the cruiser was severely damaged. *October Revolution* was also damaged on this day, when four attacks in all were made—but not sunk. She lived on until the Stuka Geschwader of the Richthofen Air Fleet was withdrawn from the north and sent to operate on the road to Moscow at the end of the month.

Rüdel had attracted attention in higher circles with his unique successes in the north. He was awarded the Knight's Cross of The Iron Cross. An astonishing career had now begun in earnest. He was to go on to the end of the war, with only brief leaves from the front, to complete a record that almost certainly will never be equalled. Today's radar-aimed and heat-seeking missiles, which require only a few seconds to home in on an enemy aircraft, make it next to impossible for such a record to be duplicated. I thought of this as Rüdel neared the end of his story about that September day so long ago. Ursula was spreading before us on a coffee table peach and cherry cake . . . and cream . . . and offering beer, wine, or cognac (but Rüdel doesn't drink). What a contrast in time and place! "It was the heaviest flak I ever saw in all my combat in the war," Rüdel concluded.

Rüdel was a controversial figure in postwar Germany. He didn't make apologies for Germany's attack on Russia in 1941 and thinks war with Communist Russia was inevitable, that Russia eventually would have attacked Germany. I asked how he viewed Hitler retrospectively, more than 30 years after the end of the war. It was a hard question, for Hitler almost idolized Rüdel and made him Germany's premier war hero. He often ordered him to stop flying, to avoid further risk, etc.

And Hitler, of course, was a master psychologist who could be most charming, reasonable, convincing, and winning. Rüdel doesn't condone atrocities or mass murder, of course, but he points to atrocities committed by the Russians and others in World War II, criticizes aspects of the war crimes trials, etc. Whatever their extent, any by the western allies at least didn't approach in magnitude the shocking mass murders of Jews and eastern peoples by the Nazis.

One must remember, though, that human nature is such that no one likes to admit he has given his all, long risked his life, lost a leg, family members, and close comrades, and seen his native land divided and crushed—all in the name of an evil cause. For most individual German soldiers, sailors and airmen, their cause was Germany's cause, not the Nazi cause, for they were mostly young and fought for their country as duty calls.

Rüdel was married by his father, a Protestant clergyman, during the war. His father and mother, who died in 1952 and 1960, are buried in Bavaria. His son teaches in Dusseldorf. For a family born in what is now a part of Communist Poland, the postwar decades have, of course, been a bitter harvest.

But Rüdel's spirit was undaunted to the end. He was active physically, a strong mountain hiker, swimmer, etc. In 1953, in Argentina, he was the first man ever to reach the summit of a 21,000-foot mountain peak. He still walked and climbed the Alps in his mid-sixties, on one good leg, when I last saw him.

I asked him about that one-of-a-kind medal Hitler had made for him near the end of the war. "It's locked up in a bank in Rosenheim," he said. He estimated its worth at perhaps 30,000 marks. That was in 1978, and considering the rise in the value of precious metals, it may be worth more today. Hitler's genuine fondness and careful attempts to flatter Rüdel and impress him obviously exerted a strong, positive image in his mind. And perhaps Rüdel was more candid than some today who refuse to admit their past feelings about a man responsible for the lives of so many millions. Rüdel gave his all, with remarkable bravery and loyalty, for his country and its leader, throughout the war—and became a national hero. Praised everywhere in the process, accomplishing unprecedented, heroic deeds, rewarded by his country's government, how does one get all this in proper perspective?

Taking leave of the friendly face and sure voice of the Eagle of the Eastern Front—and Ursula—on a starry fall night, I walked back full of thoughts to the hotel, with agreement we would meet next morning. With my companion, Harold Ligon, who had not eaten, I took a table in the hotel dining room. It was late and there were few guests. A group of youngsters from Wörgl or nearby Kufstein was enjoying a Saturday night party. They were about Rüdel's age when he joined the Luftwaffe in 1936.

Over gulasch suppe we watched the happy, joking faces of the young Germans and Austrians and listened to their music. There was an occasional yodel—and soothing Hawaiian music. They were fine-looking young people, carefree, happy, and lighthearted. Did they know who lived 200 meters away, or about his unbelievable military record? Could they ever really comprehend the mood, emotional impact, and flood of influences that inundated Rüdel's generation of young boys and girls in Germany and Austria? Would they understand if that young man of 1936—with only one leg, an immobile right hand, and an indomitable will—told them why he had given his all so enthusiastically for the Germany of 1933-45? Would they, as a group, ever possess the patriotic spirit, sense of purpose and unity—and destiny—their counterparts of the 1930s had shown? Two destinies of different times that night, two hundred meters apart.

I visited Rüdel again three years later in 1981, at Kufstein, across the Bavarian border. Prince Frederick Karl of Prussia and I had lunched with Gerhard Barkhorn in Tegernsee. It was the first meeting of these two war veterans. It was late in the afternoon when, driving from Tegernsee, we reached Rüdel's home.

He was thoroughly tan, without a shirt, on his balcony overlooking the valley and the Kaiser Mountains. We listened again to Rüdel's views on the war, Germany, and his flying career. They were unchanged. We had not come to argue politics so we devoted our time primarily to Germany's present-day plight (division) and what the future might be. Rüdel showed Fritz Karl his many Stuka models and some of his decorations, and we enjoyed the sun on the balcony. I clarified some of the details and observations concerning Rüdel's career and his most famous mission. It was dark when we left and it was very plain that Rüdel and Ursula had found happiness in their charming house near the Thiersee.

In December of 1982, Rüdel and Ursula went hiking through the mountains, as they often did. When he came home, he was feeling badly. Ursula urged him to call the doctor. The doctor advised him to go to the hospital at once. Protesting, Rüdel agreed to do so. The next day Ursula visited him. He was cheerful and feeling better. He was completely lucid and spoke clearly. There was no hint of what was to come. Later that day he suddenly went into a coma. Ursula rushed back to the hospital, but he never recovered. He fought death for days and days before heart and body finally gave in to the inevitable. His death had followed that of Sir Douglas Bader—in many ways his counterpart on the allied side—by three months.

In 1983, publisher David Lindsay and I called on Frau Rüdel to offer condolences. Rüdel's special Mercedes was still there, though Ursula said it was too big and powerful for her and she didn't plan to keep it. Lindsay and I met Ursula's parents, there visiting, and we all drove over the mountains to a restaurant on the other side, overlooking another lake and a most picturesque valley. It was, as fellow publisher Lindsay remarked, a fairy-tale view.

There we heard of Rüdel's last days, the end of a living legend, as the sun shone down on the terrace on which we dined in the Austrian mountains. Until the end Rüdel held to his course, proud to have fought for Germany.

On this same trip we met with Ursula Barkhorn, General Barkhorn's daughter, who had visited me with her parents in 1982, just months before they were killed in an automobile accident. And so it happened that Douglas Bader, Gerhard Barkhorn, and Hans Rüdel all died within a few months of each other. The famous eagles of the Second War were passing on earlier than one had expected, and much history was dying with them.

Of all the pilots of the war, however, Rüdel holds a special place in the estimates of military historians studying the air war. What he did in the air was so incredible he should have been celebrated as another Graf von Luckner. But, as fate would have it, this young pilot of the late 1930s was destined to fly for a Germany led by Adolf Hitler. Only that prevented Rüdel from being the most celebrated flier of the Second World War.

So he died in relative obscurity, though his funeral was nevertheless a major event. A squadron of German fighters passed over his grave just as he was being interred. It was a coincidence, officially. But it also appropriately recognized the final rites of Germany's greatest pilot by those who admired courage. Rüdel would have appreciated the gesture from an air force he had been a part of, in another world, long ago.

Chapter 5

Scramble at Guadalcanal

American armed forces checked the Japanese advance across the Pacific in June 1942 at the battle of Midway. In August, U.S. Marines landed on Japanese-occupied Guadalcanal and began a six-month struggle that finally brought American forces their first major land victory over desperately resisting Japanese land, sea, and air forces.

Guadalcanal is an island in the Solomons few had heard of before the war, and one no American commander would have selected as the site for a decisive military struggle. Yet because of its sudden strategic importance, for many months it was the scene of a critical struggle between the air forces, fleets, and armies of the two countries.

The Solomons are two parallel rows of islands—Choiseul, Santa Isabel, and Malaita, and just below, on a parallel northwest-southeast course, New Georgia, Guadalcanal, and San Cristobal. Toward the northwestern end of the chain is the large island of Bougainville, and then New Britain and New Ireland. Guadalcanal is located northeast of Australia.

Following up sensational war-opening victories, the Japanese had advanced steadily southward and eastward across the Pacific. They established a major base at once-German Rabaul, on New Britain, and New Ireland, and then reached out to the hot jungles of Guadalcanal in June 1942. They landed a small troop contingent and began constructing an airfield. They also disembarked troops at Tulagi, across the channel on nearby Florida Island.

Concerned about a Japanese envelopment of Australia, the American reaction was the first U.S. assault on an enemy base. The initial plan called for the landing of a Marine division on August 1. When it was discovered the Japanese were building an airstrip on Guadalcanal, the task became urgent. Nevertheless, delays postponed the American landing until August 7, which was just in time, since the airstrip would have become operational that month. Quick progress was made by the landing force, outnumbered Japanese retreating into the surrounding jungle.

On August 12, the first U.S. aircraft, a PBY, landed on what was to become Henderson Field (named after Major Lofton R. Henderson, commander of Marine dive bombers at Midway). It brought Lieutenant William S. Sampson. U.S.N., who pronounced the field operational.

Marines had been designated to furnish Henderson's initial fighters. Pilots were to be transported to within flying distance of the field by the carrier *Long Island.* The need for airpower at Guadalcanal had quickly become critical because of a naval disaster at Savo Island. The very day after ground forces went ashore, a Japanese task force steamed southeast down the island chain's "Slot" and surprised the U.S. force screening the landing operation. Sunk were cruisers *Astoria, Quincy, Vincennes,* and *Canberra.* *Chicago* was heavily damaged.

The Savo Island disaster instantly changed the naval balance of power. American forces pulled out; they included a carrier force and its needed fighters. (The Japanese admiral nonetheless missed an inviting opportunity when he turned away after this stunning victory; he was only six miles from still-unloading U.S. transports.)

When American naval forces withdrew, transports dumped their supplies on the beach—as many as possible—and departed also. Those ashore, left to their fate, looked anxiously to air support.

It was slow in arriving. The first Marine squadrons sent to Guadalcanal were VMF 223, commanded by Captain John L. Smith (fighter squadron), and VMSB 232, commanded by Major Richard C. Mangrum (dive bomber squadron). Smith's pilots were inexperienced and he wisely exchanged some of his green fliers for more experienced veterans in a nearby squadron. Because of this and other delays it was not until the afternoon of August 20 that *Long Island*, escorted by cruiser *Helena* and destroyer *Dale*, launched the two Marine squadrons into the wind 200 miles southeast of Guadalcanal. Nineteen Grumman F4F Wildcats and 12 Douglas SBD Dauntless dive bombers headed for Henderson Field. At 5:00 that afternoon, Smith landed the first American fighter on Guadalcanal.

That very night the heaviest land fighting of the campaign to date occurred, and gunfire could be heard by the aviators only 3,000 yards east of Henderson Field. This was the Battle of the Tenaru River, sometimes called the Ilu River, or Alligator Creek. The Marines won handily; the Japanese attacked with only 900 men, having underestimated the strength of the invading American force.

This proved to be the first of a long series of enemy attacks on Henderson Field, and for Smith's fighter pilots a foretaste of most difficult operational conditions and dangers. The military situation deteriorated from August until October, when it reached crisis proportions; pilots and crewmen nevertheless carried out daily attacks against often-superior enemy forces, living in tents on the edge of the field. They had only meager rations (at times, only Japanese rice) and were regularly subjected to enemy strafing, naval bombardment, and shelling from Japanese Army howitzers. Many constantly suffered from the malaria-carrying mosquitoes and from dysentery.

Enduring this ordeal on the ground, they nevertheless shattered the myth of the Zeros' aerial invincibility. For the first time in the war, U.S. fighters intercepting from Henderson Field exacted a heavier toll of attacking Zeros than they themselves suffered.

Flying the F4F Wildcat, the best American-built fighter available—which did not in many performance comparisons equal the Zero—Marine pilots intercepted large invading flights of aircraft from August 21 onward, seldom hesitating to dive into enemy formations outnumbering them substantially. From the military and psychological standpoint, this exerted a positive influence on the ground struggle.

In the October crisis, speculation about American withdrawal began to creep into official conversation; it was Marine air strength based on Guadalcanal that spelled the difference between victory and defeat.

Marine fighters and dive bombers, supplemented by a very small U.S. Army fighter force and by reinforcements of carrier fighters that flew in from time to time as the struggle intensified, produced most of the Japanese air and sea losses in this crisis period.

Had it not been for the efforts of these aggressive U.S. air units, the Japanese could and would have landed heavy troop reinforcements on the western end of Guadalcanal. As it was, the enemy suffered heavy losses in attempts to do so. That the Japanese were unable to reinforce Guadalcanal, even with naval superiority during much of the campaign, proved the key to victory. Although often outnumbered two to one by the enemy's air forces at Rabaul and Buin, Marine pilots achieved and maintained control of Guadalcanal's air throughout these bitter months. That enabled Major General Alexander A. Vandergrift's 1st Marine Division to win the ground struggle.

Captain John Lucien Smith was born and educated in lower school in Lexington, Oklahoma. He attended the University of Oklahoma, graduated in 1936, and joined the Marines. He served two years as an artillery officer, after which he was ordered to Pensacola, Florida, to begin training as a Marine pilot. After pilot training, he flew dive bombers for a time, then was transferred to a fighter squadron that had just been ordered to Wake Island.

However, war intervened. Wake fell before the squadron, on the way, arrived; it was therefore put ashore at Midway. There Smith learned his trade as a fighter pilot. He was ordered to Pearl Harbor before the Battle of Midway and given the task of organizing Marine Fighter Squadron 223, destined to be the first ordered to Guadalcanal.

Soon after landing there on August 20, as the first, he also became the first American to shoot down an enemy Zero. Cruising with a flight of four Wildcats at 8,000 feet over Savo Island, Smith sighted six Zeros 2,000 feet above him. Despite the enemy's advantage, he attacked, and his was the only victory of the day. That interception revealed the presence of American fighters at Henderson Field.

The grim nature of the sustained aerial campaign that followed is reflected in statistics: In less than two months, all but six of Smith's 21 pilots (19 aircraft) became fatalities or casualties. Of the surviving six ordered out of Guadalcanal on October 13, many, including Smith, had been shot down and injured, but had returned to duty.

It is Smith's exciting mission of August 30, nine days after his first victory, with which we are now concerned.

It is 4:30 A.M. when Smith awakes in his tent and pulls on his field shoes and khaki shirt and trousers. Outside, first traces of light are beginning to distinguish green palms on a muggy morning. VMF 223 has been in action nine days. Already six of its original 19 fighters have been lost. The air battle is increasing in intensity

71

as the Japanese react strongly to the arrival of U.S. fighters on Guadalcanal.

After breakfast of coffee and captured Japanese cookies (somewhat similar to vanilla wafers) in the mess tent, he walks outside to his blue-and-white F4F Grumman fighter at the edge of the field, and then warms up the engine. The roar can be heard for miles in the jungle's morning stillness. Leaving the F4F, he makes his way to the Ready Room tent in a coconut grove between the beach and lone runway. It's just past five A.M.

Squadron 223's first orders this morning are to maintain a standby until dawn plus 30 minutes. In the Ready Room, pilots await a radio warning from a network of coast watchers (Australian and native) on the islands to the northwest. In recent days the Japanese have been attacking Henderson Field each morning.

After a time, Smith and other VMF 223 pilots return to their fighters and continue to wait. Thirty minutes past dawn, no message has yet come from the warning system. Pilots gather in the small shack that serves as Operations and settle into a game of cards. The sun rises in the eastern sky to reveal a mass of dark cumulus clouds over the blue-green waters of the Slot and Sealark Channel. There is still no warning at 8:00.

Eight Marine pilots, flying Wildcats, are on duty. A number of Army pilots, some flying slower P-40s, are also available. (Later that same day, the remainder of Marine Air Group 23's flight echelon will arrive, badly-needed additional fighter and dive bomber strength.)

Smith glances intermittently at the clock as he plays. Since scoring the first Marine air kill in the Solomons August 21, he has shot down four more enemy planes to become an ace. He's the first American fighter pilot to achieve five kills at Guadalcanal. An hour passes and it's past 9:00.

The telephone ends the waiting. An excited voice reports a large flight of Zeros "on the way," a "large flight of Betties" following—all at medium height. All pilots, including Army pilots, are ordered to intercept. They bolt from the shack, running toward their aircraft—not a second to lose.

Smith had earlier told his pilots they would rendezvous 10 miles east of Henderson Field. Then, in combat formation with height, they will return to intercept the enemy. As he runs to his fighter, he notices very high banks of cumulus to the north and west. It's clearer in the east. This will allow an orderly join-up, by which time he hopes radar will have picked up the direction of the enemy. (Henderson Field boasts one of the early radar sets; the exact direction of an enemy strike can't be accurately determined, however, until attackers are already at the northwest end of the island—10 minutes away.)

A shotgun shell fires. The Pratt and Whitney engine roars to life. Smith had signaled Corporal Erving Yach, his crew chief, as he sprinted up to the big fighter. Yach is now busy helping him with his harness and gives him spirited words of encouragement. Smith waves him off, applies throttle, and heads for the end of the runway. It's almost 10:00 A.M.

Moments later, the roaring Pratt and Whitney lifts the fully loaded Wildcat off Henderson Field's runway. The stubby Marine fighter skims over the palms heading east. Smith watches as Lieutenant Charles Kendrick, his wingman, and other pilots lift safely off behind him. They follow the eastern heading at maximum climb. Below, Cactus Control (Base Operations) has received no further information. Smith decides to bluff over the radio, which might confuse the enemy as to his strength. He presses the mike button and reports in as the commanding officer of one squadron, then another, and another. The Japanese monitor radio transmissions; this may lead them believe several squadrons of U.S. fighters are forming up over Henderson Field.

Only eight Marine fighters, however, climb into the blue east. The Wildcats reach 10,000 feet. Superchargers of the two-stage engines cut in. Pilots carefully check guns. Each Wildcat carries six .50-caliber Browning machine guns and 1,850 rounds of ammunition—armor-piercing, ball, and tracer. The P-40s, following, are armed with four Brownings or 20-millimeter cannon, though limited by a lower ceiling.

As the Marine fighters continue their climb above 10,000 feet, the P-40s break off, but continue to keep the F4Fs in view. The Army pilots have no oxygen and can't operate much higher than 12,000 feet.

Cactus Control now reports coast watchers have lost the enemy in heavy cumulus clouds to the west. They're sighted again, only to be lost once more. Found again, they're now reported very close to Henderson Field! Smith looks at his altimeter: 15,000 feet. He orders a turn to the west, to intercept the enemy over Henderson Field. The F4Fs wing into a left turn. The P-40s below follow.

Cactus Control radios: "We're pretty sure they're in the area now!" Smith levels off and points his nose straight for Henderson Field, almost due west. But the enemy isn't in sight. He's cruising at 165 knots in scattered clouds that move in from the west. They begin to obstruct vision. At times Smith can't see the Army P-40s below at 12,000 feet. The eight Wildcats approach Henderson Field, the pilots "rubbernecking" to guard against surprise. (While bombers are also expected, fighters will be at a higher altitude; Smith seeks enemy fighters first, since the Zeros are sure to be positioned above, to dive on the Americans attacking the bombers.)

The Wildcats cross directly over Henderson. Still no sight of the enemy! Momentarily, Smith has lost sight of the Army fighters below.

Suddenly a voice comes in loud over the radio receiver: "Zeros over us! Jumping us! We're right north of the field!" Frantically, Smith scans the sky to the north. There they are—22 newly painted black-brown Zeros! They're already making it hot for the lower P-40s. Two parachutes billow in the sky below. Instinctively, Smith banks into a diving right-hand turn, ordering the others to follow, and heads for his outnumbered Army comrades.

The battle is 3,000 feet below, and two surviving P-40s are carrying on a twisting, turning dogfight with the more numerous Zeros. Smith orders each Marine pilot to select an enemy fighter. They pick up speed fast as they dive downward and Smith quickly checks the light circle on his fixed gunsight. His first four Wildcats are now well ahead of the second four; he eases back on the stick at better than 300 knots, drops left wing, and banks into a left turn behind one of the four dark Zeros. He can see the red rising-sun ball on its wings, straight ahead; his finger grips the trigger button.

Behind, at great speed, the other three blunt-nosed Wildcats of lead flight curve down on other Zeros in precision flight. The enemy fighters are making over 200 knots, banking slowly left, oblivious of the danger. The F4Fs close in rapidly. The range is down to 900 feet.

Smith closes . . . 800 . . . 700 . . . the enemy's wingspan now fills the sight. Press the trigger button! White smoke streaks back from six guns, the F4F vibrates, and tracers mark a gunnery pattern converging on the Zero ahead. The enemy aircraft sheds pieces and smoke. Smith holds the trigger down until his prop nears the Zero's rudder. Then a flash! A yellow ball of fire fills the sky; the burning fighter wings over, trailing black smoke, and plunges below. Smith pulls up to avoid debris. Victory number six!

So well co-ordinated has been the attack that the other three Wildcat pilots all achieve surprise. Three other Zeros burst into flame and plunge earthward. Four victories for pass one!

The Zeros had overwhelmed the slower U.S. Army fighters and shot many down, and now the second flight of Wildcats takes its revenge. They dive into the remaining Zeros and several trails of dark smoke soon mark the fall of burning aircraft. The enemy, like the P-40s, have received a surprise from above. Zeros now scatter widely.

Smith, checking his rear, has all his pilots in place; all report their victories. The four F4Fs begin a slow climb, seeking Zeros that have scattered, but none come in view. Enemy bombers haven't been sighted, either from the ground or by American fighters. All eyes scan the sky to the northwest; they are expected any second.

Ten o'clock, ahead, a lone speck emerges from a cloud. Smith watches the enlarging object closely until he identifies it. Zero! He pushes the throttle forward, dips his right wing, and with right rudder banks into a turn behind the lone Zero. His wingman and the other two Wildcats follow. Because the Zero had been climbing, his speed is reduced; the Wildcats quickly close the gap.

Smith, eyes on the sight ring, hand on the trigger, watches the wingspan of the Zero grow wider as he rushes up from behind. In seconds he's in range; he presses the firing button and his shells immediately register—fragments of his victim's aircraft fly backward, a veritable shower. The cowling of the Zero glances off Smith's canopy but causes no damage. The Zero emits yellow flame and suddenly blows up in an orange flash. The enemy pilot has no chance. Victory number seven!

Smith now has two victories in less than five minutes. But the Wildcats still haven't located the bombers. Smith radios: "Charge your guns," and points the blunt nose of his F4F north, over the water, to get a general view; he searches the sky for the unsighted bombers. Seeing nothing, the four fighters execute a left turn, then another, which puts them on a southward heading—toward Henderson. And then Smith spots a suspicious object dead ahead.

Twelve o'clock, on collision course, the low-wing silhouette grows larger. Smith, in the lead F4F, points his nose directly at the oncoming bogey and intensely studies the silhouette. At this instant someone yells: "Bandit!" Smith hardly has to change course. He's automatically on a firing pass! The enemy fighter gets bigger and bigger in the sight.

Suddenly light flickers from the Zero's wings—a death message from the enemy pilot! Smith presses the trigger in reply. The two fighters are closing at 500 knots. The F4Fs behind Smith follow, pilots watching; it's the division leader's fight.

The Zero comes on, wing guns still flashing. Smith maintains his fire. Neither loses nerve but the Zero begins to trail smoke. Pieces fly backward and it breaks up under the impact of so many hits. The enemy fighter explodes.

Smith rams the stick forward, diving beneath and through the debris of the enemy fighter. Some of the pieces of this Zero strike the F4F of his wingman, Lieutenant Kendrick, and it leaves a vertical smoke trail as it plunges down toward Henderson Field below. Victory number eight!

The sky is now clear of Zeros, but, Smith's four-plane division is no longer intact. Both his and Lieutenant Kendrick's F4F have been hit by many pieces of his last victim's aircraft, and the flight has been scattered. The clouds are closing in, making joining up difficult. The ceiling is also lowering. (The cloud buildup Smith observed to the west earlier in the day is now moving over Guadalcanal.)

Smith dips his left wing and banks into a spiraling left turn, descending to 9,000, 8,000, 7,000, 6,000 feet. He glances around, looking for Kendrick.

"Kendrick, where are you?" he transmits. "I'm short of fuel, circling the north shore, west of the field," comes the reply. "Wait there. I'll join up and we'll go in to the field together," Smith orders. The lower he descends, the heavier the clouds. Scud is everywhere. Where is Kendrick? He's down to 3,000 feet, 2,000, 1,000! His fuel gauges show an adequate supply; he therefore wonders if Kendrick's tanks are leaking. He's flying east along the north shoreline, now down to 800 feet. Still he doesn't sight Kendrick. He continues east, a few hundred feet above the shore, and left, ahead, detects two single-engined aircraft. One could be Kendrick. But *two*? He banks left at full power, and begins to close. Visibility is poor, so he can't positively identify the aircraft, though he's within 700 feet. Closer . . . 600 feet, 500 feet. Zeros! The two, in close formation, have likely been strafing the field while the air battle raged above it.

Smith grabs the silver-colored handles of his gun chargers and maneuvers the nearest Zero into his sight. He's already within 300 feet! The Zero is only a few hundred feet above ground, and Smith, alone, knows the other enemy pilot ahead will circle behind to get on his tail once he opens fire. And the Zero's turning radius is smaller! Nevertheless, pointing his wing guns at the Zero on the right, Smith once again presses the trigger.

Tracers mark his shells' path toward the victim. The Zero staggers under the weight of the close-in fire. The stricken enemy pilot pulls straight up. Smith yanks back on the stick and maintains fire. The Zero begins to trail flame and smoke; its left wing suddenly lifts and it noses over, to the right, into a dive. The canopy flies off and it goes straight into the ground a few hundred feet below. No parachute—nor was there time to use one.

Remembering the other enemy fighter, Smith S-turns and searches the sky behind, but the other Zero has apparently had enough or is low on fuel and disappears. Victory number nine!

He follows the coast east, not sure of his exact position, and resumes the search for Kendrick. But no plane, friend or foe, is in view. Then, ahead, he recognizes the Lunga River.

He circles it to identify it positively, then sets a homeward course that should lead him to the field. The clouds on all sides have lowered considerably and navigation is difficult. Kendrick surely has returned to the field. In a few minutes, his dead-reckoning navigation proving true, familiar landmarks appear. Ahead, low, beyond the palms . . . Henderson field! Smith's tension eases.

Cactus control reports everyone else down; Smith's stubby fighter descends in a left turn, speed 75 knots on the approach, and settles steadily to touch down. Slowed, canopy back, he turns off the runway and taxies to the edge of the trees.

A group is waiting. Kendrick is down and has told crewmen and pilots about the dogfight. As Smith taxies into the crowd, someone yells above engine noise—how many victories? Smith holds up four fingers and smiles. There's an extra-appreciative smile from Corporal Yach.

Among those waiting is Lieutenant Colonel Ray Scollins, who reports that 14 of the 22 Zeros have been shot down in the battle. The bombers turned back because of foul weather, and only Zeros reached Henderson Field. Four Army P-40s were lost, however, and several other Army fighters badly damaged, but no Marine pilots were lost.

It was an important aerial victory, though more hard fighting lay ahead; Smith would shoot down 19 enemy planes before being recalled from Guadalcanal, then the highest-scoring American air ace.

As leader of the first Marine fighter squadron at Guadalcanal, the first to shatter the myth of the Zero's invincibility, his performance in the summer of 1942 was one of the great individual air combat efforts of World War II, and an inspiration to pilots who followed him. He was awarded the Medal of Honor by a grateful Congress.

The destruction of four Zeros on August 30, when outnumbered, is impressive because Smith was up against the best—highly-trained and select pilots responsible for stunning Japanese victories in the opening phases of the war, and generally superior to many of Japan's late-war pilots. Smith wasn't flying an F6F Hellcat or an F4U Corsair, both of which later enjoyed a wide performance margin over the Zero, but the slower F4F.

The citation accompanying his Medal of Honor reads, in part:

"For conspicuous gallantry and heroic achievement in aerial combat above and beyond the call of duty as Commanding Officer of Marine Fighting Squadron Two Twenty-Three, during operations against enemy Japanese forces in the Solomon Islands Area, August-September, 1942. Repeatedly risking his life in aggressive and daring attacks, Smith led his squadron against a determined force, greatly superior in numbers, personally shooting down sixteen Japanese planes between August 21 and September 15, 1942".

"In spite of the limited combat experience of many of the pilots of this squadron, they achieved the notable record of a total of eight-three enemy aircraft destroyed in this period, mainly attributable to the thorough training under Major Smith and to his intrepid and inspiring leadership."

"His bold tactics and indomitable fighting spirit and the valiant and zealous fortitude of the men of his command not only rendered the enemy's attacks ineffective and costly to them but contributed to the security of our advance base. His loyal and courageous devotion to duty sustain and enhance the finest traditions of the United States Naval Service."

Ironically, Smith had been ordered to leave Midway, just prior to the climactic battle there, to form VMF 223. At the time, he felt he had missed an opportunity to participate in the air war. In three months, however, over the sand and coconut palms of little-heard-of Guadalcanal, he helped as much as any one man to check the Japanese advance southeastward across the Pacific.

Smith survived the war by 27 years. He retired from the Marine Corps as a colonel in 1960 after having served as an aide to the Chief of Naval Operations in the Pentagon. He was employed after his retirement by one of the aviation industry's firms and died unexpectedly in 1972.

Chapter 6

Into the Sea Off Malaita

The most famous American Marine fighter ace to emerge from World War II was probably Joseph Jacob Foss, of Sioux Falls, South Dakota.

Foss shot down more enemy planes in the Pacific than any other Marine and was the first American fighter pilot to equal the record of Captain Eddie Rickenbacker of World War I, credited with 22 enemy aircraft and four balloons. Foss would go on to fame and success after the war, being elected governor of South Dakota and later commissioner of the American Football League.

His combat duty was performed during the most rugged period of air fighting in the Pacific war. He arrived at Guadalcanal on October 9, 1942, just four days before then top-scoring Marine ace Captain John Smith was withdrawn from combat. He succeeded in shooting down 23 aircraft in little more than two months.

As executive officer of Marine Fighter Squadron 121, Foss played a leading role in the crises of October and November 1942, when things were blackest at Guadalcanal. The contribution of VMF 121 in the defense of the island is apparent in statistics. The squadron set the record for the most enemy planes downed in a single tour. It wasn't a cheap accomplishment. Of 40 who arrived with the squadron in October (flying 400 miles from carrier *Long Island* to Henderson Field), half were lost in a hundred days.

Six days after Foss landed, the naval outlook had become so grim that Admiral Chester Nimitz, commanding the Pacific Fleet, admitted: "We are unable to control the sea in the Guadalcanal area." He added: "Thus our supply of positions there will only be done at great expense to us. The situation isn't hopeless, but it's certainly critical."

Nimitz spoke the day after Foss and other pilots had these grim realities brought home to them by shells from Japanese battleships, which boldly stood off shore and bombarded Henderson Field and other installations. That bombardment killed several of the pilots, including Foss's old instructor at the Pensacola Naval Air Station, Ed Miller. U.S. stock sank lower. On the morning of October 15 (after Henderson Field had been shelled for the second successive night, this time by enemy cruisers), Foss and other pilots could see enemy transports lying off Tassafaronga 10 miles distant, unloading Japanese troops and supplies, unhindered.

Samuel Eliot Morison notes in *The Struggle for Guadalcanal* that Secretary of the Navy Frank Knox, usually optimistic, sounded bleak on the 16th. He refused to make a prediction about Guadalcanal, adding, "But every man will give a good account of himself . . . everybody hopes we can hold on."

The situation remained critical through October and into November. The Japanese determined upon one more massive attack.

This last great Japanese effort to land large-scale reinforcements on Guadalcanal was turned back in a series of fierce air and naval battles. They culminated in the Battle of Guadalcanal—perhaps the fiercest single warship engagement of the war.

Coincidental with the Japanese failure to retake Guadalcanal, the fortunes of war were shifting in favor of the Allies in all theaters. This same month, Field Marshal Erwin Rommel's Afrika Korps was beaten at El Alamein. The elite German Sixth Army, which had failed to capture all of Stalingrad, was encircled.

That point in the war in the Pacific, November of 1942, is the period of time with which we are concerned in this chapter.

In their final effort to retake Guadalcanal in November, the Japanese decided to commit an entire division—their largest troop commitment thus far. Because losses in transporting troops to the western tip of Guadalcanal had become excessive (because of U.S. Marine, Army, and Navy airmen), the Japanese resorted to the use of cruisers and destroyers to send in the men and supplies. According to Captain Tameichi Hara, Imperial Japanese Navy, in *Japanese Destroyer Captain*, 20 Japanese destroyers were used between November 2nd and 10th to land the Japanese Army's 38th Division on Guadalcanal. It was the job of U.S. airmen on Guadalcanal to hinder this reinforcement as much as possible, since the U.S. Navy had lost control of the waters in the Guadalcanal area.

Marine pilots at Guadalcanal's Henderson Field were well aware of Japanese ascendency at sea. The American carrier *Hornet* had been sunk October 26th in the Battle of the Santa Cruz Islands. Carrier *Enterprise* had been damaged, as had the new battleship *South Dakota*. As a result, Admiral William Halsey, commanding American naval forces in the area, had fewer capital ships with which to oppose the enemy than he had had several weeks earlier. And Halsey was soon to lose two cruisers and four destroyers, plus other cruisers and destroyers damaged, in the murderous Battle of Guadalcanal on the night of November 12-13.

The Marines were soon aware that enemy reinforcements were landing on the western end of Guadalcanal. General Louis Woods, who had just relieved Major General Roy F. Geiger, commanding the First Marine Air Wing at Henderson Field, was informed as early as the first day, November 2.

When a dive bomber scout reported on November 7 that 11 Japanese warships had been sighted in the biggest reinforcement so far, north of Florida Island, steaming toward Guadalcanal, Geiger and Woods and every Marine airman knew what had to be done.

The enemy's intention was to land this large contingent of troops after dark. An air strike had to be launched immediately so the enemy warships could be bombed before arrival, in daylight.

Colonel William Wallace, commanding Marine Air Group 23, of which VMF 121 was a part, and Major Leonard ("Duke") Davis, commanding officer of VMF 121, brought word of the sighting to the operations hut of Fighter 1 (an auxiliary fighter strip that had been built southeast of Henderson Field). A strike composed of F4F fighters escorting SBD dive bombers was ordered. Foss would lead eight of the Wildcats (F4Fs), each of which would carry 200-pound bombs. The SBDs would carry 500 or 1,000-pounders.

Saturday afternoon, November 7, the sky at Guadalcanal was overcast. Scattered thunderstorms flashed in the area. Foss and his fellow Marine pilots were scrambling "on the double" to take off as soon as possible, hurrying between tents below the tall palms of once cultivated groves. Eight thousand miles away, in the United States, attention that afternoon was turned to football. The 1942 season was coming to a close. Would Illinois, Iowa, or another team win the big Ten championship? Would Georgia or Georgia Tech (both undefeated) win honors in the Southeastern Conference? On this same day in North Africa, however, U.S. and British troops were landing in North Africa.

Foss, a farm boy (his father of Norwegian ancestry, mother Scotch-Irish), had graduated two years earlier from the University of South Dakota. He had excelled on the college boxing and track teams and was an excellent marksman. His father—before he was killed in an automobile accident in 1933—had taught him to shoot.

The young captain had no idea that Saturday afternoon that he was destined to receive the Medal of Honor from President Franklin D. Roosevelt. The task that faced him now was to act as an air decoy—to draw antiaircraft fire while SBD dive bombers dropped their heavier bombs on Japanese warships.

That Saturday most Americans were preparing for parties or dances and complaining about the shortages of gasoline, tires, and sugar. Foss was strapping on a life preserver and flying gear and hurrying out to his well-camouflaged Wildcat, just off the end of the runway at Fighter 1 under the palms. He had first become interested in flying when a squadron of Marine pilots performed an airshow at Sioux Falls in 1932. Fascinated, three years later, in 1935, Foss paid $5 for his first plane ride. In 1937, he paid $65 (on the installment plan) for his first flying lessons in a Taylorcraft.

At the University of South Dakota, he completed a Civil Aeronautics Authority flying course, and when he graduated he had logged a hundred hours. In 1940, soon after World War II began but before the United States became a participant, Foss hitchhiked to Minneapolis to enlist in the Marine Corps Reserve. Of 28 men applying that day, two were accepted. Luckily for the United States, one of them was handsome, dead-serious Joseph Foss.

Now, two years later, Foss was fastening his seat belt in a bluegray Grumman Wildcat on the other side of the world. Number 13, which had been on the side of the fighter, had been changed to 53 by superstitious crewmen.

"Clear!" The prop, engaged, begins to spin and smoke belches from blue stacks. Other props are beginning to turn and soon the Wildcats are taxiing to the end of the runway. Seven SBDs, led by Major Joseph Sailer, Jr., and three TBFs, led by Lieutenant Harold H. Larsen, are carrying the Marine's big bombs. Twenty-three Marine fighters are taking off, as well as eight P-39 fighters.

All pilots have been told that enemy warships must not be allowed to further reinforce Guadalcanal. Earlier in the week, Japanese warships succeeded in landing sizable reinforcements east of U.S. forces. Since the enemy's major strength is on the western tip of the island, they are obviously preparing a double envelopment of the American foothold from both sides. Back in the United States, on this very day, November 7, an Associated Press dispatch reports:

"The Japanese landed troops and reinforcements earlier this week to undertake a squeeze maneuver . . . So far, American positions to the east of the airfield are unchanged . . . The threat has only been checked, rather than eliminated."

Newspapers also told Americans of Japanese attacks in strength the day before. Pilots flying north toward the enemy fleet today will be fighting the battle of the Marines on the ground as surely as they are fighting their own.

Foss roars down the runway and lifts into the gray; it's 2:00 P.M. and soon he and the other Marine fighters are climbing north into an overcast sky, leaving behind the white coral sands of the Guadalcanal coast. According to the latest sighting reports, the Japanese force is due north of Florida Island. Florida Island is soon in view ahead. Foss checks his instruments and charges his guns by pulling up three levers on each side of his seat, letting them snap back. The six .50-caliber machine guns are loaded with armor-piercing, incendiary, and tracer ammunition—tracers in every fifth slot in the belts.

In 20 minutes the Wildcats are at 10,000 feet. Foss scans the sky ahead and regularly looks behind. The SBDs are nearby and all the pilots' eyes are fixed on the surface of blue now visible north of Florida Island.

Thirty minutes after takeoff, the fighters are still climbing. They reach 15,000 feet, still below the overcast. As altitude increases so does vision, and Foss can now see 20 miles. No ships! Florida Island is now far behind; the dive bombers and their fighter escort continue climbing.

Foss sees only empty ocean ahead, right, and left. And then . . . he's the first to see them! Not ships. Left hand on the throttle, right on the stick and still climbing, Foss studies suspicious specks to his right, ahead. Then he pushes the radio transmitter button: "Bandits! Two o'clock."

Other Marine pilots also detect the silhouettes of six float-type Zeros. They're descending, banking from right to left. Foss orders dropping of bombs by eight fighters preparatory to combat, and instinctively banks slightly right. The other fighters stay with the

SBDs, who continue north toward the expected Japanese fleet ahead. He eases his throttle all the way forward, keeping his eyes fixed on the six descending enemy fighters which apparently haven't seen the eight F4Fs approaching rapidly from the south and above.

Foss can now distinguish the dusty, gray-green paint and the red rising suns on their wings. He's closing rapidly, and the enemy, having turned southwest, are oblivious to the approach of death from behind. He pushes the stick forward. The enemy fighters are rapidly descending too—the Wildcats are still undiscovered.

Foss focuses his attention on the Zero farthest left. Other Americans concentrate on other victims. The Zeros continue to cross to the left. Foss banks hard left and realizes he'll have to make something of a deflection shot, turning inside the enemy. Finger on the trigger, a quick glance behind—other Wildcats are fast closing on the other Zeros.

The selected enemy's wingspan grows wider. He must wait until the Zero is well in range. Still the enemy aircraft make no move and now the Zero's wings fill the sight ring. The Wildcat shudders from the recoil of its six guns and tracers streak on a converging course into the Zero on the left. For an instant nothing happens as the .50-caliber shells pummel the stricken aircraft. Foss holds his 70-degree angle. Suddenly the Zero simply disintegrates! Its fuel tanks have exploded, and pieces of debris litter the air. Foss maneuvers to miss them and watches the Zero fall to the sea.

Surprised, he notes a parachute opening below. The pilot survived. Other Wildcats are following Zeros in power dives. Several Zeros fall, burning. Foss recognizes friend "Danny" Doyle chasing a Zero to the deck. As he glances up from his altimeter—7,000 feet—up ahead he now sees the enemy fleet! The ships, leaving white wakes in their paths, are in three parallel lines, with an outer screen warship on each flank. They're steaming due south. Three ships form each column, the center column being slightly ahead of wing columns—a cruiser and 10 destroyers! Visibility is excellent and Foss watches the bombers above flying north to attack. Now he gathers his fighters together by radio and they climb once again for precious altitude.

Only six, however, have joined him and the enemy fleet is not far away. Foss will assemble them and lead them in a simulated bombing approach. Their decoy attack will divide antiaircraft fire between the Wildcats, the SBDs, and the TBFs, the latter armed with torpedoes.

Doyle, who dived to the deck after a Zero, is missing. But the time has come. Foss presses the mike button: "Reverse order—attack!" Reverse order means the seventh plane in formation will attack first, etc.

The warships below begin to spread out as the seventh fighter, at 10,000 feet, peels off right. Foss will be the last of the seven to wing over.

As the Wildcats go into dives, Foss notices a speck in the sky ahead approaching rapidly from the north. Friend or enemy? Foss watches, converging, as the other F4Fs dive on the fleet. Now the silhouette reveals an enemy two-seat floatplane!

Foss banks sharply right and yet the enemy aircraft passes so close he barely misses him. The enemy pilot cuts his throttle; his light aircraft seems to "brake" to a stop. Foss, still turning right, notices a gunner in the rear cockpit aiming straight for 53. It's a shrewd maneuver. The enemy pilot attempted to ram, then chopped his throttle to slow down enough so that his rear gunner could hit Foss in the turn.

Holes rip through the Wildcat's cowling and wings. One round smashes into the canopy, leaving a hole the size of a walnut. Momentarily outmaneuvered by the enemy firing away, Foss absorbs many hits. Recovering, he rams the stick full forward. The Wildcat drops steeply down. His fighting instinct taking over, he then pulls back on the stick and begins a fast climbing approach.

He'll make a belly attack. Steeper and steeper he climbs at full throttle and with the momentum gained in the dive. The enemy fills his sight ring. He must fire quickly; the Wildcat won't hold this climb angle long. Again, tracers prove the .50-calibers perfectly aimed. Shells rip into the exposed belly of the two-seater, and soon smoke begins to trail behind the brownish-green aircraft. Foss's second victim of the day explodes also, and he watches two chutes billow. Victory number two, after a close call! His aircraft is damaged, but how badly? He looks below, now directly over the enemy fleet. Ships are turning in every direction and the F4Fs and other attackers dive on them. One enemy destroyer sends up a column of smoke. The cruiser has also apparently been hit.

Then Foss's thoughts are interrupted. Out to his left, below, something is moving—another enemy two-seater! Foss glances at his engine gauges before attacking, for he wonders about possible engine damage. They are in the green.

He curves into a diving left turn as he eases forward on the throttle and watches the enemy silhouette grow larger in sight ring.

Wind whistles through the hole in the canopy and creates considerable vibration, but Foss concentrates totally on the two-seater, his speed building up in the dive.

He's approaching the lower enemy at a slight angle from left, behind, and this enemy gunner in the rear seat doesn't see him. Closer and closer; he presses the button and for the third time today the six guns roar and the Wildcat shudders and a stream of metal smashes into the enemy ahead.

The large two-seater disintegrates as Foss keeps firing, now at point-blank range. The enemy's wing goes up and there is another explosion. He pulls clear of the remains and smoke. Victory number three!

Down below he can see Wildcats circling, having delivered their attacks on the enemy ships. He points his nose southward and radios VMF 121 fighters his position and orders them to join him. An F4F approaches, shot up badly. He signals him to move in closer and he will escort him home—two cripples. They head south.

As he eyes worsening weather ahead, south, once again his eye warns him in time. Behind, converging fast—fighters! At this instant his engine begins to miss. That rear gunner's shells have taken a toll. With a weak feeling in his stomach, he rams throttle all the way forward. They'll run for it. The engine responds, but unevenly. He looks back: unmistakably Zeroes—many of them, converging fast on the two cripples.

Foss, now desperate, looks to the clouds ahead. The worsening weather may be his only chance. Just then his engine cuts out—silence. Now it roars back into action! Every few seconds it cuts out, and then cuts in again. Foss pushes the stick farther forward; both are diving down to the closest cloud. The Zeros come on, more than a dozen of them. Foss feels for his comrade, also trying to reach the cloud bank. It draws nearer, and the Zeros behind draw closer—too close. He must get out of the line of fire . . . now! He pushes the stick forward and dives almost straight down into the nearest cloud. The milky gray rushes forward and envelops him just as the Zeros arc in range. He slows his dive in the cloud, with a still-missing engine, hoping the enemy won't be able to follow. The altimeter reads 7,000 feet, then 6,000 feet. As long as he's in cloud he's safe.

As the altimeter hits 3,500 feet, the engine cuts out completely. It resumes; the instruments on the panel jump back and forth. Rain spatters the canopy. Suddenly Foss plunges out of the bottom of the cloud, at 3,500 feet over water. He glances behind and sees

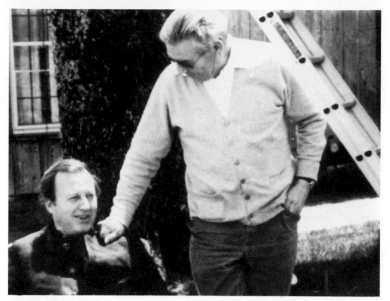

General Gerhard Barkhorn (right), 301 air victories, discussing air combat with author, May 1982, Asheville, NC.

Admiral P. D. "Percy" Gick on south coast of England, 1986, in front of harbor he built upon retirement in 1964. This picture was made 45 years after attack on *Bismarck*.

Author and Sir Douglas Bader at Bader's country home outside London, September 1978.

Lieutenant D.B. "Dick" Law, Royal Navy, seen in the western desert in front of a Wildcat four years before he flew the mission described in this book.

Sir Douglas and Lady Joan Bader at their home, outside London, shortly before Bader's death.

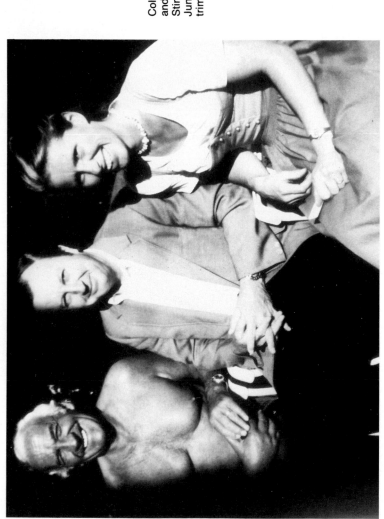

Colonel Hans Ulrich Rüdel, author, and Frau Rudel at Rüdel's house on Stimmersee near Kufstein, Austria, June 1981. Rüdel, at 65, was still trim and fit.

Air Vice Marshal Johnnie Johnson, top RAF fighter pilot scorer with 40 WWII victories, author, and Colonel Erich Hartmann, top scoring fighter ace of all time with 352 victories; author's publication party London, 1968.

Colonel Erich Hartmann (right) with Wing Commander Stanford Tuck, 1968. Hartmann's wife, Usch, is at left. Publication party at Bad Godesberg.

Colonel Werner Schroer in wartime flying uniform. He is wearing Knight's Cross with Swords and Diamonds, won in summer of 1943 after 84 victories.

Captain Joseph Foss shot down 25 Japanese airplanes during WWII (photograph by Brown Brothers).

Lord John Kilbracken (center) in front of Stringbag in flying uniform, 1944.

no Zeros in sight. (Unknown to him, the Zeros have caught his fellow cripple and shot him down.)

Tropical rain suddenly comes down hard and spatters the front of the canopy with such impact that visibility is almost nil. However, Foss dimly makes out, left ahead, the shoreline of an island.

It has to be Malaita, a long island in the southern Solomons, since Foss knows he's still northeast of Florida Island. He's down to 2,500 feet and the engine gauges are all red. Five or six miles to the coastline; rain still heavy—he'll try to make it to the island, then decide what to do.

Foss banks slightly left and the F4F—engine intermittently running and stopping, holes in wing and fuselage, battered by the rain—inclines downward and finally reaches the coastline palms of Malaita Island. Through the rain, to the left, Foss catches a glimpse of a small village. He aims his dying engine toward it. If worst comes to worst, he'll find human beings there.

But he can't remember if this part of Malaita Island is controlled by the Japanese or Americans. As he approaches the shore and banks right to fly along the coastline, his engine seizes. He's at 1,500 feet.

He must ditch. Canopy all the way back! The airframe is vibrating. Will the rainy weather that saved him from the Zeros prevent his rescue by the people in the village? Altimeter 1,000 feet. He banks right; he'll go into the water about a mile from the village shore.

He can see the swell and maneuvers to skid along the swell in a smooth ditching, as Marine and Navy pilots are trained to do. But the battered Wildcat reacts sluggishly to the controls and Foss is suddenly just over the waves. Back on the stick! A big swell rises up in front. Too fast! He eases farther back, but the Wildcat slams into it with a crunching sound. The canopy slams forward and closes. Foss wonders for a split second whether he'll bounce, flip over, skid along the water, or sink. To his dismay, the Wildcat is rapidly settling. Suddenly water is over the wings and sloshing up toward the canopy. The fighter is sinking fast, the canopy is still closed, and Foss is strapped into his seat.

Frantically, he reaches up to pull the canopy back. It's stuck. Now the waves are closing over the top; the Wildcat is sinking! He unbuckles his parachute cheststrap but forgets to unbuckle the leg straps. As he struggles to get the canopy open, the parachute remains strapped to his legs, begins to soak up water, and starts filling the cockpit. Everything around him becomes dark green.

He's under the surface, sinking farther and farther, and he can't open the canopy.

Panic! He lunges desperately at the canopy handle and yanks it back with superhuman strength. The desperate heave breaks it open. Foss jerks himself clear. The parachute, however, to which he's still attached, rises first. It pushes his head down. He's swallowing water and gasping for breath. In these seconds he realizes clearly he has only a few more to live unless he surfaces. The chute pulls him up and breaks the surface. He fights desperately to get his head out of water to one side. Instinctively, as the act of a trapped man, he pulls the cord of his Mae West. The life preserver suddenly inflates. It shoves his upper body around the chute to the surface. He gasps free air at the last second.

It's minutes before he regains normal consciousness and is able to effectively breathe, after heaving up much water. He's a couple of miles off Malaita. He rests, at last, to regain his strength, shaken from the close call of almost being entombed below in his fighter.

He remembers briefings about tides in this area, and a warning that tides between Florida and Malaita run at 14 knots. If the tide's against him, he'll never be able to swim to shore. He can only glimpse the shoreline above the waves, every so often, and so he rests, momentarily, trying to determine which way the tide is running and what he will do.

He can't determine which way the tide is running but decides he'll start swimming, now, while it's still daylight, while he can still see the shore ahead. He swims slowly to conserve strength, but keeps at it. His strokes get heavier and heavier but he swims on. He worries about sharks, prevalent in these waters, and remembers to break one of the emergency capsules that are supposed to keep sharks away.

As he continues to swim, he notices the dye in the water remains around him. Discouraged, he realizes he's making little progress. Doubts about being picked up race through his mind. If he had been on a morning mission he would have all day to be spotted by aircraft above. But it's now about 5:00 P.M. or later, not much daylight left. The rainy sky also minimizes chances search aircraft will see him in the water.

For a long time he swims on toward shore, but it becomes obvious he's making no progress. Yet he refuses to accept that agonizing conclusion. He swims on and on. Light is failing and he's been in the water a long time. The shore is still about two miles away; he realizes he'll never make it.

And so he relaxes, again, and breaks another capsule to keep sharks away. This could be the end, and he has the satisfaction of knowing he shot down three enemy planes on the mission, if it is to be his last. He wonders if the enemy fleet was stopped, how much damage was done. He thinks about the tents back at Guadalcanal, the primitive conditions—now they seem luxurious as he floats in choppy water and darkness descends over the Pacific.

His thoughts drift back to the United States, 8,000 miles away.

A wire service reporter, writing this day thousands of miles on the other side of the world, repeats a Russian communique: "On the battlefield northwest of Stalingrad, where the Russians are pressing the Germans hard to relieve Stalingrad, Nazi and Russian artillery maintain a fast duel." (This was the early prelude to a massive Russian counterattack that cut off the German Sixth Army besieging Stalingrad.)

In newspapers in the United States on this day, advertisements are urging Americans to: "Sell your idle tires to Uncle Sam now." The newspapers also reported stock market gains, a reaction to the victory of Field Marshal Bernard Montgomery at El Alamein. Investors and fortunate citizens back home are making money. Foss is fighting for his life under a darkening sky in the fast-running, chilly waters between two of the Solomon Islands, far, far away in the Pacific.

It's dark. Foss has stopped swimming to conserve his strength. The rain has stopped, but all is silent around him except the splashing of the waves. No lights are to be seen, even though he looks in the direction of the village every time the water lifts him high enough to see the shore. Time passes, and Foss is sure he is in a losing game. He wonders how long his Mae West will remain inflated, how long he can float before he attracts sharks. He breaks another capsule of shark preventive. There have been so many jokes about these capsules. He wonders if they work. So far, he has escaped the attention of the dreaded creatures.

He's not sure he saw it! In the direction of the shore. Again—a small light! The waves hide it, and it goes on and off. He comes alert and tense. He's sure now he saw a light.

And now also, for the first time, he knows something is moving in the water close to him. Every so often it cuts through the water on one side or the other. It comes to him suddenly—sharks! He breaks another capsule but, unmistakably, sharks are around him. Perhaps they've been there all the time and he has been unaware of them. His thoughts race back to the light. It keeps appearing, in the direction of the village. The sharks make him frantic and he cares less whether Japanese or Americans are in control of the village—if he can just reach shore.

The light is closer, and it's moving! A boat? Foss hesitates to utter a sound. He treads water and keeps his eyes fixed in the direction of the light. It steadily comes closer. Now a black object is visible ahead, moving toward him. Still Foss remains silent. It's some kind of boat—it looks like a native canoe, coming straight for him.

He watches as the bow approaches within 10 feet. Have they seen him? How could the boat approach so close? Now the bow is on him. The boat is passing almost directly over him. He ducks his head under the water momentarily. He raises it and listens. The language he hears sounds like broken English. It's utterly dark, and the light is now shining in the other direction. He realizes at this moment that he's between outrigger and canoe itself. Heart throbbing, Foss still remains silent, watching, just a few feet away. He sees figures moving in the boat, but still he can't understand the language being spoken. Suddenly, one of the men in the boat speaks, loudly and clearly: "Let's look over here."

Foss shouts back: "Right here!" The light flicks off. Foss sees a couple of natives pick up clubs and lift them menacingly. He yells: "Friend! Birdman! Aviator! American!"

Foss can't understand the jabbering. But the natives, now directly over him, don't club him. One of the men in the boat leans over in his direction and holds out his arms. He reaches out to grip the outstretched arms of Tommy Robinson, an Australian sawmill operator, who pulls a South Dakota fighter pilot into the canoe.

A native adds a helping hand, and they lift him into the bottom of the boat. Foss looks up and realizes a priest is also in the boat. "I'm Father De Steinberg," the priest says. Just at that time a flying fish smashes into the light and knocks it out. Had that happened earlier, Foss might never have seen the boat. But he had seen it, and has been rescued, and relief and thankfulness well up inside. He asks:

"Where are you from?"

"We're from Buma Mission." Buma Mission is the small coastal settlement he saw from the air.

Slowly they make their way to shore, Foss explaining what had happened that day in the air and asking how they had known he was out there in the water, two miles off shore. A native had seen him crash and had excitedly exclaimed: "There's a birdman out there in the sea!" As a result of his sighting, several canoes started out from shore in search of the pilot, who might have survived.

The boat finally reaches shore, and once ashore, Foss at last relaxes and talks to Robinson and Father De Steinberg. The priest offers Foss his bed, and, emotionally and physically worn out, Foss accepts. Soon he's sound asleep.

Morning revealed a beautiful village and island. Foss decides that if he survives the war and has the time, he'll someday go back and visit this island. The feel of land, the smell of foliage, the security of earth below his feet joined with the beautiful scenery make him thankful he's alive. But Foss knows he should get back to Guadalcanal, and so next day he spreads out his parachute, which had been picked up with him, in a clearing on the island.

It was Sunday, and Foss wondered if his comrades would be looking for him. He didn't have long to wait. A sleek American fighter flew down the coastline only hours later and spotted the chute. The pilot radioed Guadalcanal. Back at Operations on Guadalcanal, Jack Cramm, an old friend, hurried to take off in a PBY-5A to investigate the parachute sighting. Later in the day, Cramm landed the PBY-5A off the coast opposite the little village. Taxiing in to shore, he soon learned it was indeed Joe Foss who had survived and awaited rescue.

Foss thanked his rescuers profusely, bade them goodby, and boarded the PBY-5A for the return to Guadalcanal. Now he learned that one of the Americans' heavy bombs had hit the Japanese cruiser the day before, that two pilots had put torpedoes into her side. The P-39s that had also taken part in the strike had shot down five enemy planes. Marine fighters had destroyed nine, including the three Foss shot down. Two others had been accounted for by the other U.S. aircraft. A fellow Marine pilot in his flight, William P. Marontate, had scored three kills. Three American fighters had been lost.

Foss was soon back at Guadalcanal, enjoying the "luxury" of a very primitive fighter base. Asked about injuries and physical condition, he declared himself ready to fly again.

As a result, on the very next day, Monday, the 9th of November, he was ordered back into action.

Unknown to Foss at the time he treaded water in the dark off the shore of Malaita Island, there was a danger he never encountered because he was unable to swim to shore. Off the coast of the village the water was infested with crocodiles. At this particular spot along the coast they were notorious and deadly. Had Foss been able to swim to shore, he would likely have encountered them.

And so Foss had been lucky in many ways to survive the ditching of his crippled fighter on the afternoon of November 7, considering all the dangers involved.

He remained on operations at Guadalcanal until just before Christmas, when he received a short leave. He returned to combat on New Year's Eve and remained until February, when ordered out of action. By then, he had shot down more enemy aircraft in the Pacific—26—than any other Marine would destroy in World War II! (Foss returned to combat later in the war, but added no more victories to his record.)

Unknown to him at the time, his effort of November 7 was to count heavily in earning him the nation's highest award, the Medal of Honor. Six months later, at the White House, on May 18, 1943, the following citation, in tribute to his gallantry, was read aloud to a distinguished assemblage:

"For outstanding heroism and courage above and beyond the call of duty as Executive Officer of a Marine Fighting Squadron at Guadalcanal, Solomon Islands. Engaging in almost daily combat with the enemy from October 9 to November 19, 1942, Captain Foss personally shot down twenty-three Japanese planes and damaged others so severely that their destruction was extremely probable.

"In addition, during this period, he successfully led a large number of escort missions, skillfully covered reconnaissance, bombing and photographic planes as well as surface craft. On January 15, 1943, he added three more enemy planes to his already brilliant successes for a record of aerial combat achievement unsurpassed in this war.

"Boldly searching out an approaching enemy force on January 25, Captain Foss led his eight Marine planes and four Army planes into action, and undaunted by tremendously superior numbers, intercepted and struck with such force that four Japanese fighters were shot down and the bombers were turned back without releasing a single bomb. His remarkable flying skill, inspiring leadership and indomitable fighting spirit were distinctive factors in the defense of strategic American positions on Guadalcanal."

After the citation was read, the Medal of Honor was personally presented to Foss by President Roosevelt. In his tour of duty at Guadalcanal, Foss had made three dead-stick landings on Henderson Field in planes crippled by enemy fire in addition to his ditching.

In addition to the Medal of Honor, Foss was awarded the Distinguished Flying Cross by Admiral William F. Halsey for heroism and extraordinary achievement in shooting down six Zeros and one bomber during the crisis at Guadalcanal in October.

In 1943, after being ordered from Guadalcanal, he was returned to Marine Headquarters in Washington, thereafter to be sent on a tour of Navy preflight schools and naval air stations where Marine pilots were training. He helped sell bonds in a nationwide tour of the United States. His second tour of duty in the Pacific began in February 1944, when he resumed combat flights around Emirau, in the St. Matthias group. But enemy planes were scarce. He failed to add to his illustrious record.

The importance of the aerial effort by Marine pilots in the Solomons in this period of the war is difficult to overestimate. In the time Foss served, the Japanese made three major attempts to retake Guadalcanal.

Though the attacks of pilots on the afternoon of November 7 didn't stop Japanese reinforcement efforts, losses inflicted on warships and transports by U.S. pilots were becoming so exorbitant the Japanese were forced to abandon reinforcement efforts.

The enemy later admitted U.S. air strength at Guadalcanal became so formidable it became impossible to deliver sufficient troops and supplies to Guadalcanal. Shortly after the battle between Japanese warships and American fliers on November 7, the Japanese committed even heavier warships. The result was two battleships and a number of other warships lost.

The climax came November 14, one week after the mission described in this chapter. The Japanese attempted to send in large-scale troop reinforcements in a major convoy. All afternoon on the 14th, every plane on Guadalcanal that could fly was loaded with bombs and attacked transports of this convoy. The day produced the greatest slaughter of Japanese troops by American airmen in the campaign. By evening seven transports, ranging in tonnage between 5,000 and 9,000 tons, had been sunk. Another four were crippled and managed to make Guadalcanal only to be beached there, where they were gutted next day by the same pilots who had hit them the day before, and by the destroyer *Meade*.

It's estimated that only 4,000 Japanese troops out of the 10,000 in that convoy reached Guadalcanal. Many were drowned, though many were later rescued from the water by destroyers. Out of the entire convoy, only five tons of supplies—260 cases of ammunition and 1,500 bags of rice—were put ashore.

This, according to Bob Sherrod, in *History of Marine Corps Avi-*

ation in World War II, was as significant as any victory Marine aviators achieved in World War II.

When Marine airmen finally won the struggle for control of the waters around Guadalcanal, American forces on the island realized the tide had turned and that the Americans were on Guadalcanal to stay.

Foss retired as a brigadier general in the South Dakota National Guard after transferring to the U.S. Air Force Reserve in 1946. After being twice elected Governor of South Dakota—in 1954 and 1956—he was in 1960 named Commissioner of the American Football League, later to merge with the National. He resides today, in good health, in Paradise Valley, Scottsdale, Arizona.

Chapter 7

Hartmann: The Black Sea

The greatest fighter pilot in the history of aerial warfare is Colonel Erich Hartmann, who survived the war. In recent years his record has become of interest to more and more people. Seeking a quiet and simple life near Stuttgart, the ranking German ace is nevertheless the object of calls or queries from historians, the news media, the curious, and admirers. This interest comes as much from his former enemies as from comrades and countrymen. The highest scoring fighter pilot of the war achieved an incredible 352 kills.

After the war and 10 years of Russian prison brutality, Hartmann again served in the German Air Force, retiring in the 1970s. Until the 1980s, still the same personality as in the war to a remarkable degree, he continues to fly as a civilian instructor. He leads a contented, quiet life, looking ahead, not to the past. He isn't constantly on the move, hyperactive, or demanding. He affects no celebrity personality. He is the same calm, candid, quiet-spoken individual wartime comrades agree he had always been. What distinguishes him strikingly from many famous military heroes is that he projects absolutely no pretense, bravado, glamour image, stuffiness, or superior air. Yet he was the most successful pilot ever to fly fighter aircraft.

Russian prison life—10 years of it including beatings, isolation, starving diets, and the most brutal treatment—left its mark on Hartmann. But he never broke under the pressure and never signed a "confession" that he was a war criminal, as his tormentors demanded. Perhaps never again after that ordeal did he have quite the same youthful freshness—naturally enough. That hardship and crushing defeat produced a sobering effect. Probably only his parents and wife could accurately measure the full difference.

Consider the roller-coaster ride fate gave this young fighter pilot. He was born in 1922 in Wurttemberg and just 20 years later, in late 1942, he was ordered into combat on the eastern front. In the next two and a half years he became a national hero and idol, honored everywhere, highly decorated, celebrated in the press, praised by his government, church, the mayor of his home town, etc. He had just turned 23 when the war ended. From such a personal and career pinnacle he descended instantly to the depths. He found himself in the degradation of Russian prisons, accused of being a criminal. He was told he would never be allowed to go home again until he confessed. He was unable to communicate with his wife and family. In 1947 his son, whom he had never seen, died. Five years later, while still in prison, in 1952, his father, whom he revered, died. When finally returned to a faithful wife who had waited a decade, mother, home town, and family, the world was a different world. Germany was divided, his wartime effort less appreciated because of revelations about atrocities, opportunities limited. He was only 33, with more than a lifetime of hard experiences behind him. Such a turnaround, such a stark reversal of one's destiny, would have broken the spirit of many. Hartmann survived remarkably well-rounded and well-adjusted to the postwar world.

In this book of memorable missions of fighter pilots of Germany, Britain, and the United States over water, German chapters necessarily feature Luftwaffe pilots. In the U.S. armed forces in World War II there was a large naval air force of bombers, fighters, reconnaissance and supply aircraft, and many carriers. Many naval fighter aces emerged from the war. There was a formidable (if lesser) naval air arm in the British Navy. But the Luftwaffe did most of the marine flying for Germany in the 1939-45 war. Thus it was possible to recreate a mission by Hartmann, who had flown several unusual and dramatic missions over the sea. In more than 1400 missions during the war, some exciting ones had taken place over water, though Hartmann was too young to participate in the Battle of Britain and was never stationed in the Mediterranean.

So one day in the late 1970s I was on my way to Stuttgart once again, and from Stuttgart turned south on 27 along winding, hilly roads and through the innumerable small towns of Wurttemberg. From this area more Germans have emigrated to America than from any other in Germany.

Hartmann's white masonry home is two blocks from "Hartmann Strasse." One would normally conclude the street is named after this eagle of eastern front. It isn't. It's named for his father, a most popular doctor, who died in 1952 while Hartmann was still in a Russian prison camp.

Hartmann wore a blue jacket and pants with sandals. His hand shook slightly. "Too many cigarettes," he smiled. When asked how many he smoked a day, he estimated 40 to 50. His blue-grey eyes are clear and he moves easily, with what seems a natural calm. We are friends of some years, the three of us, and relaxed around a large glass table on red oriental rugs covering a marble floor. There's greenery everywhere inside, and outside in the garden, on the other side of a picture window. Red velvet draperies match a red shaded Chinese lamp in the corner. (Erich's father took the family to China when he was a baby and they stayed four years; in the room are mementos of that period.)

Behind me is a large white bookcase. A circular stairway leads to Erich's desk, located on a sort of balcony, behind an iron rail. Usch says retirement for them is beginning to be very busy. "The telephone rings and rings," she says. "Always someone wants a picture or an autograph, or wants to talk to Erich. And so many write for pictures or autographs. Unless they send the postage we can't comply with all the requests." Usch is still thin, trim, and attractive with dark hair and eyes; her memory and interest are so much a part of Hartmann she's almost necessary in any serious interview. She remembers things Erich no longer recalls—she kept all his letters from the war and kept abreast of everything, and still does.

"We never talk much about the war these days," she tells me. "Old comrades like to get together, of course," Erich says. "But this thing about 'if only I had done this or that,' it's wasted time. We're interested in now, the present and the future. The past is past. It's over," Hartmann says.

Hartmann always expresses keen interest in the depth of America's determination to resist Communist expansion. How realistic, how firm is U.S. policy and resolve? He understands the Russians well, having spent 10 years in captivity there. And one senses quickly that he dreads the thought of a Russian takeover of West Germany.

Finally, we get around to the war years. I ask him to think back over his hundreds and hundreds of missions. Had he flown over much water, or experienced an especially interesting mission over the sea? Usch remembers: The most nerve-wracking time during the war involved a long flight over water by Erich and his now-famous crew chief, Bimmel Mertens.

"It was in the summer of 1944. I had a map and followed the progress of the Russians advancing in and around Sevastopol. I knew Erich was there. I was very worried as they came nearer and nearer. It was the worst time for me. Finally he got out in the nick of time."

Erich recalled: "I had to fly out. I put Bimmel and my other crewman behind me in the single-seat 109. We had to fly from near Sevastopol across the western Black Sea to a place just north of Constanza in Romania. It was a close call. We just got out in time before the Russians took our airfield. But we made it—I think that was in May of 1944." It was a flight of more than 200 miles over water, and marked the final retreat out of Russia in the south in 1944 for the German Army.

As we talked about flying in the Black Sea area, Hartmann recalled one really memorable mission flown over water, one on which he almost lost his life and ended his combat career before it reached the halfway mark. It had occurred a year before the flight to Romania, in May of 1943. That was a time of comparative calm on the eastern front in the south. The great Russian offensive that cut off and decimated the Sixth Army, Germany's best-equipped, had ended in February and March. The German Army struck back and recaptured Kharkov (the counterthrust of Field Marshal Erich von Manstein). In the three months that followed Kharkov's recapture, a relative lull settled over the front.

Little did Hartmann know at the time that this would be the last such lull of the war in the east. Contrary to popular belief, Germany was not forced on the defensive permanently at El Alamein or even at Stalingrad. The month many Germans recall as the one after which Germany never really recovered the initiative is July of 1943. That month the German Army's last eastern offensive, Citadel, betrayed to the enemy by Ultra decoding, failed to achieve its objectives after very heavy losses. It was this month that Sicily was invaded and Mussolini fell. This month Hitler's insomnia returned—to remain. The series of 1943 disasters began in May. Axis forces surrendered in Tunisia. Germany's U-boat campaign faltered that same month, amidst heavy losses and few sinkings.

All this Hartmann wasn't aware of on that May 8th morning, 1943 (two years to the day before Germany surrendered unconditionally). Nor did he know that six weeks earlier Mussolini had urged Hitler to end the war in the east, and that Stalin, irked that there was no second front in Europe, was not unreceptive to peace talks. One Soviet diplomat had hinted Germany could even keep Poland in a settlement. But Hitler was gambling all the way and that doomed Hartmann—to aerial combat fame and 10 years of imprisonment.

JG 52, the Luftwaffe's most successful Jagdgeschwader in World War II (with over 10,000 aerial victories by war's end), was stationed in southern Russia in this last lull of the war the spring of 1943. Gruppe III, Hartmann's, was based on the airfield at Taman, a short distance from the Black Sea and not far from Kerch in the Crimea. Taman was a windswept, forlorn base in desolate, desert country. The airfield's radio towers looked down on a flat, brown sandy soil. Its bunkers were well camouflaged and dug deeply into the ground. A line of low hills stretched around the horizon. ME 109s and other aircraft were dispersed widely over the field. Dark tents served as squadron headquarters. The diamond-shaped emblem (cross inside) of JG 52 was prominently displayed atop a bunker near the radio towers.

Hartmann was housed in the town of Taman, two kilometers distant. It was a primitive billet, but the best available. He and several other pilots shared a one-story white masonry house with a Russian family. They all slept in the same big room; it was full of fleas. Hartmann kept flea powder in his boots but that didn't defeat the fleas.

As usual, the pilots rose early on the morning of the 8th, dressed, and were driven to mess in town by a halftrack. From there they drove to the airfield for the day's orders. This was a sparkling, clear spring day and the sun rose shortly in a solid blue sky. Commanding Officer Gunther Rall was absent that day, the aerial war being relatively quiet.

The drama, in fact, was not to begin until 1800 hours (6 P.M.) that afternoon. In the air fighting the day before, Hartmann had bagged his 12th and 13th aerial kills—a Lagg-3 and a Lagg-5. The young ace was at the very beginning of his aerial career, though it was well into the fourth year of the war. Pilots not on duty spent the morning playing cards, relaxing, and talking. After lunch, Hartmann was one of those who flew briefly. But the afternoon passed quietly.

The sky was still clear, the sun low on the horizon, and all seemed peaceful. Suddenly, a roar of engines . . . growing louder! Everyone dived for cover. Six to eight greenish Ilyushin (IL-2) ground-support Sturmoviks came thundering over the northern edge of the field, quite low. These attack bombers German ground forces had learned to dread. (During Citadel, two months later, a large formation of these IL-2s caught tanks of the 9th Panzer Division in the open and claimed 90 in less than 30 minutes!) Hartmann's one thought as he saw the enemy roar past overhead was to go after them. Mertens must have had the same idea, for almost before the noise of their flight across the field had faded, Hartmann—running hard—was nearing a new ME 109G-14. Bimmel and another crewman were revving up the engine as he leaped on a wing and into the cockpit. Other pilots were in the same race. Within seconds, sand was swirling and blowing backward as the German fighters raced over the brown sand and pulled up, heading south after the slower bombers. The Russians had only strafed the field in one lightning pass, causing limited damage, obviously having dropped their bombs elsewhere. Now they were heading out over the Black Sea—but followed already by 109s with straining engines, their pilots determined.

Hartmann was nearest the trailing enemy two-seater. Within minutes he could clearly see the gunner in the rear seat facing him, his single machine gun pointed directly at him. The ME 109 was fast closing; Hartmann had taken off with no flaps and had little altitude to gain. The Il-2s were hugging the earth. It had been perhaps the fastest takeoff of Hartmann's career. Now out over the Black Sea, he maneuvered slightly to close with the Sturmovik, now steadily growing larger in his gunsight. Other 109s were closing on other bombers as the sun sank to the horizon. Roaring up from slightly below, Hartmann was at last within gunnery range and opened fire with his two 20mm cannon and two 7.92 machine guns. The noise was deafening as the guns let go and the 1150-horsepower Daimler Benz engine roared at full throttle. Hartmann saw hits. He was expecting his 14th victory any second.

Suddenly blue smoke began to fill his cockpit. He now had trouble seeing his target ahead. The engine began to miss—rougher and rougher! Disgusted that this would happen at just that moment, Hartmann banked to one side, trying to see better. The smoke increased and his engine temperature gauges told him he had already a very hot engine. Quickly he turned it off to prevent a fire. No power—and over the sea! Hartmann turned north toward Taman. Could he make it?

The smoke in the cockpit thinned with the engine off. Fortunately for him, it wasn't the same malfunction that had overtaken the Luftwaffe's Star of Africa seven months earlier. Hans Marseille was also in a Messerschmitt that day. His engine caught fire. The smoke was so thick Marseille couldn't stay in the cockpit, yet he was over British lines. Desperately attempting to remain in the smoking aircraft long enough to reach his own lines, Marseille waited seconds too long. When he rolled over to drop out, he must have been faint. Whatever the reason, the rudder struck him as he fell and broke his back. They found him in the desert sand of North Africa shortly afterward, parachute unopened. The burning engine of his brand-new 109 had caused his loss to the Luftwaffe and Germany.

Now Hartmann, destined to be the leading German ace on the eastern front, was fighting for his life in another brand-new 109 with smoking engine. And he was without enough altitude to glide very far. For the first time, Hartmann realized he might not make it back to the coast. He need only glide a few kilometers; he could see the shoreline by Kerch in the distance ahead. He tried to hold precious altitude, but to avoid stalling was forced to drop the nose. He noticed whitecaps on the surface. The water seemed to rush up closer and closer. It was all happening very fast. Hartmann knew he couldn't jump. He was too low. He would belly it in.

His speed was now down to 150 kilometers. He checked his seatbelt and braced himself for the shock. Through the windscreen the sea's surface rushed to meet him. The 109 smacked into four-foot waves and bounced along the surface. It didn't flip over, but slowed to a mush and settled in the water. Hartmann had uncranked the top of the canopy. (There was always the danger that a crash-landing fighter would flip on its back and trap its pilots.) He quickly unbuckled and stepped out of the cockpit onto the left wing, still above the water. He was surprised that the fighter, with its heavy engine, floated so well.

But now he also realized how little time he had before darkness. It was after 6 P.M. Yet the 109 continued to float and Hartmann sat on the side of the cockpit and took stock. What to do? The fighter was slowly settling and he knew it would be only a short time before he was in the water. He had worn his Mae West, thankfully, and would float. But would they find him in the gathering darkness? He decided to keep his shoes on; they were valuable and hard to replace. They would be soaking and heavy but his Mae West would keep him afloat. Now the fighter began to sink more rapidly;

the wings and fuselage were filling with water. His feet went under as the wing sank so he plunged into the surface to be free of the sinking fighter, which now went down fast. The water was cold—it was early May—and he sank all the way down to his neck because of his clothes, boots, etc. He guessed the time to be about 6:30 now, and it was fast getting dark. No one had flown overhead to mark his position or wave to him. He was only a very small object in heavy waves. He hoped the yellow dye marker, now seeping out and marking his position, would be visible in the darkness. Could he survive through the night if they didn't find him in the darkness?

Two or three of the enemy bombers had been shot down, but not his target; he wondered if his attacking comrades had seen him go down. The waves splashed around him and as he rose and fell he could sometimes catch sight of a boat plying back and forth near the shore. The rescue boat from Kerch? Had they seen him go in? It didn't seem so. The boat came no nearer. It was deathly quiet. Occasionally he heard planes returning, but they couldn't see his head below in all the waves. By now they were all back at the field. What were his comrades thinking? Perhaps that his 13th victory had proven unlucky—and was to have been his last? Or did they know he was only a kilometer away from the rescue boat?

As always in his career, Hartmann kept his cool and didn't panic. He knew he was in a crisis, but somehow felt he'd be found and rescued. He clung to that optimism even as darkness deepened and the only sounds were the lapping and splashing of the water around him. That lonely silence continued as the night lengthened. His watch had stopped. He no longer knew what time it was, but he realized he had now been in the water for over an hour. And no one was even near him, though he still caught sight of the rescue boat from time to time as a wave lifted his head. That gave him encouragement. The rescue boat hadn't given up, but why didn't it come on out toward his position, which he estimated to be no more than a kilometer off shore? It would be tragic to remain unfound so close—so close that he could see his would-be rescuers and lights on the shore.

The night was crisp and clear and the stars now shone down on the Black Sea as he continued to wait and drift. He could see the yellow dye he had released around him in the water. But he had no light—and began to realize how important that might be. Most fighter pilots who fly over water have a small light in their jacket which lights up automatically when they're in water. But

Hartmann didn't usually fly over water—the Germans controlled the Black Sea—and that precaution he hadn't taken when he scrambled that afternoon. Only the dye, then, would pinpoint him in the water at night! Perhaps the boat would have a searchlight that would help locate the dye. But would it be visible in the dark? Such questions ran through his mind.

Another hour passed. He had been in the water now over two hours and the cold was beginning to affect him. His movements were getting slower but he still refused to give up hope. He couldn't tell whether he was drifting inland or out to sea, and he still glimpsed the rescue boat from time to time, and the lights ashore. Every now and then, he thought the rescue boat was nearer. Was he fooling himself? He restrained an inner feeling the boat was coming closer—until he became more sure. After a few minutes, he saw it *was* heading his way at last! The important thing now was to make himself heard or seen when it came nearest to him on this outward sweep. He glimpsed it only when lifted by the waves. Steadily it approached. It had a searchlight; he could see it sweeping the surface some distance away. Would they see him? Could they spot the dye on the surface? His excitement grew as he prepared to take advantage of his chance—his chance to live, to fly again.

Slowly but steadily, the boat came on; it was now maddeningly close. He could see it so well, and its light, and even hear voices, and still they didn't see him. Though weak, he began making all the noise he could. Yet he was but a small speck in a heaving mass of water. An arc of light finally swept over the trail left by his dye marker. His rescuers saw the yellow! The boat turned and began to follow it. Someone spotted his arms, waving weakly but frantically. Whether they heard his shouts, he didn't know. But now the bow of that lifesaving rescue boat pointed toward him. Hands on deck prepared to help him in. Wonderful relief; the tension now began to tell, the tension and cold. Until now, he wouldn't admit to himself how weak he had become (after this 132nd mission of some 1405 he would fly before the war ended).

Now he was pulled aboard by friendly hands and got a lusty greeting—smiles on every face, but no one he knew. It was close to 9:00 P.M. Hartmann knew many in Gruppe III at Taman had given him up for lost. The boat seemed to take forever to travel little more than a kilometer. Yet it was luxury to Hartmann, and a warm drink helped. As he reached shore, he thanked all hands and he commandeered a car back to the field. At 10:00 he arrived at squadron headquarters, still soaking but in high spirits; a tumultuous reception followed from fellow pilots. Dry clothes, tea, and cognac warmed him up. The cold water had stopped his watch—but not Erich Hartmann.

That narrow escape (and perhaps the day Hartmann went down behind Russian lines three months later) were among the closest brushes with death in Hartmann's wartime flying career. Had he not been found that night, the name Erich Hartmann would be known by few today. Thirteen kills in the Luftwaffe, in the east, was not a spectacular accomplishment. Gerhard Barkhorn was to go on to 301 victories and Gunther Rall, their commanding officer, would shoot down 275. When he was shot down and captured three months later, on August 20th, Hartmann's score had risen to a more impressive 90 victories. He would have been remembered if lost on that date as a promising young Luftwaffe ace. But he would not have become the greatest name in the history of fighter warfare. And his victory total would have been surpassed by dozens of other pilots.

What saved his life May 8th? Perhaps it was his decision to quickly shut off the engine when the cockpit began filling with smoke. Marseille had had altitude over Egypt to fly on, but Hartmann hadn't. Had his engine caught fire, he would have had to jump at dangerously low altitude and risk fatal injury from the fall or ride in a burning fighter—both likely to have been fatal. That same choice just two days later faced one of Hartmann's comrades. His engine afire, Acting Group Captain Ehrenberg jumped over a shallow part of the sea near the coastline. The water where he landed was only shoulder high. Ehrenberg drowned. His aircraft had been hit and was burning so badly he had to get out immediately. Hartmann's former commanding officer, Walter Krupinski, also was forced to make a similar choice about this time. He rode his aircraft down—luckily, it wasn't burning—and landed along the shoreline in sand. The landscape was rocky and treacherous. The sand may have saved Krupinski's life—and a second career in the Luftwaffe years later, as an ally of the western democracies he had opposed in the Second War. (Krupinski went on to achieve 196 victories by the time of Germany's surrender in 1945.) Ehrenberg had jumped at 500 meters to escape a choking smoke and might have been trapped under water in his chute. When his body was dragged up from the sea (his parachute came up first), doctors found no broken bones.

Hartmann was not to remain at Taman long. In less than two

months he and his Gruppe moved northward to take part in the last great German offensive of the war in the east. He then flew daily from Ugrim, where in 12 days he shot down 22 enemy aircraft, the first spectacular indication he was to become one of the Luftwaffe's greats.

At 60 in 1982, Hartmann rarely looked back to the war's turbulent, triumphant, and disastrous days for himself and Germany. On another long night we three—Erich, Usch, and I—talked into the early morning. Hartmann warned that the East German Army was very good. He's not sure how good the new Luftwaffe is; he has been retired some years. But he warns that the West must not underrate the East Germans and Russians—for whom he, interestingly, has no hatred. He recalls that the average Russian, even Russian guards in prisons, were often sympathetic in dealing with him and other prisoners. "After the war, when many soldiers of the Gross Deutschland Division were prisoners in Russia, they were interned in a town which they had occupied during the war. Many Russians somehow managed to invite them into their homes and help them in innumerable ways," Hartmann recalled. And he added: "When we first went into Russia, the people welcomed us. The political people who followed us ruined the atmosphere."

Would he stay in his home town if the Russians invaded West Germany? Hartmann thinks he would. He knows the language, might be able to get along, and hates to think of leaving his birthplace. Maybe, he says, he would go to America, which he visited often while serving his second tour of duty in the post war Luftwaffe. But basically he now lives such a quiet, peaceful life, staying near home almost all year, he is and would be reluctant to leave. Today he won't shoot a deer or a bird. He notes that war is full of ironies. "In the war my country awarded me the diamonds and I was acclaimed for shooting down 352 aircraft. The next government says war is criminal." He cites another truism of war: "Aside from mass murder, the crimes committed by the winning side are forgotten. Crimes committed by the losers are crimes." But in all this philosophy, Hartmann is good-humored and resigned. And Usch shows no bitterness to her husband's former enemies. She says: "All fighter pilots are the same the world over."

She and Erich were married in 1944, and were together only briefly before the end of the war. Erich surrendered to U.S. forces, who later, incredibly, turned him over to the Russians, assuring him the Russians would treat him properly as a prisoner of war!

That cost him 10 years of his life. Yet he isn't bitter. They have a daughter who is now a very grown-up girl. "Yet, she's a baby, you know," Erich says. "Each generation is different and has a different world to grow up in," he adds.

Looking back on the war, he expresses admiration for the late Gerhard Barkhorn, the second highest scoring Luftwaffe ace of the war with 301 victories—51 fewer than Hartmann. No one else, however, came close to Hartmann's record.

We looked out over the garden and I noticed the sliding roof over their heated swimming pool. "I built it myself," Hartmann said. One doesn't doubt he could do it, or anything else he puts his mind to. And the greater the length of time since the end of World War II, the more Hartmann's remarkable 352-kill record is appreciated. He entered combat after the easy-kill days for German pilots were, to a large degree, over. His aerial triumphs were compiled in two years, while many of his comrades spent twice that time in combat. Also, Hartmann's total would probably have been higher had he not been removed from combat—against his will—on a number of occasions.

The Russians appreciated his talents so well that they put a price on the head of the ace they called the "Black Devil"—10,000 rubles. They captured him during the war once, on that August 20th, after he had been shot down behind their lines. Hartmann feigned injury so realistically that he managed to take his guards by surprise and suddenly bolt from a moving truck carrying him to the rear. Then he cautiously walked back to his own lines for a day and a night, and resumed his flying career. He found his own lines by following a Russian patrol!

Such confidence and adaptability were the secrets of Hartmann's survival. He possessed a rare combination of caution, sound tactics, and a cool head, plus exceptional flying ability, good eyes, and expert markmanship. He did it like no one else ever did it. Yet he remains unaffected. Certainly there will never again be such a total of kills by a fighter pilot in aerial warfare. Today's aircraft are fewer and super-sophisticated, with heat-seeking and other modern guided missiles.

The days of Hartmann's style of air fighting are gone forever. But Hartmann doesn't think the days of fighters are over, and doesn't think the days of the single-seat fighter are past. "They say two men are needed today in fighters. I don't agree. One man is better. Two make for complications. Two eyes, ten fingers, and one brain—that's still best."

Chapter 8

Schroer: B-17s at Sea

During the many years air historians have been analyzing the records of the world's greatest fighter pilots, several great aces have remained relatively neglected. One who has not received widespread publicity is the Luftwaffe's Werner Schroer, who died in 1985. Yet his record in some ways is the most interesting of all the world's fighter pilots. Part of the explanation for this is that Schroer lived in Rome for many postwar years. Therefore, writers visiting Germany often missed seeing him.

I recall, when I lived in London in the 1960s, that a British air historian spoke to me about Schroer. "In some ways he is the most interesting of the surviving German fighter pilots," he remarked one day, adding also that he was a most likeable man—a man of culture. Hans Ring, the German air historian, confirmed that view. I was determined to look Schroer up. But when I lived in Germany from 1961 to 1965, and on many visits to Germany after that, I always found him in Rome. And when he was in Germany, I was out of the country.

Finally, in the early 1970s I made the trip out to his home in Ottobrunn, outside Munich, and soon found myself in solid agreement with my fellow historians. Here was a great ace whose record is indeed unique. He was one of only eight German fighter pilots to have scored more than 100 victories against British and American opponents. He flew both from Western Europe and in Africa, and after Hans Joachim Marseille, achieved the highest number of victories there. Of the top six German scorers who flew against western opponents, Schroer had the highest victory total of any still alive, 114. Kurt Buehligen had 112, Adolf Galland 104. Three with high West totals no longer alive at that time were Marseille (158), Heinrich Bär (124), and Joachim Muncheberg (102).

With such an outstanding victory total, one would assume Schroer had flown at least four or five hundred missions. (The greatest ace, Erich Hartmann, flew 1400 missions in recording his 352 kills.) Schroer flew only 197 missions from which he was credited with 114 victories! Twenty-six were against four-engine bombers. Compare this with the number of missions flown by the other German fighter aces who shot down many western foes: Marseille—383 missions; Bär—1,000 missions; Buehligen—700 missions; Galland—425 missions; Muncheberg—500 missions; Egon Mayer (who also shot down 102 aircraft in the West)—353 missions. Schroer's percentage of victories per mission flown is by far the highest of all the top aces with more than 100 victories against western airmen. (The only other German ace with more than 100 kills in the West was Josef Priller, with 101 victories in 307 missions—11 four-engine bombers.) Mayer and Muncheberg failed to survive the war. Bär and Priller did, only to die relatively unappreciated by millions of countrymen. Bär was killed in a lightplane crash in Brunswick in 1957 and Priller died in Upper Bavaria in 1961.

Of all the German fighter aces, one whose life would have made a unique book because of his personality and record was Bär. He was the Luftwaffe's leading jet ace, with 16 victories in the ME 262. He had much experience and many victories in all three German theaters—96 in the East, 45 in North Africa and 79 in Western Europe. A singular tribute is paid his character and charisma in the official Society of Fighter Pilots listing of *Ritter kreuz Trager of World War II* in this sentence: "His personal charm and wit are hard to forget." (I keenly regret not having been able to interview Bär and Mayer. Priller died just months before I arrived in Germany to live for four years, in 1961. And Muncheberg, also greatly admired, would have been a fine subject for a book. Like Bär, he was a leader with charm and charisma. These were Germany's great aces of the western front.)

Fortunate it was that the Luftwaffe ace with the best percentage of kills to missions against the West was still available to recall his experiences until 1985. It wasn't until 1978 that Schroer and I sat down together and looked back over his career and selected a mission to recreate. He had flown many over water, from

France, Africa, Rhodes, Greece and Crete. For him, then, and for this book about over-water flying, the task was easy.

While this book was in preparation, after our meeting in Munich to select one of his most memorable missions, Schroer entered the hospital for triple bypass heart surgery. Fortunately, I was in Munich at the time (1979) and I visited the hospital one Sunday afternoon just before he was operated on. I urged him, while he had the time and was slowed down for rest and recovery, to write a book about his varied and dramatic experiences and accomplishments. He gave me that easy smile of his, and with the softest of voices, said: "I don't think there would be much interest in that in Germany today." I disagreed, and pointed out there would be considerable interest outside of Germany, as well as in Germany. "Fighter pilots were all very young men when the war began," I said. "Thus, they can't be involved in politics or actions of the state. They were just young, patriotic men doing their duty for their country—as young men have done for centuries. That's what's nice in writing about them."

Schroer smiled again and said maybe he might write a book together with another leading ace. I told him he himself had lived enough experiences to fill a book and then some. If two of them decided to write, it should be two books; there would be ample interest in both. This was the end of the summer of 1979, a time-world away from the youthful, tumultuous war days of 1939-45. Schroer's hair was now grey; he had lost much of it, at 61. But he approached his operation with the same quiet calmness and courage of his fighter pilot years. One of his thoughts, on the eve of surgery, was about his sons. "They find it hard to understand that I didn't know about war crimes," he smiled. "They've said to me: 'You must have known!' I've explained I knew nothing about such things."

Some day, of course, Schroer's sons and all of today's young idealistic Germans will realize how naive it is to assume fighting troops, or pilots at the fronts, knew about war crimes taking place in secrecy behind the lines. The intelligence services of the Allies had only a vague idea of what was going on, though all had agents in Germany seeking such facts. How then were unsuspecting young men, fighting for their lives at the front, dependent for news on a state-controlled media, to know about such things? Most of them, even if they had heard rumors about crimes, wouldn't have believed them. A controlled press would have denied them. One hopes sons of such greats as Schroer will never be forced to live through a similar era. And almost surely they will not, for today in Germany the press is free and society is open, the state far from all-powerful, as it was in 1939-45. But in a way, one wishes that for a fleeting week or month, today's young Germans could see how it was in the 1930s and '40s. It is surely unfair to a wartime young man like Schroer, lionized by his countrymen when the nation was fighting what most believed an inevitable war, now to be individually held accountable for the crimes of his government. Schroer as a war hero was proudly married by the mayor of his city, hailed as an example in every corner of the country, and decorated with the highest awards, a national celebrity. Yet until his death he went largely unrecognized on the streets, having to "explain" why he didn't shirk the time-honored obligation to country!

On a cold winter afternoon in Munich, in 1978, it was dark at 5:00 P.M. The blue streetcars outside rumbled by periodically as I waited. I had decided to eat early, so I could write while the Schroers talked and ate. I had started a rare cigar, at peace with the world, when the Schroers arrived. Werner appeared aged and grave until he smiled, and perhaps this had something to do with his heart condition. He was one of the great aces who seemed to carry a heavy burden after the war. There was little of a carefree, happy demeanor about him. But his green eyes (a small scar over the right eye) lit up readily with a quick and friendly smile. Ilse is trim, brown-eyed with brown hair, and attractive. They had just celebrated the 44th anniversary of their first meeting. He had already told me about their long and happy marriage, how on so many mornings he had awakened to find a small gift at his bedside.

They met in Mulheim when he was 17 and she was 15, in dance school, in 1935. They were married during the war, in 1943. The Burgemeister of Mulheim made the Stadhalle available, so large was the crowd. He had already been awarded the Ritterkreuz, the first from Mulheim to be so honored. The Luftwaffe gave him three weeks leave. He started home for the wedding from Rhodes.

For those pilots who had flown in Africa, it was obvious in 1943 Germany was losing the war. Schroer had shot down 61 enemy aircraft in the African campaign, second only to Marseille, but had been evacuated to Rhodes as Axis forces began their last retreat. The small area in Africa still controlled by the Axis, in Tunisia, was shrinking and the war there was less than three months from its end. Thinking more now of his upcoming marriage than the hopeless situation in Africa, Schroer loaded his tan ME 109s, with gifts, foods, and—most delicate of all—a set of china. Goods were still plentiful and inexpensive in Rhodes in 1943.

He took off for Italy via Crete with a wingman, course due west over the Aegean Sea, on February 11th. He had no warning of enemy aircraft in the vicinity, and expected to encounter none. But before reaching Crete, the two ME 109s chanced into a flight of two slower twin-engine British TFX Beaufighters, which had in recent weeks been attacking Axis shipping with success in the Aegean and Sea of Crete. Schroer was hesitant. His fuselage and wings were loaded with china and wedding presents, yet there was ammunition in his guns and this was the enemy. He and his wingman were flying at the same low altitude as the brown Beaufighters off to the right; the 109s were much faster. The Beaufighters were, in addition, highly vulnerable—carrying torpedoes. It took Schroer only an instant to decide.

Banking right, he curved in behind the two slower radial-engine bombers, who had not seen the German fighters; they were only 300 meters distant. Schroer's 109F was armed with three 20mm cannon and two 7.2 mm machine guns. In seconds he was behind his first unsuspecting victim and the distance had decreased to 100 meters. Schroer opened fire, aiming at the right wing, which almost instantly streamed smoke and dropped. They were just above the surface and Schroer watched the ten-ton Beaufighter and its three-man crew plunge into the green out of control. Poor devils! His wingman still with him, left, Schroer pulled up, turned left, and came back down behind the other Beaufighter, which soon came within range. His wingman was yelling: "Get the other one!" He pulled in very close, opened fire, and was dumbfounded to see that Beaufighter explode immediately. A lucky victory—but rotten luck for these three victims. Schroer now worried about the china, wine, and wedding gifts carefully stored in every spare corner of his fighter. Had they been broken?

He was near Crete and would soon find out.

He touched down on the island German forces had captured at such great cost in 1941, to be greeted by a Captain Dullberg, fighter commander on the island. Dullberg found Schroer's story hard to believe. Schroer offered to fly him to the spot. Air-sea rescue craft had been alerted, but found no survivors. Schroer and Dullberg then took off and found the wreckage 17 miles east of Crete. They radioed that location in, but also saw no survivors.

Upon landing, a question still on Schroer's mind was how many pieces of his wedding china had been broken. Inspection showed four of eight plates smashed, and seven of the cups. The biggest serving plate was unbroken. Schroer bought other gifts as replacements, and after spending the night on Crete and celebrating his weird victory, next morning began the flight to Foggia, Italy. News of his strange combat, with china aboard, had preceded him. An Italian correspondent had sent the story to Italy and German newspapers picked it up. Ilse had therefore read about her wedding china's rough treatment before her Werner reached Mulheim! From Foggia, Schroer flew northward to Munich, where he left his fighter. From there he took the train home for his wedding. It took place March 2nd—four days before Rommel's last ill-fated attack in Africa, on the Mareth Line.

Schroer returned to the Mediterranean after leave, flying from fields in Sicily and Italy. On Sicily, serving as Kommandeur of Gruppe II, in J.G. 27, three months later, Schroer had another fateful encounter over the sea. Before I asked him to describe that mission in detail, we discussed the history of J.G. 27 and its greatest ace in Africa, Hans Marseille. Schroer had known Marseille well. I had talked to Marseille's commanding officer, Oberst Eduard Neumann, about the great fighter ace of J.G. 27 on several occasions. I had once traveled to Köln to question Marseille's wingman and had talked to him again in Munich in 1973. I had questioned Adolf Galland and others about Marseille and his amazing record. He had often shot down five or six (or more) aircraft in a day. So I wanted to ask Schroer, too, as fellow pilot of J.G. 27, about Marseille.

"Marseille was a genius in shooting, in estimating distances, in innovating," he said. "He would lower flaps or even lower the undercarriage to gain in a turn. He studied and learned everything about the aircraft. He pioneered completely new techniques in air fighting.

"I remember that the English over Tobruk would go into a defensive circle to defend themselves against our attacks. It was effective in a way. They were always at 2,500 meters and we would approach at 3,000. This happened day after day. We were having trouble with this defensive tactic and Marseille decided to do something about it.

"One day—he had figured this out—he dived low and under them and suddenly came up inside the middle of the RAF's defensive circle. He shot two of the English aircraft down—they were Hurricanes—and scattered the formation. Then the rest of us had targets to go after, and we scored heavily that day. That was typical of Marseille. He went in alone and produced the victory.

"I remember that he went into a spin after shooting down the two Hurricanes that day. But he recovered nicely—it was part of his plan. It was late; it always was when we met the Hurricanes over Tobruk. We used to worry about getting back with enough daylight to land. We had to fly from Gazala to Gambut and then to Tobruk. This was in 1941. We were very short on parts and aircraft. In fact, we used to play cards and gamble to see who would get to fly. We had an absolute feeling of superiority.

"At that time Marseille was a Lieutenant and I was a Sergeant. He was in the 2nd Squadron and I was in the 3rd. At one time, over a period of some four weeks, we had only two serviceable aircraft. We were all eager to fly and morale was very high.

"But Marseille, he was in a class by himself, no doubt about it."

Schroer usually flew the ME 109 but once flew the FW 190. New models of 109s or FW 190s, or special production models, were constantly introduced during the war, versions incorporating the latest technological developments. "I remember that in February of 1945, just three months before the war ended, I got a specially built FW 190D-9. It was better than the P-51 Mustangs American pilots flew. It climbed better. It had a supercharger, as the Mustang did. It was a very fine fighter. They were being introduced into the geschwadern—I was leading J.G. 3 (Udet) at that time— only one at a time. We never got another. By giving the most successful pilots the first of the most advanced fighters, the Luftwaffe probably helped some of them survive."

Schroer shot down just about every type of British and American aircraft. In Africa he usually opposed Hurricanes and Spitfires. In Italy and Sicily he began to engage P-40s, Boston (Douglas A-20) light bombers, and the B-17 Flying Fortress and B-24 Liberator heavy bombers. When transferred to home defense in northern Europe, he then took on P-38s, P-47s, and P-51 Mustangs. He respected the Thunderbolts and Mustangs most, as well as the Spitfire—which in northern Europe he met only nearer England, not deep in Germany where Mustangs, with their far superior range, penetrated daily in the war's last year.

The mission Schroer especially remembered took place over the Mediterranean Sea at the end of May in 1943. It contained an element of mystery. Schroer took a chance in ordering that it be flown.

Axis forces had surrendered in Tunisia early that month. The

Allies were looking north to Sicily and Italy. U.S. B-17 bombers began flying missions from North African bases to the heart of Italy (which would surrender in a matter of months.) The German High Command had initially thought defending Sicily would be hopeless, but partly changed its view and sent troops and air units to the island.

Schroer was there at this time as Kommadeur of Gruppe II, J.G. 27, with the rank of Hauptmann. His 109s were based at Trapani, on the northwestern tip of the island, 100 kilometers west of Palermo. The Luftwaffe didn't have enough long-range reconnaissance aircraft to comb the entire Mediterranean. The few FW 200 Condors were employed primarily over the Atlantic (but had been roughly handled lately by British fighters catapulted from ships). There were only a limited number of BV 138s flying, mostly over the Atlantic and in Rumania. AR 196s had been operating in the Mediterranean, but they were not suitable for attacking bombers. Nor were the Condors, nor the Blohm and Voss flying boats.

A special problem for Schroer's fighters at this time, then, was locating enemy bombers. The B-17s were fast enough to evade anything but fighters, and were very heavily armed, with 10 machine guns. B-17 formations were flying almost daily from North African bases to Italy, bypassing Sicily and German fighters to the west of the island. Schroer's communications officer repeatedly received alarms by radio when Italian targets were being hit. But all the fighter unit had to go on was the target attacked, the time the B-17s had dropped their bombs, and the direction they were flying when they left the target. This hadn't been enough for J.G. 27 to effect interceptions. Fuel was so short that Luftwaffe orders were not to fly unless on necessary missions or against specific, located targets. Of course, it was purely guesswork or conjecture whether the B-17s would change course several times on their way to Italian targets and how far they would miss Sicily to the west on return flights to North Africa. Schroer and his communications officer, Werner-Stahl, puzzled long over the probabilities. Werner-Stahl theorized that the big bombers were coming as close to Sicily as they dared to reduce flying time. He estimated they would stay just far enough off shore, to the west, to remain unseen, fly low, and depend on mathematical odds (very much in their favor) that no German fighters would happen to be in that airspace at the time they passed. Even had German fighters been alerted by boats or reconnaissance aircraft as the bombers passed west of Trapani, it would then have been impossible to overtake the B-17s before they reached the safety of the North African shore—and protecting fighters—only about 150 kilometers from Sicily. The only chance of interception for J.G. 27 was for the fighters to take off when the Italians reported a target bombed, estimate the time and place the U.S. bombers were likely to pass on the return route, and be there, hoping to make contact.

Schroer and Werner-Stahl had discussed this theory for days. They were ready to try it—or Schroer was—when May 31st dawned clear and bright over the Mediterranean with excellent visibility. Schroer ordered his pilots on ready status. Their camouflaged pale brown 109s (with yellow noses) were run up early by crewmen that day for the possible mission. But the morning passed quietly and lunchtime came without reports from Italy. Schroer and II Gruppe pilots lounged in the squadron room (a commandeered Sicilian house) not far from the grass field. On warm days like this, pilots wore only light blue shirts with blue trousers. Rather than solid leather helmets, in this climate they wore a light, netlike covering over the head, with earphones attached.

At 14:08 a call came in from Naples. The city had just been bombed by a large formation of four-engined American bombers. Schroer and Werner-Stahl began measuring distances on squadron maps. From Naples to a point west of Sicily, where the bombers might pass, it was 400 kilometers. The best hope was for an intercepting fighter force to fly northwest—and soon—for earliest possible interception and enough time to engage the bombers over some distance. Schroer gave the orders and soon pilots were scrambling to dispersed fighters. Following a timetable, in 20 minutes 20 German fighters lifted off the dusty Sicilian field and pointed their yellow noses west by northwest. Schroer feared the consequences from higher headquarters if they didn't intercept, so it was with continuing trepidation that he led the Messerschmitts upward on course 300 degrees this spring afternoon.

Radio silence was maintained and they leveled off at low altitude after leaving the coastline of Sicily behind, southeast. Schroer was thankful for the good visibility. The formation held position as minutes dragged by. All eyes were searching various arcs of the sky, mostly right and ahead. They remained low, about 30 kilometers from the Sicilian coast . . . nothing. They flew on, still looking.

Then, ahead, low, greenish-colored aircraft—big bombers—came into view. Simultaneously, the first spotter shouted excitedly over the earphones: "Da sind Sie!" Schroer had sighted the enemy at the same instant. He could make out about 60 four-motored bombers close to the water. Obviously, they had left Naples some minutes before Trapani received the alarm, and had the fighters delayed takeoff, they might have missed them. Schroer radioed to his pilots the position of the bombers ahead, moving from starboard to port. Flushed with excitement, he ordered pilots to attack as they wished—"Bitte, alle Ankommen! Jeder grief an wie er will!"

The four-engine Fortresses were surprisingly low. Schroer estimated their altitude at 40 meters and as some of them now saw the German fighters, they dipped even lower. The tactic they were using was designed to deny the Germans an attack from beneath, to force the fighters to come in from above. From above, the many defending guns could be more easily trained on the faster fighters— from tail turret, fuselage "waist" guns and overhead fuselage turret. On-the-deck flying eliminated one attack approach and simplified the bombers' defense.

Schroer pointed the yellow nose of his lead fighter downward, banking into a left turn. He would approach from behind at high speed. Other 109s singled out their targets and banked left in descending approaches. The speed of the fighters reached 500 km., 550 km., 600 km. As they neared the American bombers, the B-17s began to close ranks to concentrate defensive firepower.

There are ample targets for each fighter, since there are three times as many bombers. And it's obvious that not all the bomber crews have seen the German fighters or heard radio warnings. U.S. Fortresses have been flying such missions for weeks and their crews have become lax. In some tail turrets there's still no gunner as the gap between them and the oncoming fighters fast closes. The big bombers now began to fill the sights of the fighters. Schroer picks out a straggler to the rear and in seconds has him squarely in his sights; he presses the firing button. He has underestimated his own speed and zooms over the big green Fortress far too quickly. He might as well go for the leader. The formation commander is more than a kilometer ahead of the rear bombers, many of which are now being attacked by the German fighters. Without altering course much, Schroer flashes over other bombers and maneuvers to approach the lead aircraft.

He sees no rear gunner, and is closing at a slower 300 km. This time he won't overshoot; he banks carefully into firing position to the right rear, above, and puts his finger on the trigger. The Fortress is now in range and he aims deliberately at the right wing engines. The three 20mm cannon and 7.2s send a trail of shells into the two right engines and both begin emitting black smoke! Schroer had been dead on target. As he flashes by on the right, the big Fort banks left. At the same time, others splash into the sea behind. But the smoking leader doesn't lose his precious altitude and heads straight for the mainland—Sicily! The pilot obviously knew his position exactly and knew instantly what to do. Schroer banks above the B-17 and watches heavy black smoke trailing behind. The Americans know they'll never make it to Africa, and hope now to land in Sicily, where the crew will become prisoners. (Perhaps that B-17 can be repaired and utilized by the Luftwaffe.)

The green bomber neared the shoreline ahead, low over the water. Schroer flew alongside until he noticed that his fuel was low. "Achtung, Benzin!" he radioed fellow pilots. They must return to Trapani. The sea behind was a sight to remember. Eight of the big four-engined bombers were down. Radio alerts went to Italian air-sea rescue to come out and pick up downed airmen. Though Schroer should have been heading toward Trapani, somehow he couldn't leave his victim, so he stayed close. They were both headed in the same general direction anyhow. The two aircraft crossed the shore and the smoking B-17 made for a large grass field. Still trailing black smoke, it successfully accomplished a forced landing in a big green field not far from the coast. Eleven Americans hustled out of the bomber, which was about midway between Trapani and Palermo. Italians at the scene quickly took the Americans prisoner; their treatment at the hands of the Sicilians wasn't gentle.

Schroer had written down the numbers on the bomber's side and flew straight back to Trapani. He landed at 15:10 and—amid congratulations from all sides, especially Werner-Stahl—called Luftwaffe headquarters in Palermo to ask about the crew of the surrendered bomber. An Army general had been aboard. That meant, to Schroer, the U.S. Army might be inspecting the Italian coast for possible landing sites. He inquired about the American pilot, who was alive and well—a captain. Schroer decided to meet him and flew to Trapani. A short time later he found the American dejected and exhibiting considerable anxiety. He had heard gossip about tough Luftwaffe interrogation and wondered what might happen to him there. Schroer reassured him and offered him a drink!

The B-17s had been making the Africa-Italy run for weeks now. They had felt safe—too safe. After a time, the two pilots became friendly and when the captured American departed, he was in a much better state of mind.

Field Marshal Kesselring, the theater commander, heard of the attack and was pleased with the interception, but headquarters asked who had authorized the flight! It was all explained and Schroer was officially forgiven—but only after more admonitions and warnings about unauthorized takeoffs. The score for that May afternoon was eight B-17s shot down and one forced to crash-land. No German pilots or planes were lost. Many of the downed bomber crewmen were fished out of the sea by Italian rescue boats. Some, unfortunately, had not been saved.

"I didn't fly again that day." Schroer recalls with a smile. "Our planning had worked. We had a celebration that night. It was a special mission I'll always remember. We took a chance flying it. If I had found nothing, higher command would have had me on the carpet."

There had been other memorable flights over this same part of the Mediterranean for Schroer. After his wedding, he was posted to Tunisia, where British and American armies were fast closing in on Axis forces from south, north, and west. In the final days all hope of escape was gone for most Germans. U.S. Fighters had caught big, slow German transports shuttling between Tunisia and Sicily on several occasions and slaughtered the vulnerable craft. The sea lanes were all but cut off for the Germans and Italians. At the very last minute, Schroer and other Luftwaffe fighter pilots fitted two ground crewman into the single seat of the 109, sat on top of their passengers, and flew to Sicily. Schroer had flown from Bone, west of Bizerte, to the field he was now operating from, Trapani. And he had gone back again after the first trip and brought out two other ground crewmen. These were desperate days and those who couldn't get out knew they would be captured. The four ground crewmen Schroer evacuated successfully were greatly envied at the time by comrades left behind. But the war for those captured was over. Who were the lucky ones, after all? Few of those evacuated could envision the extent of Germany's destruction and defeat two years later.

Schroer had not foreseen the tragic end ahead for Germany. In fact, he admits he was very much impressed meeting Hitler two months later at Hitler's headquarters in the east. He and seven other aces were decorated by the still-convincing dictator. They had to wait two days until Hitler found time to see them. Finally, at 2:00 A.M. on August 2nd. 1943, they were ushered into the Fuhrer's presence. They had tea around a circular table after Hitler had presented them the Knight's Cross with Oak Leaves. Schroer at that time had been credited with 84 aerial victories. Hitler greatly impressed all the young pilots. He was friendly, calm, amazingly knowledgeable about the air war, and even about the details and the nature of the ammunition they were using. He told them how he would rebuild Germany's destroyed cities, expressing deep concern over the cities' fate at the hands of Allied bombers. But the fighter aces were surprised when Hitler spoke of the new ME 262 jet as a revenge weapon, a bomber. One had spoken up and told Hitler the 262 should be used as a fighter. Hitler understood their sentiment. He replied that Germany was already producing enough fighters but that fuel was short. The newly decorated aces left much impressed by Hitler's personality, his knowledge of the air war, and his calm confidence. "But I didn't know anything about mass killing of Jews or others at that time," Schroer emphasized, "or about so much else."

At the end of the war, Schroer was detained as a prisoner by the Allies for three months. Released in August 1945, he returned to a completely shattered nation in which people were horrified by tales of war crimes and were struggling for their very survival. It was a most difficult time for the couple who had been married in such fanfare and public acclaim two years earlier. But one of the bright spots for Schroer was the kindness of an American officer, Paul Cook, who was on occupation duty in Germany. This Coloradan met Schroer one day purely by chance when he offered him a ride. They immediately liked each other. Cook soon realized Schroer's value to his captors and made him his intelligence officer. That eased the hard years for Ilse and Werner, to a degree. And Germany began to get on its feet again in the next few years.

Schroer held an executive position with the international air and space firm of Messerschmitt-Boelkow-Blohm in the 1970s, and in the '80s, after one retirement, accepted another job. One son is a lawyer in Hamburg and the other lives nearby. Ilse and Werner Schroer enjoyed a quiet life. The great ace of Africa and the West, with the best victory per mission percentage of all Luftwaffe pilots who downed 100 or more allied aircraft, was seldom recognized by his countrymen on Munich's streets. Even more ironic, he had missed a pension by only a few months! But comrades and historians appreciated Schroer's unique flying record. Schroer still had his logbooks and victory confirmations—which invariably came only months after a combat, from Berlin, after a thorough evaluation of the claim.

He gave me copies of several, plus an interrogation report

from the Luftwaffe interrogation center at Oberursel—three pages of information about the crew of a Liberator downed in July of 1943. He gave me a copy of the newspaper article by the Italian correspondent on Crete who wrote the story about his engagement with Beaufighters while his 109 was loaded with china and wedding presents. "We still have some of the china," Schroer said, with that quick smile, during a talk one day in Munich. That day we also talked about death and hospital bills. Hanna Reitsch had just died, the famous flier of prewar, wartime, and postwar Germany. "Too much fear," Schroer remarked solemnly, "doesn't remain in the clothes. It remains in the body." We were sitting in room 339 of the Deutscher Haus Centrum on Loth Strasse and Schroer was contemplating an operation. He was looking through a huge window so typical of German buildings built in the first half of the century. I asked how much the operation would cost. He turned to me and smiled again, and I noticed in the sunlight how grey the hair of the once-young eagle was. "I had nine and a half years of military service. One needed 10 to get a pension. So I must pay for this operation myself," he said quietly, still smiling.

His answer reminded me instantly of a meeting I had had 10 years earlier in downtown Munich with one of the greatest fighter pilots of World War I, Joseph Jacobs. Jacobs was then about 80 years old and still working for a living, and I asked why he had no pension. He said (and he was one of Germany's World War I heroes) that only regular officers got pensions, adding: "You see, I was only a reserve officer." Jacobs died only a short time before I visited Schroer in the hospital. The great First War pilot who had flown with von Richthofen had served only a few years during that war. But Schroer, one of his country's greatest heroes in the Second World War, had served nine and a half years in the military, accomplishing almost unparalleled feats in the air. It hadn't been quite enough. He survived, to pay for the operation.

But in February 1985, his heart finally stopped. He died at 67, almost unknown, but one of the greatest pilots in history.

Chapter 9

Trapped by Zekes: Rabaul

The most formidable Japanese base in the South Pacific in World War II from 1942 to 1944 was Rabaul.

Rabaul is located on the northern tip of New Britain Island, at the northwestern end of the Solomon Islands; it lies about 400 miles north of the eastern end of New Guinea. Simpson Harbor at Rabaul is one of the finest natural harbors in the Pacific, protected by massive hills on three sides—among them, five volcanoes.

This great military base in the Bismarck Archipelago had once been the territory of Japan's World War II ally, Germany. German colonial possessions, including this archipelago, were seized by Australia and Britain in World War I.

The Australians administered the former German territory between the wars and until January 23, 1942, when onrushing Japanese forces captured New Britain and moved on southeastward.

Japanese militarists had long appreciated Rabaul's potential, particularly its magnificent harbor and strategic location. They quickly set about to make it the principal Japanese base in the South Pacific, from which their naval and air forces could operate against New Guinea, Australia, the Solomon Islands, and southeastward. Rabaul became the headquarters of the Imperial Navy's Southeastern Fleet and Eighth Army. A hundred thousand civilian and military personnel were sent there, including an army of 75,000.

Around Rabaul five military airfields were constructed: Laukani, Vunakanau, Rapopo, Keravat, and Tobera.

The complex's importance as a naval base was rivaled only by Truk, the main Japanese fleet base 695 miles to the north. From Rabaul came practically all of the striking forces that fought the battle for Guadalcanal and control of Solomon waters for the better part of a year.

From its harbor and airfields surrounding it sortied most of the Japanese air and naval strikes against American forces island-hopping up the Solomons after U.S. forces achieved victory on Guadalcanal in February 1943.

By late 1943 U.S. airpower had closed in on the great base and was strategically disposed to conduct a major offensive against it. American troops had successfully completed a landing on nearby Bougainville (Empress Augusta Bay), though the Japanese were entrenched on both ends of this long island. A U.S. air base, Torokina Field, was now in operation on Bougainville. In addition, numerous American air bases were in operation down the Solomons chain to the southeast. To the west, General Douglas MacArthur's forces were advancing along New Guinea and now controlled the western tip of New Britain itself.

The American air offensive against Rabaul began late in 1943 and from then until February 19, 1944, the most intense series of aerial encounters of the war up to that time took place. The Japanese fed into Rabaul hundreds of extra fighters in a desperate attempt to check the American air offensive.

In January 1944, the reorganized 2nd Carrier Division of the Japanese Navy, under Rear Admiral Takaji Jojima, was ordered to fly its planes to Rabaul to bolster tottering defenders (the 26th Air Flotilla). They arrived January 25.

The 2nd Carrier Division's Air Staff officer was Masatake Okumiya, one of Japan's greatest fighter pilots and most aggressive combat leaders. The more than 100 planes of the carrier division flown from Truk to Rabaul strengthened the enemy's defenses considerably, bringing to over 300 the number available for defense of Rabaul. These carrier reinforcements were the best of Japan's carrier fighter pilots.

American air attacks on Rabaul continued all through January, the enemy often sending up as many as 75 or 100 defending fighters. American forces included fighters, dive bombers, and torpedo and heavy bombers. The torpedo bombers concentrated on shipping in Simpson Harbor, and on some raids were highly successful in spite of bitter opposition. On January 17, five Japanese ships were sunk by SBDs and TBFs. The U.S. attackers lost 12 aircraft in this battle, one a TBF that struck a Japanese ship after its torpedo run.

A week later, on January 24, another sizable force of torpedo bombers, escorted by fighters, attacked shipping in Simpson Harbor. The torpedo bombers carried 2,000-pound bombs with delayed action fuses, and once again five Japanese ships were sunk. It was just after this attack that planes from the enemy's 2nd Carrier Division arrived at Rabaul.

Despite this reinforcement, the continuing fierceness of the U.S. aerial assault and success of dive bombers and torpedo bombers forced the enemy to withdraw most of his ships from Rabaul. And the air battles were exacting a very heavy toll of defending fighters.

In January's intensified air battles, many of the top United States Navy aces were also shot down. Lieutenant Robert M. Hansen, USMC, credited with 25 kills, was lost in a crash pulling out of a strafing run on Cape St. George. Major Gregory Boyington, USMC, credited with 22 kills in the Pacific, was shot down off Rabaul and taken prisoner.

One of the war's top-scoring Navy aces, Lieutenant Ira C. Kepford, was among the handful of U.S. fighter pilots stationed on the newly won base at Bougainville during this air struggle. Kepford and his comrades of VF 17 had been at Bougainville only a short time when the assault reached its climax. The navy had already lost a number of its pilots, who were operating under far-from-ideal conditions.

Japanese troops were still sniping at them from the jungle. They were living in tents in a sea of mud. In these circumstances many were flying several flights to Rabaul a day!

It was a stark contrast to Kepford's recent college days at Northwestern University, where he had joined the Navy. He had been blocking back on Northwestern's football team and was inducted at halftime during the Northwestern-Purdue game in 1941.

At Bougainville, the Muskegon, Michigan, athlete confronted a life vastly different from his college days. Bougainville was the end of the American supply line; American pilots had to make out with delicacies such as ram's tongue. Needless to say, the reaction of Navy pilots, who rated "chow" by carrier standards, was less than enthusiastic.

Bougainville was dusty and dirty—or rainy. It seemed always hot. The coral dust was a problem for equipment and crew chiefs, and caused frequent trouble in the big radial engines of the F4U Corsairs VF 17 pilots were flying. Pilots usually wore only shorts, a summer flight suit, and tennis shoes on missions.

In spite of these difficulties, VF 17 was to compile one of the outstanding records of all combat fighter squadrons in World War II. And Kepford, the Northwestern halfback, was to emerge from his tour as the fifth-ranking fighter ace in the U.S. Navy.

His most memorable mission, and one which almost cost him his life, occurred on February 19, 1944. To that day we now turn.

The duty officer shook Kepford awake early Saturday morning, February 19. He was flying the day's first mission. He dressed in a lightweight flying suit and white tennis shoes, and after a quick breakfast at the "chow" tent, he reported to the briefing shack a short distance away under the palms.

Leading the early morning mission was the executive officer of VF 17, Lieutenant Commander Roger Hedrick. He conducted the briefing. Twenty planes would participate in the day's first mission, a strafing attack on—of course—Rabaul and surrounding military installations. Hedrick estimated Japanese fighter opposition would be quite strong; it was known that the enemy had recently received major air reinforcement—the 2nd Carrier Division.

One of the targets to be given particular attention was the concentration of antiaircraft guns on a volcanic slope jutting into the harbor at its upper end near Lajunai Field.

The weather officer forecast good weather. The squadron would split, 16 fighters doing the strafing and four acting as top cover. Kepford was one of the top cover.

An ammunition truck hustled the pilots to squadron headquarters, where a second briefing took place to ensure complete understanding and cooperation among divisions of the squadron. After that, a truck deposited the pilots at their Corsairs near or under the palms, each wearing a Mae West, pistol, and emergency medical kit strapped under the left arm. (Parachutes were left overnight in the planes.)

Leading the four-fighter division to act as top cover was Lieutenant Merle ("Butch") Davenport. Earlier, Kepford had been Davenport's wingman but had graduated and was now second-in-command of the four-unit division, flying number three position. Ensign Don ("Red") McQueen, of Chicago, was flying his wing.

The squadron's call name was "Hog" and the flight leader's code name was "Big Hog." Kepford was flying F4U 29, and therefore known on the radio that morning as "Hog 29."

Dark-blue Corsairs roared to life and taxied out to the end of the runway. In minutes they were taking off into a clear sky. The twenty F4Us climbed at 170 knots over the hills and palms of Bougainville, course 320 degrees. It was 8:00 A.M., and the sun, behind, was rising, basking the ocean, left, in shimmering silver. The sun was so bright that looking back, the sky was only a bright blur. Ahead, a haze slightly reduced visibility in the direction of Rabaul but the light nevertheless painted the tips of waves to the west silver.

The squadron continued to climb into the northwest until superchargers cut in at 17,000 feet. Shortly, the coast of New Britain appeared ahead, and pilots began to tense—every attack of late had produced a strong reaction.

The Japanese had lost an estimated 300 aircraft since the American aerial offensive against Rabaul had begun, but steady reinforcements enabled them to send up strong intercepting forces. They were known to receive warnings of incoming attacks from Bougainville coast watchers.

The coast of New Britain, ahead and below, is now quite close. Kepford is suddenly distracted and disturbed by wingman Red McQueen's flying. Puffs of white smoke shoot backwards from his engine stacks and he's falling behind. Kepford eases his throttle back to have a look into his wingman's cockpit. As he does, McQueen motions to him. He gives the sign for coral dust in the carburetor. He must turn back. Worse, Kepford might have to turn back also—no singles are allowed to participate in attacks on Rabaul.

Squadron Leader Hedrick is informed by radio. Big Hog directs McQueen to return to base and orders Kepford to shepherd McQueen home. As McQueen's blue Corsair banks away and down, headed back to Bougainville, Kepford requests permission by radio to accompany the attackers and not McQueen. McQueen, he says, is in no danger of attack. Hedrick relents and gives him permission to remain with the squadron, but only until it's over the target area. (This will give him official credit on his flying record for completing the mission.) Kepford banks into position with Davenport and his wingman; top cover is now but three fighters.

They cross the New Britain coast. Kepford makes out the big base ahead and scans the sky in all directions for enemy fighters. It's apparently quiet. Now they approach the big harbor and enemy airstrips. Davenport and his wingman see him waggle his wings and give them a good-by kiss. He banks into a sweeping right turn, disappointed in being forced to abandon the mission minutes before the strafing.

As he turns right, New Ireland, the long island above Rabaul and running northwest-southeast, lies straight ahead of him. Kepford, a lone American fighter in an area where many enemy fighters can appear at any moment, nevertheless can't force himself to turn back all the way and forget the whole thing. He'll sneak over New Ireland for just a few minutes and see what's below as his comrades dive on Rabaul.

Kepford also wants to look at the enemy's Buka Island base, a few miles from the northern tip of Bougainville. Alone now, continuing to bank slowly right, Kepford constantly rotates head: right, left, behind, up and down, searching a very bright sky for bandits.

Throughout his flight training, as a cadet and afterward, instructors had drummed into his head the vital necessity of constantly searching the sky. The advantage invariably lies with the pilot who sees his enemy first and has time to prepare his attack—or avoid one, as circumstances dictate. This vigilance is now rewarded. Ahead, below right, Kepford's eye catches sight of motion, something moving just above water: a dark aircraft, moving in his direction from one o'clock, just above the surface.

Bandit! It's a darkly-painted single-engine enemy floatplane, very large, flying straight toward Kepford, well below.

A quick glance behind; Kepford pushes the stick forward, and slides off to the left slightly. He'll use superior altitude, execute a 180-degree turn to the right as the enemy approaches below, and dive straight down on him in a near-vertical pass.

The enemy aircraft comes on, unaware of the blue, gull-winged Corsair above. Kepford waits until the enemy is about to cross under, then rolls into the dive. If all works well, he'll fire almost straight down, and the enemy pilot will fly into his shells.

The dark silhouette flies on almost directly below. Kepford pushes right rudder and wings over into a steep dive. The F4U plunges downward with increasing velocity; Kepford must ease back on the throttle. Now his gaze is fixed on two yellow circles on the sighting glass. The enemy should appear at any moment, just above the cowling, flying into the Corsair's line of fire. The dark silhouette streaks out from under the nose of the F4U, in the sight circle—in range!

Kepford squeezes the trigger and tracers streak almost straight down as the staccato of six guns shakes the Vought fighter. The enemy flies through the chain of fire, the Corsair's guns tearing open holes all along the top of the fuselage. Kepford is almost on top of him but there's no more time to watch; he must pull out or hit the water. He pulls the stick back hard, blood drains from his head, and his line of vision races forward over the ocean, the advancing cowling obscuring the stricken Japanese below.

The ocean rushes up; the Corsair curves through the bottom of its arc and levels off very low over the water at high speed. Kepford glances back at the dark enemy aircraft, banking, streaming smoke. It smashes into the ocean! Kepford, easing back on the throttle, sees the fatal oil slick spread on the surface—a quick victory.

He banks into a sweeping turn, heads south, picks up the mike, and proudly presses the transmitter button: "Big Hog from Hog 29. Scratch one. Returning to base." As he pulls back on the stick to climb back up on the return flight, he hears a reply on his radio: "Prove it!" He realizes, with chagrin, that no one has seen him down the enemy plane. Wing cameras are not reliable in conditions such as those at Bougainville. Therefore, he may not have film to confirm his victory claim.

The altimeter gains in his southward climb and he continues to search the sky in every direction; in the direction of Squadron VF 17's Rabaul attack he can see nothing. But ahead he sees aircraft above . . . and freezes!

His heart pumps. If they're enemy fighters, between him and Bougainville, they have a tremendous altitude advantage and greatly outnumber him—at least 20. The dots grow larger. Now there are 30! He tensely studies the silhouettes coming on, . . . not friends—Zekes!

Kepford's first hope is to escape enemy eyes by being unobtrusive; perhaps the enemy won't notice him below. Pushing the stick forward, throttle all the way forward, he noses down toward the waves, angling slightly away from the oncoming gaggle. The Zekes are now unmistakable in the bright sunshine; they continue to fly straight ahead, as if they don't see him. Will his luck hold? Kepford nervously picks up the mike and radios VF 17: "Bogeys at five o'clock to your position!"

Hedrick immediately replies: "Where?" Kepford: "Repeat, five o'clock to your position."

There's no more time to talk. Four Zekes ahead peel off and start down. Kepford is discovered. He can't accept four-to-one odds and fight because there are 30-odd Zekes above, any one of which could get him in the end. All have the critical altitude advantage. He must run for it. He stands the F4U on its left wing at full throttle and turns away from the diving Zekes. But that means he's now headed north, away from his base. The big 2000-horsepower Pratt and Whitney engine roars and sweeps him rapidly along over the waves . . . but the diving Zekes are gaining. One is far ahead of the other three. He closes so fast he only has time for a short burst. Then the dirty green enemy skids out in front . . . for an instant. Kepford seizes his chance and opens fire. Hits register on the enemy's tail. He has shattered the Zeke's stabilizer and it falls to the sea. The other three spread out behind, one left and two off to the right.

They're boxing him in, to prevent him from turning back. Whichever way he turns, he'll turn into one or more, who will have a head-on shot at him. The Zekes gain and tracers streak by on the right. Unless he can shake his pursuers, he'll be splashed in a matter of minutes. He glances at the throttle quadrant. A copper wire and notch prevent the knob from going farther, the wire only to be broken in an emergency. It injects water into the engine, adding power. This is such an emergency! Kepford thrusts his left arm forward, gripping the throttle hard and the wire breaks. The engine seems to pause, then roars, and Kepford can feel an extra surge of power. It's temporary, but it's his only chance.

The F4U vibrates heavily; it rockets across the coast and over the trees. Kepford is now heading northward across New Ireland, directly away from his base. The Jap pilots hang close. He glances behind, right, then left. Are they still gaining? Tracers streak by his wing. Something slams into the Corsair from behind. They're still in range!

The engine howls and vibrates and the airspeed indicator continues to increase. His wings waxed and polished to give him a few extra knots, his engine on emergency power, Kepford is making well over 350 knots. The Japs stay behind, as if tied on.

Whump! Whump! More hits. Kepford feels the Corsair shudder. He's desperate now, almost frantic, and zigzags in an effort to throw the enemy pilots' aim off. Ahead, he sees the water. He has crossed the island and is headed northwest. If he doesn't turn back soon, the chase can only end in his ditching. He won't have enough fuel to get back to his base.

He glances back again. The three Zekes are still there, but not closing. They're no longer hitting him. On a pad on his right knee, his navigation pad, he jots down the time and notes the fuel remaining. He'll fly on northwest on emergency power a little longer, but then must turn back. Right now the enemy is still too close. A turn in either direction will bring him into range of an enemy fighter. He must lengthen the distance between them as momentum from their dives continues to slacken.

His earphones come to life; Big Hog is calling. Hedrick wants the position and direction of the Zekes.

"Still five o'clock from you," Kepford replies. Then he adds: "Many bogeys—this looks like it!"

Kepford gains slightly. He breaks out in a heavy sweat. Looking back, he can see the Zekes in almost the same position. The big Pratt and Whitney has been on emergency power for what seems ages. Soon he must turn into the enemy and give them their opportunity. His hands now tremble on the stick, his feet are jumping on the rudder bars.

For the first time in the war Kepford is totally overcome with fear. He's trapped, getting farther and farther from his base every second. And now the engine begins to overheat! It's throwing oil out over the canopy, a brownish-yellowish film. The engine gauges reflect high temperatures.

Strangely, Kepford's thoughts race back to the past, about his family, his mother's face. He thinks about his father, the day in the far-distant past when his father took away his air rifle! His thoughts go back to the campus at Northwestern, to his brother, now a Marine sergeant. He thinks of friends, and then of Lieutenant Commander Tom Blackburn, the squadron commander.

His feet—in tennis shoes—are already soaking wet. The white Keds have turned green! He can't understand this. Can his tennis shoes really be green? It puzzles him, even in this desperate situation, and he realizes perspiration draining from his body has discolored them!

The engine has just about spent its maximum power and the enemy fighters are slightly farther behind. He's finally leaving them!

Now he must turn one way or the other and fight his way out. Kepford hopes high engine temperatures are only the result of emergency power. If the enemy shells are responsible, the engine could soon be red-hot.

Another glance behind—the Corsair is definitely stretching the distance. Two enemy fighters to the right are still in position, but farther back. So is the lone enemy fighter left, behind. Kepford begins to fake a little to puzzle his pursuers. He banks slightly right, the enemy immediately following. Then he "slips" out of the turn. The Japanese take a moment longer to straighten out from theirs. They lose just a little. Kepford fakes to the right again, and invisibly rudders left, sliding out of the turn unobtrusively. The Japanese lose a little more distance in the cat-and-mouse maneuver.

Kepford decides to ease back slightly on the throttle. He's out of firing range. Back on the manifold pressure about two inches

. . . the engine seems to run more smoothly. It's still rough and vibrating, however, and Kepford, too, is still shaking. Now he must turn and head for home. He'll reverse course, turning left. There are two enemy planes to the right, and if he turns right, they'll both meet him. To his left there's only one to cut him off. Another consideration is torque—he can turn left quicker than right, since he'll be turning against the propeller. There's a chance one or more of the pilots behind him, opening fire in a turn just over the waves, might not keep his eye on the surface carefully enough and dip a wing. So he'll make it a sudden, violent turn.

He kicks left rudder hard and pulls the stick back into his stomach in the sharpest turn his body and the aircraft can stand. The F4U stands vertically on its left wing and begins a blood-draining arc left. Specks dance in Kepford's eyes, his vision dims—the first sign of a blackout. He pops the stick forward slightly, lessening the pull of gravity, and the blood flows back into his head just enough to sustain vision.

Stick back again—the Zeke on the left, behind, cuts him off in the turn. Twinkles appear on the leading edges of the green enemy's wings. Tracers streak by as the enemy pilot turns inside him. Kepford holds the stick in, the tracers shoot past, and the Corsair shudders on the verge of a stall.

The enemy pilot continues to fire and turn, barely above the tops of the waves. Kepford can see him out of the left corner of his eye, guns winking fire. A splash behind! The left wing of the enemy fighter has hit the water and the Zeke is cartwheeling. Its guns, continuing to fire, throw tracers into the sky; it cartwheels along the surface of the ocean, its wings breaking off.

Thankful relief! The enemy fighter that should have shot him down in the left turn is eliminated. Kepford, headed back to New Ireland again, looks to his left, behind. Were the other two enemy fighters able to follow? Apparently not. They're either staying with their crashed comrade in the sea, or realize they can't catch the Corsair. In the turn left, Kepford increased the distance from the Zekes behind, right, so he eases back on the throttle.

His fuel gauges, after so much all-out flying, are low. He must throttle back and lean the mixture if he is to reach base at Bougainville. The engine gauges are still red, but the engine runs smoothly. Looking behind and seeing no Zekes, he eases back a little more on the throttle.

Ahead, on the horizon, is New Ireland. If he can get safely over it, he'll feel more secure.

Meanwhile, at the base at Bougainville other pilots of VF 17 land. The last thing heard from Kepford was an excited transmission that many bogeys were attacking him.

The island airstrip resembles a T, the strip itself being crossed near the end by a taxiway. Near one end of the taxiway is a large tree, under which sits Kepford's crew chief, Moore, and ordnance man, Dineen. They're waiting despite suggestions from other crewmen that No. 29 must be down. Kepford is overdue but Moore keeps repeating:

"Mr. Kepford will get back."

Kepford roars in over the coast of New Ireland, headed southeast, crossing low, on the very tops of the palm trees. His worry now is fuel. He has the mixture control on very lean, which causes the engine to again run rough and hot. He figures his chance to get back is only 50-50. The solitary F4U crosses the opposite shore of New Ireland out over the blue Solomon Sea—still 200 miles from base. The morning sun is still bright, and everything at the moment seems a strange anticlimax.

The Corsair grinds along minute after minute, and loud roar of the engine becoming the only monotonous sound. There's no radio chatter; all the other pilots have long ago landed. Kepford flies on, fuel gauges gradually approaching empty.

Bougainville! The long island comes in view ahead. With gasoline dangerously low, Kepford stays to the right of enemy positions on Buka and northern Bougainville. He will turn slightly left shortly, to approach the U.S. base on the west coast, halfway down the long island.

After what seems a long interval over water, with gauges touching empty, Kepford catches sight of Empress Augusta Bay. He has a few gallons of fuel left. He can't contact the tower by radio. No one knows he's approaching. Therefore, he must circle the base and get a green light from the tower, clearing him to land.

He's just above the water and approaches from the sea. He can see activity on the base, though no planes are taking off. In a slow left turn, he sees a green light from the tower—just in time. He drops wheels, turns onto the base leg, and then turns another 90 degrees onto the approach. He slows the big Corsair to 100 knots, eases back on the stick, and waits for her to bump on the dusty coral runway. She bumps, settles, and rolls, and he approaches the intersection of the runway and taxi strip—near the big tree.

His crew chief and armorer have recognized No. 29 and dash to the battered blue fighter and jump on the wing. Moore looks at his pilot with a grin, but Kepford is again shaking all over as the tremendous tension drains out.

The crewmen find holes in the wing, in the flaps, and through the elevators. Kepford climbs from the cockpit, shaky, suffering from genuine shock. He speaks only briefly and softly to crewmen and fellow pilots as he walks to the squadron tent. The skipper and the flight surgeon, Lieutenant Lyle Herrmann, meet him there. A glance at Kepford and Blackburn knows he's in no condition to be interrogated. But Kepford insists on telling the intelligence officer what happened, though Blackburn and Herrmann urge him to relax.

Herrmann pours him four ounces of medicinal brandy and offers him two large pills; Kepford takes them. The flight surgeon insists Kepford eat and he gets food and coffee.

Then, still early, Kepford—totally exhausted physically and emotionally—falls asleep.

He sleeps all afternoon, all night and most of the next day. When he awakens, his tennis shoes are still green!

The last time the Japanese scrambled a major force of fighters to oppose the American aerial offensive against Rabaul was February 19. Fifty enemy fighters intercepted the American torpedo planes, dive bombers, F4Us, P-40s, and F6Fs.

American pilots took a heavy toll, shooting down 23. The next day, remnants of decimated Japanese fighter forces at Rabaul were withdrawn to Truk, where, ironically, carrier pilots from U.S. Navy Task Force 58 had just wrecked over 300 Japanese planes—intended reinforcements for Rabaul.

The Americans didn't realize immediately that the Japanese had pulled back, that the important enemy complex of bases was virtually abandoned, and that the long and bitter aerial struggle had been won.

The Japanese had lost 400 to 500 aircraft in their defense of Rabaul, not counting the 300 knocked out at Truk.

The long struggle hadn't been as costly for the Americans, though it had cost the nation some of its greatest aces. One of the most significant results of the victory at Rabaul was the impression it left on Japanese pilots, and on air staffs. The strain on the higher staff officers during the last days at Rabaul was unbearable. They saw the weight of the American attack increase day by day, and witnessed the growing futility of the Japanese defense.

Despite the most strenuous effort and the commitment of carrier pilots, the air staffs realized now that even their country's best

Army and Navy squadrons couldn't stop the mushrooming American aerial offensive. To many, the tremendous weight of the American attack, the increasing numbers of U.S. planes, and the improved performance of the American aircraft, convinced them the war was lost.

A Japanese air staff officer who served at Rabaul, Masatake Okumiya, noted that when the battle was finally over it had become clear to the Japanese who had watched it from the beginning that a great gap existed between the industrial potential of Japan and America. This produced a growing spirit of defeatism reaching into the highest military circles. The Rabaul air battle, more than any other fighter battle fought from land bases during the war, broke the back of Japanese air power.

The once-powerful Japanese bastion at Rabaul was to be bypassed. New Zealand infantry landed on Green Island, little more than 100 miles from Rabaul itself. On March 6, a 5,000-foot coral airstrip was completed on Green, and a week later American fighters arrived.

On March 20, the 4th Marine Regiment landed on Emirau Island, in the St. Matthias Group, northwest of Rabaul. This completed the encirclement of the great Japanese base and cut it off from Truk, 600 miles to the north.

Thereafter the mighty Japanese air and naval base—from which so many fleets had sailed toward Guadalcanal in that bitter campaign, and from which so many heavy air raids had been mounted against the Americans in the Solomons—strangled to death.

Kepford's use of water injection for extra power was one of the earlier U.S. demonstrations of this device. Shortly afterward, in May of 1944, the Navy issued a release to the press entitled: "Top-Scoring Navy Fighter Pilot Credits Water-Injection Device on Plane's Engine with Saving His Life."

The Navy had only recently installed the water-injection device in their fighters and there was still some debate over its merits at the time of Kepford's mission. His experience was confirmation of its value.

The Navy described Kepford's use of water injection as follows:

"The twenty-five-year-old pilot, whose home is in Muskegon, Michigan . . . found himself in a position that is a nightmare to every combat pilot.

"He was only fifty feet over the water and three Zekes were close on the tail of his plane—two on the right, astern, and one on the left. If he pulled up, he would be at the mercy of the Zekes; the same if he turned right or left.

" . . . It was then that the pilot flicked the water-injection switch. The resulting spurt of speed carried him far enough ahead so that he left the streaks of tracers . . . ."

Kepford ended the war with 17 confirmed aerial victories. He was awarded two Navy Crosses, the Silver Star, three Distinguished Flying Crosses, and the Air Medal.

The Navy's fifth-ranking fighter ace was discharged shortly after the war ended, in 1945, and married Esther M. Kraegel, of Superior, Wisconsin.

In search of a job, he answered a newspaper advertisement of the Rexall Drug Company. The company, after giving him various tests, hired him. He eventually rose to president of the Liggett Drug Company, another of the many successful fighter aces who disproved the theory that war heroes generally fail in postwar civilian life.

Chapter 10

D-Day over Normandy

The second front in Europe in World War II was opened with the cross-channel invasion of Normandy by British, Canadian, and American armies the morning of June 6th, 1944. Looking back on the largest amphibious undertaking in the history of war, it's clear there was little chance it would fail. The Allies had overwhelming naval superiority, and it had been shown at Salerno and Anzio that support from naval guns on a coastal battlefield was usually decisive. The Allies also enjoyed overwhelming dominance of the air. German estimates of the ratio of aircraft that could be engaged ranged from 20 to 1 to 50 to 1.

Germany was already pressed hard on two fronts, demands from which were consuming most of the army's divisions. Other divisions were tied down with occupation and defense duties from the northern tip of Norway to Greece in the Balkans. So the German commander-in-chief in the West could hope to employ 40 divisions at best, and these were to cover a coastal front hundreds of miles long. Several times that number were committed to the eastern front. Halfway down the boot of Italy, steady fighting engaged another 20 German divisions. At least that many were engaged in occupational and defense duties in the various parts of conquered Europe. German estimates were that the Allies had up to 75 divisions deployed or nearing readiness in England (this was an overestimate); thus one can understand the bleak briefing Field Marshal Gerd von Rundstedt gave Field Marshal Erwin Rommel in December 1943, when Rommel arrived to assume his duties as commander of Army Group B, consisting of Fifteenth and Seventh Armies, positioned to oppose the upcoming Allied invasion.

Rommel had less than a year to get ready. He did much in that time, including lifting morale. But it was a hopeless task, for only considerable sea or air power could have checked the Allied landing and turned it into a much-magnified Dieppe disaster. (The Luftwaffe had won the air battle at Dieppe in August 1942.) The astonishing thing about the great Allied invasion was that the German Army would manage to contain Allied landing forces in a limited area for more than two months in the face of devastating air and sea power. To do that required almost superhuman courage on the part of the elite ground units, some of which were virtually annihilated by an avalanche of sea, air, and ground fire concentrated on them.

In the very first days of the invasion, naval gunfire often proved decisive in silencing big guns or artillery concentrations. German Army commanders had hoped to employ these guns to fight off warships and assault troops. Many shore batteries were solidly encased in thick concrete, invisible from the sea. In their planning, therefore, Allied commanders decided to include in the invasion armada every type of naval vessel, including 16-inch gun battleships. The channel was a dangerously small body of water, in close proximity to enemy air bases, for battleships. The Luftwaffe early in the war demonstrated off Norway and Crete—and Malta, too—that aircraft could sink even the most formidable naval vessels if they came within close range. Thus every officer at Supreme Headquarters in England knew the RAF and USAAF must chase the Luftwaffe out of Normandy's skies if the big ships (and others) were not to be highly vulnerable to air attack. By D-Day, therefore, two months of massive air attacks on Luftwaffe fields on or near the French coast had rendered most of them inoperable. Luftwaffe fighters and bombers had been moved back at least to Paris. As a result of this and overwhelming Allied numerical superiority, during landings the Luftwaffe was unable to cause major disruptions.

Another role was also assigned Allied fighter pilots, in addition to that of maintaining supremacy over Normandy. It's one little appreciated even today in accounts of the events of June 1944. That was artillery spotting for the gun batteries of warships lying off the Normandy coast. Royal Navy pilots who flew as spotters flew the famed Spitfire—but it wasn't called the Spitfire in the naval service; it was the Seafire and known as "the Spitfire with a hook." When it went into operation with the Royal Navy in November 1942, it was the fastest medium-level fighter carried by carriers—and it stayed in service on carriers until 1954. The Seafire was not only a formidable air combat fighter (it was, of course, a Spitfire modified to land on carriers) but an excellent spotter. Its speed enabled pilots to pinpoint targets and yet not tarry above them too long. During the great seaborne assault on France in 1944, Seafire pilots often flew from over their targets back out to sea between salvoes from parent ships. As we shall see in this chapter, German antiaircraft fire was often quite effective and pilots not prepared to take this into consideration frequently paid for their recklessness.

To have watched the Allied naval armada off the coast of Normandy from above during the days of the cross-channel assault was an unique opportunity. To have worked with the big ships of the British and American navies in gunnery action, silencing enemy artillery, and to have called in targets and corrected aim, was a never-to-be-forgotten assignment. Only a limited number of British and American pilots were assigned to this task. Spotter aircraft operated in pairs and there were only a limited number of pairs in operation at any one time. Some 150 fighter pilots—not all of whom survived—monitored the great seaborne expedition from a privileged site in the sky, looking down on a military struggle that would decide Europe's fate in 11 months.

The Allies' Air Spotting Pool, operating from Lee-on-Solent (between Portsmouth and Southampton) flew Seafires, two RAF Spitfire LVB Squadrons and a U.S. Navy unit (17 pilots) flying Spitfires—VCS-7. By the 1st of June its strength had reached 101 Seafires and Spitfires in five naval and two air force squadrons. These spotters would direct the fire of the Allied navies' big guns in the invasion attack. Most of them had by that time been in training for at least three months to learn spotter techniques.

Basically, the weaver in the pair would fly about 2,000 feet above the spotter, who flew at an altitude between 4,000 and 8,000 feet. The weaver's job was to protect the spotter from surprise bounces by enemy fighters. This spotter-and-weaver system proved its value from the first day in Normandy, for Luftwaffe fighters sometimes took a keen interest in spotters—though the Luftwaffe was seldom seen over the channel. Luftwaffe fighters appeared over the battlefield, however, from the first morning of the invasion but were so quickly bounced and so outnumbered they could find little time to support their comrades. Instead, they were almost constantly forced to defend themselves, heavily outnumbered, and to evade ground or naval fire. But concerning a frequent claim that on D-Day the Luftwaffe was *nowhere* to be seen, spotter pilots are quick to refute it.

By D-Day, the number of aircraft for spotting duty at Lee-on-Solent had been increased by two RAF and one RCAF Mustang squadrons. As an indication of the activity of spotters, they flew a total of 435 sorties in behalf of the invading forces on D-Day. This was (according to Royal Navy historian and author David Brown) highest number of sorties flown up to that time in one day from any Allied tactical air base. Thus the role of spotter aircraft in the opening days of the landing in France was of critical importance to success on the ground; in these first days, spotter aircraft often dove to the deck and strafed ground targets (usually gun emplacements) after fire direction, about which we shall learn.

Of all Normandy's invasion beaches, the most difficult landing—one that in the morning hours of June 6th appeared to be a failure—was the American Army's assault on Omaha Beach. Omaha covered a 10 mile long stretch of coast just east of the Cherbourg peninsula, from Pointe du Hoe almost to Port-en-Bessin. On the first day a permanent lodgement was obtained only in the middle half of this stretch, and nowhere as much as two miles inland.

Things began badly in the first minutes at Omaha. Heavy bombers, which were to have shattered beach defenses, delayed dropping their bombs because of poor visibility and danger to their own landing craft. The result was that 13,000 bombs carried by 329 B-24 bombers were dropped far inland. Aerial bombing on none of the invasion beaches was what had been hoped for because of the bad weather, but at Omaha the consequences of General Dwight Eisenhower's decision to go ahead with the landings despite the weather were the most serious. German-manned coastal batteries that had survived began firing at targets in the water at 0536; it was evident from the beginning that the massive aerial bombardment had failed to silence many of the defenders' coastal guns. Also, naval gunfire designed to suppress coastal fortifications was less effective at Omaha than anywhere else along the invasion front. Various reasons for this have been offered, but it seems one certainty is that coastal guns in this area were sited to cover the beaches, not the sea, and were invisible from ships offshore. Whatever the reasons, the aerial bombers dropped their bombs too far inland, and naval gunfire missed most of its targets. Third, a barrage of

Allied rockets overshot. Thus American troops met a hail of gun and mortar fire from the first moment they approached the shore that morning, especially on the right flank. It was to require naval gunfire, during that day and the next, to open a path inland for the invaders.

So grim did the scene on Omaha's beaches seem that the German LXXXIV Corps and Seventh Army believed through most of June 6th that the American landing there had been stopped at the shoreline. The U.S. 1st Division, of General Leonard Gerow's V Corps, assaulting with two regiments abreast, took very heavy losses. Soldiers were often hit in the water before they got ashore. Survivors took cover behind sand dunes and lay there practically helpless. The debacle resulted partly because these regiments had lost practically all their tanks and heavy equipment—another consequence of the decision to invade in spite of heavy weather. Of 32 tanks launched that morning to support the regiment invading Omaha's right, the 116th (attached from the 29th Division), only five reached shore, the others foundering on their too-long, 6,000 yard run-in to the beach. The assaulting infantry was transferred from transports to landing craft 10 to 11 miles off shore (too far out, considering the weather) and at least 10 of these ferry craft were swamped on their run-in to the coast. Much of the artillery intended for the beach sank in DUKW vessels, which couldn't stay afloat with 105mm howitzers in such seas. All but one of the 105s of the 111th Field Artillery Battalion were lost along with many other field pieces of the two other artillery battalions.

Compounding this trouble at Omaha were errors in navigation. Dust and smoke from the naval bombardment obscured landmarks and many landing vessels missed their intended landing points. As a result of poor visibility, weather, and unexpectedly strong currents, on Omaha's right flank where nine companies were to have hit the beach simultaneously, the right wing assault disintegrated under heavy fire from defenders not hurt by preparatory bombing.

Another important cause of this scene at Omaha was the unexpected presence of an entire German division, the 352nd, which neither Allied intelligence nor French agents had located and reported before the invasion. General Clarence Huebner, 1st Division commander, had been told his forces would attack beaches defended by only one regiment of a static coast division. Instead, it landed in the teeth of the 352nd, placed as Field Marshal Rommel would have liked all coastal defense units placed—forward near water's edge. Elsewhere, all along the invasion front, Allied intel-

139

ligence was quite accurate. The failure of agents in France and aerial reconnaissance to find the 352nd Division, which had moved to its position from St. Lo about April 1st, is—according to the official U.S. Army history—one of the remaining mysteries of the invasion.

And so it was that on the beaches near Pointe du Hoe, Pointe et Raz, and Vierville sur Mer the scene was one of a near-catastrophe on D-Day. The German officer at Pointe et Raz assumed the invasion had been stopped. He reported American soldiers lying on the shore, seeking cover, many tanks and armored vehicles burning, and many wounded in the sand a short distance from the water. (Being heavily laden with clothes, rifle, and other gear, many others had drowned when their landing craft sank and they tried to swim to shore.) It was to take heroic action and considerable bravery to organize and consolidate Omaha, even with air and naval superiority. Warships with guns that could reach 15 miles inland were badly needed.

Flying a Seafire L III at Lee-on-Solent that June was Lieutenant D.B. "Dick" Law, of the Royal Navy, one of very few British naval pilots to fly Mustangs with the U.S. 8th Air Force later in the war. He was serving with the 34th Tactical Reconnaissance Wing, and one of three flying brothers in the war. (One, captain of an RAF Lancaster bomber, was lost over Germany. A sister also served as a WREN in London.)

Born in London in 1920, son of an Army officer (electrical engineer), Law's wartime service was to be considerably more varied than that of most fighter pilots. He flew Seafires, Mustangs (at Rodney near Norwich) and—sent to the United States after a tour of duty with the 352nd Fighter Group—even flew the Japanese Zeke in flight tests at the U.S. Navy's test facility at Patuxent. Then, ordered to the Far East, he took part in the closing campaigns in the war against Japan, flying F6F Hellcats. Thus Law is qualified to compare aircraft and theaters—to reflect on a mission he flew in a Mustang to Munich, or missions against Japanese aircraft in Far East waters, or flights from carriers. He can also look back on exciting days as a spotter for British and American battleships in the invasion of France. That is what we are to be concerned with in this chapter.

I first met Law at his London office in 1978. Still handsome at 58, blond with dark green eyes and only 11 years retired (his last assignment had been as captain of the 30,000 ton *Bulwark*), he had in postwar years become a surface ship captain to complete the full circle of an impressively varied military experience. An executive of a major aerospace company, living in Guildford, he commutes to London and is often on the south coast, where he frequently sails and visits his old commanding officer, Admiral Percy Gick (whom we met in Chapter 2). About Gick, Law is explicit: "He was the finest officer I ever served under, bar none, and the finest man."

Law's hair is grey and thinning but he is active and vigorous still, and in several meetings after 1978 he exhibited the alertness and quickness usually found only in younger men but so often retained into later years by fighter pilots. Captain Dick Law, C.B.E., D.S.C., Royal Navy (Ret.) is at his desk in Duke Street five days a week and it was there that we went back to June 1944 together.

"There was one day I especially remember," he said, when I asked about a mission over the sea. "It was on the second day of the invasion, June 7th." I asked him to tell me about it in detail. He continued:

"Special training in naval spotting for bombardment and reconnaissance was begun in February 1944 at Ballyherbert and Ayr and included practical training with ground forces. No. 3 Naval Wing had about 42 aircraft and some 60 pilots. We trained in Spitfires and Seafires. In April, two squadrons including mine got the improved Seafire L IIIs. I was Senior Pilot in 886. Two other squadrons got Spitfire LVBs, which possessed about the same performance and handling qualities as the new Seafires. On the third of June—we had been at Lee-on-Solent only a few days—white stripes were painted on our aircraft over the light blue-grey. Underneath they were painted a darker grey. Everyone, of course, knew that the invasion was near. Excitement was at a high pitch everywhere.

"We knew targets were to be the German coastal batteries, with their large caliber guns in massive concrete emplacements, and the importance of our job had been drilled into us for months. So there wasn't any let-down feeling that we were not being used in the traditional role of fighter pilots. It had been explained that only heavy naval guns could knock out the artillery emplacements we would be searching out and directing fire on, and that only if these heavy guns were eliminated could invading forces safely land and advance inland.

"Gradually we had learned the technique of bringing heavy gunfire down on a target, first from a sandtable and then with Army 25-pounders on a gunnery range. In the last phase, we spotted for a cruiser lying off the coast of Scotland. So we felt we were ready the day the invasion began, June 6th.

"On invasion day—it was a cloudy one—I was ordered to take off very early in the morning. My job was to spot for the Royal Navy battleship *Warspite*, lying off the Normandy coast behind the British and Canadian landing beaches—which were to the left of the two American beachheads, Utah and Omaha. There was a gun battery west of Trouville causing much trouble. We were to find it. We did and we directed the fire of *Warspite* down on it. The flak was heavy at times but we didn't worry much about it. My closest call was after I had called in adjustments for *Warspite's* salvoes and was flying between the big ship and the target.

"Suddenly, about 25 seconds after *Warspite* fired, I felt my Seafire shudder and heard a *Whoomph!* To my amazement, I saw a 15-inch shell, on my left, streak by quite close. It weighed about a ton. After that, I was quite careful to stay out of the line of fire.

It was a full day that day. We all flew at least three times on spotting and reconnaissance missions. Some of us, at the end of spotting, chose to go down on the deck and strafe, to help knock out guns or to strafe troops. But this could be costly, and German antitank fire got one or two of our spotters on the 6th. The German coastal guns also fired back at *Warspite* and once the battleship was straddled and slightly damaged.

"We above were looking down on this duel as if it were a giant tennis match. It was a sight hard to forget—the sea, the green hedgerows of Normandy's farms, the massive array of shipping stretched out below, and all the activity. I spotted for *Warspite* on three missions on the 6th, always until relieved by two other Seafires. My wingwan stayed above me to watch for enemy fighters. I wasn't hit or intercepted on D-Day. It was the next day that I flew a mission I'll always remember."

Law arose before daylight again on the 7th, the second day of the invasion, being scheduled to fly the first flight of the day. By now, there were 2,000 dead on Omaha Beach, though three companies of U.S. Rangers, backed by two destroyers standing close-in off shore and giving fire support, had finally penetrated German coastal defenses on the American right flank. But Omaha was still a desperately fought-over beach, the area that the official U.S. Army history described as the only one where D-Day landings produced a crisis. The morning of the 7th was clear, an improvement over D-Day. Law dressed in a black flying suit—and forgot to wear his identification tags. It was 5:00 A.M. when he reached the briefing room.

There the still-critical situation on Omaha was described in some detail. Law was to spot for the USS *Nevada*, standing off Cherbourg Peninsula (Omaha) and throwing its weight into the balance in an effort to silence a 155mm battery—and others that had been devastating Allied forces since the invasion began. The U.S. briefing officer was encouraging about German antiaircraft fire. "I want to tell you, Dick," he said, "there's unlikely to be any flak for miles." Encouraged, after writing down data for radio, courses, and times, Law departed and prepared to take off.

The briefing officer had optimistically assumed the Americans had things under control well inland at Omaha Beach. In fact, the U.S. V Corps assault had reached neither its projected right or left advance line at the end of the first day's fighting. Penetration inland averaged only about a mile on a sector of about four miles of beach. But U.S. troops were being reinforced and supplied, and on the 7th they would push another two miles inland and extend both flanks—to the British Second Division boundary on their left flank, and almost to Pointe du Hoe on their right. So it was to be another hard day of fighting on this beachhead. Destroyers, cruisers, and battleships had been assigned support roles.

Half an hour after being briefed, Law and wingman Sub.-Lt. Taylor were at the end of the runway opening the throttles of their Seafires. The Rolls-Royce Merlin engines roared in the dawn stillness and the sleek fighters soon lifted upward into the blue. They set course for the French coast, 80 miles away.

Law's first task was to establish contact with *Nevada*. She was not hard to find; there were only a few battleships in the channel. He established radio contact with *Nevada*'s gun control officer on VHF. The two Spitfire pilots were told to fly inland and locate a 155mm battery regularly firing on advancing U.S. troops, as well as targets in the channel. As Law crossed in over the French coast, the landscape down below was a patchwork of small Normandy fields, most of them green or newly planted. They were bordered by the Normandy hedgerows—rows of trees or bushes, on an embankment, which marked the fields' boundaries. Law was flying at 6,000 feet; Taylor, weaving above him, was 2,000 feet higher. Close observance of the landscape soon succeeded in locating the enemy battery. (*Nevada* had given them an accurate fix.)

Law reported: "Target located, ready to open fire." This time he wasn't in the flight path of the battleship's shells. He was to the side but could easily see the six guns. In a moment, fire and smoke from *Nevada* told him a salvo had been fired and he expectantly watched the enemy battery 6,000 feet below. *Nevada's* aim was off about 400 yards. He called in a correction and banked out to sea. Flak was now beginning to puff the skies around him, which reminded him of the forecast at the morning briefing that he wasn't likely to encounter antiaircraft fire.

Spotters had learned the day before that they had time to fly back out over the channel while ships' guns were being reloaded and readied for firing. Law's Seafire, cruising at close to 200 mph, traveled a mile in 18 seconds. That 18 seconds and mile distance—or several miles in a minute—made a tremendous difference in reducing the vulnerability of fighters over Normandy.

As was *Warspite's* bombardment the day before, *Nevada's* guns were quite impressive as Law worked back and forth with the ship's gunnery officer for 40 minutes. By that time he was satisfied the battery had been silenced. The sky thus far was free of enemy fighters, though there were six to eight pairs of spotters over the invasion beachhead at the moment and everything was "going according to plan."

It was now time for two other Seafires to relieve Law and Taylor. They looked north when they heard the radio call of their relief and sighted two small dots in the blue, heading south and toward *Nevada*, below. Law had ample fuel remaining. He called Taylor to discuss a 37mm flak battery they had observed eight miles inland, still not silenced. They agreed to dive on it in a surprise attack and silence it.

As soon as their replacement Seafires were on station, they switched on their guns, checked their sights, and pointed their noses in the direction of the enemy battery, inland. Law could soon see it plainly—and the ground personnel servicing it. Their speed increased rapidly as they nosed down into a diving turn, keeping the battery in their sights. But they had also been seen by the battery's gunners, very much on the alert, anticipating just such an attack.

"I was extremely confident we could wipe them out quickly," Law recalls, "and then fly on back to the base. Looking back now, I see that we were both grossly overconfident about the success of the invasion. It appeared to us that the whole thing was becoming a walkover because we hadn't seen much of the Luftwaffe, and had been prepared for quite an aerial struggle. That day we felt we could hardly go home without having played some more direct part in the ground fighting.''

Law is the first to admit their attack was not professional. They came roaring down at 300 mph with determination. Law's hand was on the firing button and he was lining up the guns and soldiers in his sights. "But," he says, "those gunners certainly didn't share our feeling regarding the hopelessness of their cause. They were ready and their first rounds of tracer were extremely accurate.''

Law watched spellbound as the colored balls and smoke streaked up toward him in long, curving lines before he had had a chance to fire. He heard a rapid, ominous sound—37mm hits. He jerked the stick to one side to dodge the accurate fire and pulled the nose up instinctively. But instantly he knew he was in serious trouble and danger. The engine temperature gauge had begun spiraling upward. The radiator was punctured; glycol, which kept the engine cool, was rushing out. He could smell the unmistakable stench of the vaporized glycol.

Even as all this was happening, in seconds, he was pointing his nose northward to get back to the coast as fast as possible. Simultaneously, Taylor was shouting over the radio: "Head for the beach!" He had only seconds, at most a minute. The engine couldn't operate without coolant and would likely catch fire if he didn't shut it off in time. He was back up to 3000 feet—having used the speed of his dive to pull up—but the big prop out front was turning only slowly and he shut off all electrical and fuel switches. There was smoke in the cockpit.

He would have to crash-land. He couldn't even make it back to the beach. How far inland were U.S. troops below? Would he crash-land inside German lines? He had only seconds to think, because without power, he had to keep the nose of the damaged, silent fighter down or he would stall. He was fast losing altitude and called Taylor for the last time to say he was going in. Taylor watched helplessly. Law banked into a last turn and headed for a marshy area north, as near the beach as he could get. He tightened his belt and constantly checked the airspeed. He had no power now to correct for mistakes.

He couldn't afford to let airspeed drop too low, or he would stall and plunge straight into the ground, now rising up. But he had already covered most of the distance back to the beach and saw ahead the flat marshy area. He pointed the blue-grey nose straight at it, maintaining 100 mph. As he reached the marshy area, flaps down, wheels up, he pulled back lightly on the stick to lose speed but not gain altitude. The Seafire, quiet with the prop frozen, skimmed along above the ground, losing speed. It was a silent, eerie climax to a mission, and Law waited for the fuselage to strike the ground. It seemed to take some time. Then it bumped down, and the fighter slid straight ahead with no sign of turning right or left or flipping over on its back—what pilots dreaded most, for they could be trapped inside. As the Seafire plowed through the marshy flat, Law was greatly relieved to realize this soft marshy ground was a perfect emergency landing field. He watched on both sides as the fighter, its prop now bent under, slowly came to a halt. There was no fire, hardly any smoke now, and everything was deathly still. He saw no soldiers.

Pulling himself together, Law opened the canopy, unbuckled, and jumped out of the cockpit onto the wing. The fuel tanks could burn at any moment. The rule was not to wait and see—to get away from a crash-landed aircraft fast. Now Law heard guns and firing all around him and realized that in the cockpit he had been oblivious to the constant din of battle around him. The gunfire was, fortunately, some distance away, though continuous and heavy. Scrambling off the wing, he found himself in tall marsh reeds.

Just then a FW 190 roared overhead and Law—in his own words—"ran like Hell!" He stopped when he saw reeds not far away in front of him moving. He saw them parting closer and closer to him and held his breath. Two hands opened the reeds—black hands! It had to be an American! A very tall U.S. Army corporal now peered through the tall grass, sized him up, and motioned him to come over. Relieved, Law made his way to him. The big corporal knew he was an Allied pilot; he had seen the crash-landing and knew the Seafire was Allied. He was friendly from the first. In fact, his opening gesture of comradeship was to offer Law a drink from his canteen. Law thanked him and took a swallow. It was, as he now recalls, "a very reasonable vin rose."

The corporal had come ashore only that day, a few hours before. He told Law they were in what amounted to no-man's-land. He pointed the way to the beach and they bade each other goodbye. (Law would like to know, even today, who that corporal was—and if he survived the hard fighting in the next eight weeks. He says: "He had been ashore only a few hours and he was already pretty well organized.")

Law made his way on foot northward toward the sea, passing troops, guns, wrecked vehicles, and debris of all kinds. Finally, after much querying of soldiers moving to the front, he reached the sandy beach where U.S. soldiers had stumbled ashore the morning before in a hail of gun and mortar fire. The walk back took about an hour. American soldiers noticed his head was bleeding. He had hit it on the gunsight when bellying in, and hadn't realized how much it bled. Several asked to see his identification tags because he was dressed in a "homemade flying suit." But he had no identification and no uniform. Among some, that seemed a bit strange. Tired, needing a short rest, he sat down in the sand to sort things out. He could see German shellfire—perhaps from some of the batteries he had been calling naval fire in on—still hitting the beach. Troops and equipment were steadily landing nevertheless. As Law sat there, he noticed the awful cost of battle. Dead soldiers were lying about in all directions, even as men and supplies poured ashore and moved inland. Occasionally officers came his way. Once he was surprised to see a general and made his way to him to ask directions. The general's map was different from the one Law carried, but he offered to help. Another officer drove him in a jeep back to his Seafire, to retrieve its gyroscopic gunsight, then thought to be super secret. Pilots were ordered to destroy it whenever they crash-landed. Law had neglected to do so.

With the help of the American lieutenant, they found the Seafire and removed the new gunsight after walking the last few hundred feet through the marsh to get to the crashed fighter. While removing the gunsight, with tools supplied by the lieutenant, they came under enemy fire. Hurriedly, they finished the job and made their way back to the jeep as quickly as possible. This time Law was glad to be leaving the area for good; when they reached the beach, the lieutenant dropped him off near a landing site. An LST had just landed tanks and other heavy equipment. Law saw his chance and, after thanking the lieutenant, climbed up on the LST to find its captain. He introduced himself as a naval officer, a downed Seafire pilot. The captain invited him to his cabin and agreed to take him back to England.

Law could relax at last. He reached down to his ankles and turned the valve on his G-suit trousers. At that time the G-suit was another secret Allied weapon. Sailors viewing Law curiously through the window watched, fascinated, as water began flowing out both his pants legs—a scene he still remembers with a smile today. (The water inside G-suits was pumped into the lower suit under pressure to keep blood from draining away from the pilot's head, which could black one out in combat.)

It was late before the LST got underway and after an uneventful crossing of the channel, Law and a P-47 pilot who had also been shot down over the battlefield that day were given a lift to the Portland Naval Base. Their crossing and the trip to the naval base had consumed the night. It was 6:00 in the morning on June 8th when the two pilots presented themselves to the guard at the base entrance. When they asked for assistance, he curtly asked: "Do you realize it's 6:00 in the morning?"

After they had described their experience, the guard became sympathetic. Soon there was a WREN and a car at their disposal. The car took him back to Lee-on-Solent, where Law had been given up for lost, Taylor having reported him down inland from Omaha Beach. He was somewhat irked to learn that his best friends had already divided up his things, among them his watch and squash racket. They were cheerfully returned with congratulations all around—especially for Law having brought back the prized gunsight, which he had personally carried with him since the jeep return trip to his Seafire.

"I wish I could recall the name of that American lieutenant," Law says today. "And I would like to know the name of the general. But I know the briefing officer who told me that morning I wasn't likely to be bothered by flak. He's an American and lives near Brunswick, Georgia. Since the war he has been captain of a carrier. I also had a very interesting experience with another American, a 352nd Group flying comrade when I flew with the Americans. He was a Colonel Mac McCarty. I hadn't seen him in 36 years. But some time ago he rang me from America and said his son was coming to England. I was happy to see that he got a proper welcome."

Law is still a sailor and often sails his boat near the very waters presided over, in a sense, by Admiral Percy Gick. His son is, in fact, one of Britain's sailing champions and has reached his present proficiency while working, attending to his sailing in spare time. Law is proud that his son is accomplishing something in sailing competition though not wealthy, without full time to devote to his hobby. And, as public relations director for British Aerospace, he is often flying, even if he doesn't pilot his own aircraft any longer.

At 60 (in 1980), Law was still in good health and attractive. He jogs each morning and stays trim by adhering to a careful diet. And one would never guess by looking at him that his wartime experiences had been so nerve-wracking. "Not long after the invasion of France, I was posted to the Far East," he recalls. "There I flew Hellcats and operated from escort carriers against the Japanese." To most British pilots that part of the world was all new, and Law recalls one morning the whole flight attacked the wrong airfield. But they often attacked the right one too, and Law in fact destroyed seven Japanese aircraft on strafing attacks on enemy fields in the last months of the war, operating from a carrier.

He was also one of the first British pilots to oppose famous ME 262 German jet fighter. That day stands out clearly in his memory. He was flying Mustangs from a USAAF field near Norwich. The squadron was six miles west of Merseberg at 25,000 feet. It was the 28th of July, 1944, and interestingly, they had been briefed that morning that they might get their first glimpse of the world's first jet fighter on the day's mission. So everyone was alert and on the lookout for the new twin-engine jet.

"The bombers were at 22,000 feet that day," Law recalls. "We were climbing and about 3,000 feet higher. Then we saw heavy pinkish contrails climbing at 25 to 30 degrees. They were very fast.

"The German jet fighter pilots were interested in the B-17 bombers we were escorting, not us. The Fortresses carried the bombs and the jets' job was to shoot them down. I watched an ME 262 peel off and start down for the bombers. There was little we could do. They were too fast and they zoomed through the bomber stream and on out the bottom or back up and were quickly out of range."

After such excitement and so many varied flying adventures, Law adjusted well to civilian life. He's living refutation of the myth that fighter pilots find it difficult, after wars, to adjust to civilian life. At 60 he's much fun, his smile still youthful. And he enjoys life. Dining in the Cavendish Hotel, he called the proprietor, obviously fond of Law. "This is the hotel where the Duchess of Duke Street lived," he said with a smile, referring to the television series. And he turned to his friends and added: "He's trying to live up to that reputation, but hasn't quite got there yet!"

His conversation usually returns to his first love, the sea. "You know," he said, "I had to get a special sail flown here from America for my son. He needed it for a race and he had to have it right away. So I telephoned a friend of mine in Milwaukee and explained. They got the sail off straight away, and it was the only place I could get it. My boy had it in time for the race . . . ."

His father has done about everything. The son comes by it naturally enough.

The following fascinating diary notes of another spotter, Lieutenant Michael Crosley, also with the 3rd Fighter Wing, provide an accurate picture of the pace of events for spotters over Normandy.

These notes, describing the first three days of the invasion, are reprinted through the courtesy of David Brown, who included them in his book, *Seafire*; they describe exciting hours of flying, fighting, and strafing by Lt. Crosley. Written at the time of the operation, they capture the atmosphere and feel of events of that June. Crosley was a member of 886 Squadron. At 23, he had already seen combat in the Mediterranean and was credited at this time with three and a half confirmed victories. Like Law, he flew from Lee-on-Solent. His notes follow:

June 6: "Yesterday, D-Day, we all worked very hard indeed. I flew three times over France spotting for *Warspite*, flying a total of six hours and 50 minutes. Cloud was rather low and this meant that we had to go down low and spot well inside light flak range. Four blokes were knocked down, while another bloke baled out over the Isle of Wight and broke his arm.[1] Among them were Bassett[2] and Boater,[3] of whom there is no news, and an RAF type.[4] Wallace[5]—who arrived tonight—said that his arm still ached from the handshakes the French types gave him, and also that they (the French) told him exactly how to get through the Jerry lines.

"My first flight took off at 0745 and we spent 45 minutes over France, spotting on a heavy gun position near the coast. The shoot was fairly accurate, except that *Warspite's* R/T was lousy. Sub-Lieutenant (D.T.) Keene, my No. 2, was quite good, but we were 25 minutes late in getting back. The second shoot was at an impromptu target, taking off at 1245. *Warspite* was not ready to shoot until I had to go home, but on the way home I shot up and destroyed one German staff car, which overturned in a field—one occupant got out and dashed for a nearby wood—Good Show! I also strafed a heavy lorry, which stopped and was left on fire. We were 20 minutes late in getting back.

"By this time things were warming up generally, and guns were pooping off at you and everything else too. One bloke saw our tanks shooting at eight Jerry tanks from the cover of a wood. Four Jerry tanks went up in smoke! Transport and gun carriers were reported to the ship. The third time I took off my R/T was duff, so I landed and got into another plane and followed my No. 2, 25 minutes late. This aircraft was little better than the first—my jettison tank wouldn't jettison and not all the guns would fire. I strafed a flak position on the coast which was absolutely pitted with heavy shell

holes and received no return fire. I found a beautiful target (a concentration of transport camouflaged as trees) about 20 miles inland, but *Warspite's* R/T was still u/s.

June 7: "Two trips today—both good fun. *Warspite's* R/T was still useless so I went inland and reported a new target—tanks in a camouflaged yard behind a farmhouse. I also shot up a lorry in Something-or-Other sur Orne, and it crashed into the side of a house. My No. 2 followed me but his guns didn't fire a solitary round. He was very annoyed. Second time I went in, only the Brownings fire. Blast it!

"The weather was much better for the second trip, with cloud just under one-tenth over the coast and increasing to ten-tenths further inland. As the ship's R/T was still u/s—I almost expect this now—we had a look for a few targets in the wood east of Tourville and as nothing was moving we went farther inland. About 15 miles southeast of Caen, I saw what I thought to be one of our chaps stooging along above the ten-tenths cloud with not a care in the world. I flew by on an opposite course to see who he was, as I thought it was a Mustang. Lo and behold, it was a 109—on its own, too. I opened everything up but he dived into cloud and although I chased him the closest I could get was 1,000 yards, when he finally disappeared. If only I could have been a bit faster!

"I climbed up to 7,000 feet, having lost my No. 2 in the chase, and hardly am I there but I see another (it might have been the same one) about six miles away, doing the same thing. This time I know he is a Hun, so I get in close, out of the sun, and let him have it from 200 yards to mighty close. He goes down through a cloud streaming smoke and glycol and comes out in a vertical spiral dive, hitting the deck in a bright orange flash.

"To bed: 2135 and I'm up at 0330 tomorrow. What a life!

June 8: "Our losses yesterday were pretty formidable and we have been forbidden to shoot up any lorries. The majority of our losses were to light flak, which the Germans are bloody good at. Tiny Devonald,[6] Dicky Law,[7] Val Bailey,[8] Foxley,[9] and an RAF type[10] all got shot down. Dicky Law had wizard fun: he destroyed his IFF, then called up his No. 2 on VHF after the crash and said he was OK. His No. 2[11] told him 'Walk about a mile to the East and the beach is there.' Dicky then walked out with his camera magazine and his gyro-gunsight. Wizard teamwork. Tiny Devonald got back to Devonport by landing barge this morning, but unfor-

tunately nothing's been heard of Val or Foxley.

"With Keene, my No. 2, I flew on a very early patrol and were over the beachhead at 0630. We had no joy on the ship's R/T, as usual. My No. 2 slowed down to drop his tank and at that critical moment I saw some 'Spitfires' coming in from out of the sun and above, from the northeast. I said, very bored-like, over the R/T— 'There's a bloke on your tail,' and, thank God, he broke, because just at that moment the Jerry opened fire with tracer. Keene broke well and truly, and the rest of them, eight or nine, came down after me. For a second or two I retired into the cloud above, then came down to pick off what I thought was the "ass-end Charlie." However, before I could get into range, I saw another FW 190 alongside me—upside down—and they appeared from all over the place. One bloke pulled up vertically in front of me.

"I selected the bloke who was upside down, and by now diving vertically, and gave him a five-second burst, doing about 400 mph at the bottom of the dive. There were several Spits or FW 190s following me down, so I broke up into a tight loop and did not see what happened to my target, on which I had seen about 10 cannon hits from 300 to 500 yards as he was getting away. The Franks Flying Suit [anti-G suit] had helped me no end in the turns and I was able to come down from the loop on top of the bloke who was behind me. Unfortunately, I had only a few rounds left and I was closing in on this one, right down on the deck. God knows what speed I had on the clock! My No. 2 then reported that he had been hit and was returning. As I had no ammunition left, I did so too.[12]

"I was over France again at about 1400. This time I called *Ramillies*, and just as I was finding my target we were jumped by four Spits. We ducked and showed our markings but more and more joined in until we, with our square wing-tips, were the target for about 30 Spitfires plus a few Thunderbolts. We opened the taps wide and got in a defensive circle, calling the HQ ship to tell them to lay off. I was bloody annoyed and very frightened. However, after 20 minutes of using up precious petrol, they broke off and we got down to placing a few shells on a road junction north of Caen, where there were some tanks and gun positions.

"Jerry certainly attaches a lot of importance to this spotting idea, and all movements—troops, lorries, etc.—cease when we are overhead, and they spill out into the nearest hedge or house. The Jerries joined in over the R/T and tried to give *Ramillies* a lot of false target Reference Nos, but we told them to pipe down—though

we didn't use those actual words.

"Yesterday, Campbell-Horsfall[13] was out with Commander (F)[14] and got rather badly pranged by some 190s, Commander (F) being shot down and Campbell-Horsfall being chased out to sea with no ammo left. Our one casualty today was Sam Lang who was jumped by 109s.[15] Simpson[16] and Chamen[17] were bounced this morning by a most elaborate Jerry tactic—decoys. Chamen was badly hit but got back OK."

1. Lieutenant C.L. Metcalfe RNVR (885 Squadron).
2. Sub-Lieutenant A.H. Bassett RNVR (885 Squadron)—missing, presumed killed.
3. Sub-Lieutenant A. Goater RNVR was not shot down during "Neptune," but Sub-Lieutenant H.A. Coghill (808 Squadron) crashed into the sea after flak damage on this day—missing, presumed killed.
4. Flying Officer G.R. Duff RAF (No 63 Squadron)—recovered safe.
5. Lieutenant W.A. Wallace RNVR (886 Squadron).
6. Lieutenant-Commander S.L. Devonald RN (CO 885 Squadron).
7. Lieutenant D.B. Law RNVR (SP 886 Squadron).
8. Lieutenant-Commander P.E.I. Bailey RN (CO 886 Squadron)—shot down by "friendly" AA, baled out and landed on Allied beach, setting off a land mine but suffering only a sprained ankle.
9. Sub-Lieutenant R.J. Foxley RNVR (886 Squadron)—recovered safe.
10. Flying Officer G.R. Wilcock RAF (No 26 Squadron)—missing, presumed killed.
11. Sub-Lieutenant A.E. Taylor RNVR (886 Squadron).
12. Sub-Lieutenant Keene received four hits on his Seafire's tail but returned safely; Lieutenant Crosly apparently carried only 60 rounds per cannon and 150 rounds for each of the two Brownings left in.
13. Lieutenant-Commander C.P. Campbell-Horsfall RN—Deputy Wing Leader.
14. Commander J.M. Keene-Miller RNVR—taken prisoner.
15. Lieutenant H. Lang RNZNVR (886 Squadron), who was shot down by a FW 190.
16. Sub-Lieutenant H.H. Simpson RNVR (886 Squadron)—damaged.
17. Sub-Lieutenant R.G.S. Chamen SANF(V) (885 Squadron)—undamaged.

Chapter 11

Carrier Strike on Formosa

The second-ranking U.S. Navy fighter ace in World War II typifies the citizen-soldier called upon to fight his country's wars since the Revolution. Also called back to duty during the Korean conflict, his story is, in a sense, the American story.

Cecil Elwood Harris was born into a Crespard, South Dakota, farm family in 1916. He was 23 when Germany invaded Poland in September 1939, igniting World War II. Harris had attended Northern State Teachers' College in South Dakota, and was teaching school in a small town in that state. He enlisted immediately in the United States Navy Reserve as a seaman.

He eventually won an appointment as a reserve aviation cadet and four months later—days after his 25th birthday—the Japanese attacked Pearl Harbor. He was one of those Americans who didn't wait to put aside civilian life to take up arms against the dictators.

Harris passed elimination flight training at the naval reserve base in Minneapolis, Minnesota, and reported next to the naval air station at Corpus Christi, Texas. His cadet class—its pilots desperately needed—was speedily graduated on February 11, 1942, at the darkest point of the war in the Pacific.

That spring of 1942 Harris was assigned to U.S. Navy Fighting Squadron 27, and received further training with the Advanced Carrier Training Group, Atlantic Fleet. His first combat duty came during British-American landings in North Africa, flying ground support missions from a carrier.

Early in 1943 he was ordered to Guadalcanal, where he shot down two Japanese planes—the first of 24 confirmed victories he was to score in World War II. (Few, even many who served with or under him, are familiar with his ranking as the Navy's second leading ace of World War II.)

After World War II, Harris returned to his teaching career and a small schoolhouse in South Dakota that had captured his affection, only to have it interrupted by the United States' defense of South Korea. As was the case with so many of World War II's veterans—men already trained, whose skills were needed immediately—Harris received "preference" over younger men who—in fairness—should have supplied the manpower for that conflict.

Interestingly, Harris and Joe Foss, who shot down more enemy planes in the Pacific than any other Marine pilot, both hail from the inland state of South Dakota, far from any ocean, and within whose boundaries no carrier ever sailed.

But it is with World War II that we are concerned and in that conflict the South Dakota schoolteacher displayed a coolness and effectiveness in the face of superior numbers of enemy aircraft which won for him nine medals, six of them major, all resulting from combat.

In this chapter we relate a mission Harris flew when the U.S. Navy's Task Force 38 struck Formosa. But before "flying" along on that mission, several others merit mention.

Harris won the Navy Cross for a flight 15 days later. His action was described in the Navy Cross award Citation:

"For extraordinary heroism as a Fighter Pilot in Fighting Squadron 18 (*USS Intrepid*) on Luzon, Philippine Islands, October 29, 1944.

"Quick to intercept two successive flights of Japanese fighter planes preparing to attack our bomber and torpedo squadrons as they completed a strike on Clark Field, he boldly led his division in a swift assault on the enemy planes . . . shot down one enemy plane from each flight, and put the other to rout . . . .

"Intercepting a superior force of enemy fighters . . . he engaged in a fierce dogfight . . . successively knocking down two enemy planes . . . and assisted essentially in the utter defeat of the entire enemy formation without the loss of any of our planes from enemy action . . . ."

No American planes were lost in the action described above, though Harris shot down four enemy aircraft. In all his combat in

As the blacked-out ships moved nearer Formosa that Wednesday night, Harris and the 16 fighter pilots who would fly the next morning—and "spares" who would go along—met for informal briefing. Questions were asked about Formosa's air defense; from intelligence available, the expectation was that it would be formidable. There was an air of the unknown about this strike on the big island; this was the first fighter sweep of the war against it.

Across from the wardroom on *Intrepid's* starboard side, on the first deck below the hangar deck, Harris was awakened by bugle reveille over the loudspeaker at 4:00 A.M. He crawled out of a lower bunk, shaved, donned khakis and Marine-type shoes, and in 10 minutes was in the wardroom eating breakfast. Carrier pilots enjoyed good food, and though the milk was powdered, Harris had eggs, bacon, toast, coffee, and juice.

The loudspeaker bugle soon sounded "Flight Quarters." Harris and other pilots hastened to their squadrons' ready rooms above hangar deck. Briefing began as soon as the roll was called. The intelligence officer warned that Japan's best fighter units could be expected over Formosa. Harris announced the course in; after the action, pilots would do their own navigating. The weather officer forecast good weather all day—always a welcome pronouncement for pilots flying from carriers.

Murphy pinpointed on an enlarged map the airfield VF 18 pilots would strafe on the northeastern coast of Formosa. That meant a northwesterly course to target, southeasterly course returning to *Intrepid*. Pilots were to maintain strict radio silence. Wingmen were ordered to remain close to their leaders. The squadron would climb to 15,000 feet going in. Each two-fighter section was reminded to cover the rear of the division's other two-fighter section.

Now the chaplain led the pilots in prayer, asking a "safe return." Over the loudspeaker system came the familiar announcement: "Pilots man your planes—on the double!" The pilots bounded out of the ready room, up the ladder to the flight deck, and to their Hellcats. *Intrepid* was launching the fighter sweep with two catapults, and Murphy would be the first off. After his division and the second division, (eight planes in all), Harris and his division would be launched.

Intrepid headed into the wind, knifing through the still-dark Pacific at 30 knots as the eastern sky was just beginning to whiten. The deck came alive with spinning three-blade props, yellow-blue fire shooting from stacks, crewmen scurrying back and forth. Pilots in their cockpits checked instruments and switches. Murphy braced his head on the headrest and revved up. At a signal from a deck flag man, the catapult thrust him forward, his weight pressing hard against the back of the seat. The carrier deck suddenly ended; he felt a slight mush, and began to maneuver quickly with rudder and stick. The Hellcat then began to inch upward in a slow, roaring, full-throttle climb. Soon the 2200-horsepower Double Wasp Pratt & Whitney engine provided good climbing speed.

Murphy's F6F and that of his wingman turned to clear the bow of slipstream and climbed out in front of the carrier. Two more fighters followed. Then came the first two F6Fs of the second division, then the last two. Harris was maneuvered onto the catapult by deck crewmen. When the launching officer came down with outstretched arm, the catapult rammed him forward as if a gigantic hand had pushed him ahead. He was not over the water at full throttle, beginning a slow climb.

In the lead, Murphy continued to fly straightaway. When Harris' division and then the last four planes were airborne, Murphy banked into a 180-degree turn and flew back to the carrier. As he did, each of the Hellcats turned inside him, and by the time Murphy's Hellcat passed over the carrier, flying in the opposite direction, the squadron was assembled. Murphy banked to the northwest, toward target Formosa.

Sixteen blue Hellcats climb at 150 knots in semi-darkness. The squadron is flying "finger-four" divisions, the four divisions themselves making up a "finger-four" squadron. Murphy's wingman is on his right, a section is behind, left. Slightly behind and to the right of the lead division is the second division. The second division leader's wingman is to his left, and the second section in the division is to the right and slightly behind.

Behind the second division, well to the left, is Harris' division, with Harris' wingman, Franklin Burley, on his right and behind, and his second section, led by Lieutenant (j.g.) Bill Zeimer, to the left, farther behind. The fourth division is to the left, behind Harris, with the division leader's wingman on his right and slightly behind, and the second section in the last division to the left and behind the lead section.

Intrepid is now a small, dim silhouette, falling farther behind in the grey dawn. Harris looks out on each wing, which the crewmen have waxed to give him a few extra knots of speed. With waxed wings and emergency water ejection, Harris in the F6F has a speed advantage over enemy fighters. The pilots flip on their gun switches; the stars above have now "gone out."

VF 18 continues climbing northwesterly; other squadrons of Task Force 38 planes, over an expanse of many miles flying from many different carriers, also drone upward into the northwest on climbing courses, heading for other targets on Formosa.

The silence is almost eerie, except for the roaring engine. It's 20 minutes since the squadron left the carrier when VF 18 levels off at 15,000 feet; the first stages of the superchargers go into action.

Ahead, in the distance, Harris sees the eastern shore of Formosa, picturesque green hills and mountains. Now the earphones vibrate with orders from Murphy. Harris will take his division down to have a look at the target airfield, near the coast. He acknowledges and pushes the stick forward. The four Hellcats point their noses downward and gain speed. Twelve Hellcats remain on course at 15,000 feet. The green shoreline becomes clearer, and the mountains and hills grow larger and larger.

Harris sees an open space near the shore, ahead; it must be the airfield. He banks slightly to point his nose in that direction. His wingman, Burley, to the right, and his second section to the left, are in position. He wonders whether the four fighters will achieve surprise, or whether the enemy has already picked them up on radar and scrambled fighters to intercept.

The shoreline comes closer. Harris' altimeter needle continues to drop and his airspeed increases as he descends. He must be very low to get a good look at the field. He makes out a large runway, southeast-northwest. On the eastern edge of the field is a major industrial plant.

He "rubbernecks," knowing his division is vulnerable, approaching an enemy field at a low altitude where Japanese fighters are most effective.

The coastline of Formosa is just ahead; Harris is now down to 2,000 feet. Above, Hellcats of Two-A-Day 18 are approaching north of the field, to circle left. Harris, a little ahead of the rest of the squadron, sets course to pass north of the field and also circle left.

The four cross the coast at high throttle, and with the momentum of their descent are registering 260 knots. Harris dips his left wing and they circle the field. At the southern end he gets a clear view of a large number of parked Japanese aircraft. He eases out of the turn and will pass directly over the field, strafing. This tests enemy flak. The engine loudly responds to full throttle, and he pushes the stick forward.

Above, Murphy and the other pilots will locate antiaircraft gun positions on the field. The four Hellcats are gaining speed and only about a thousand feet above the trees.

"Bandits!" comes a cry over the radio.

It's Harris' section leader, Zeimer, shouting. He's spotted five enemy bombers.

Harris looks ahead and to both sides, but can't see them. He tells Zeimer to lead the division to them, and Zeimer makes a slight pull-up, then presses into a blood-draining bank to the left. The four Hellcats, turning as tightly as possible at this high speed, are now over and behind the bombers, heading southwest. Harris sees them now—five . . . land-based . . . twin-engine. The enemy leader has four bombers stacked back on his right. Orange "meatballs" on the wings are clearly visible. The bombers appear to have taken off only moments before; they are at low altitude. The Hellcats, with superior speed, rapidly close the gap, with Zeimer in the lead and Harris' section close behind.

The division is almost down on the trees—a precarious position if enemy fighters are near. Through the sight ring Harris watches the silhouettes of the bombers grow larger and larger. Zeimer is maneuvering perfectly to be in a position to open fire on the enemy bomber last in formation, farthest to the right. Harris kicks left rudder and moves the stick left. He watches Zeimer, ahead, almost within firing range.

The bombers, caught from behind, are completely surprised. White smoke streams back from the wings of Zeimer's Hellcat as the six .50-calibers send streaking shells into the trailing brownish-green bomber on the right. In seconds smoke is streaming back. With a splash of flame, the enemy bomber disintegrates.

Zeimer whips his Hellcat onto the tail of the fourth enemy bomber, now the last in line, and opens fire almost immediately. Harris, eyes focusing on the yellow gunsight ring, at the third in line, sees its wingspan steadily widening. The wingspan fills the sight circle.

Six roaring .50 guns shake the Hellcat. The aim is accurate; the target bomber is taking hits. None of the bombers have made a move; those not hit are unaware of the Hellcats. Harris' .50-caliber guns literally tear the twin-engine enemy apart, and he watches his shattered victim wing over quickly and dive for the earth.

Left rudder and stick, and he pulls in behind the next bomber, left ahead. He opens fire immediately. Grayish-black puffs begin to fill the sky. Japanese antiaircraft guns, below, are firing on the Hellcats. Harris maintains pressure on the trigger button; the bomber ahead is badly damaged and pieces fly back. Smoke begins to stream from the fuselage. Without warning, the bomber explodes, and Harris rockets through debris and smoke. The front of his canopy and wings are covered with oil.

Easy, so far—but Harris hasn't time for self-satisfaction. A shout over the radio: "Zeros!" They are above, with the altitude advantage. Harris looks up and behind and sees nothing. The lone remaining enemy bomber is forgotten.

A Zero streaking from above opens fire on Zeimer, who is immediately hit. Harris now sees other Jap fighters, diving behind, right. The Zero pilot who surprised Zeimer dives away between Zeimer and his wingman. Harris, banking right and left, glances back. His wingman is in position. Zeimer's F6F is trailing smoke—heavy smoke; he'll have to get out. A chute blossoms—it's Zeimer. As he floats down to enemy territory below, his wingman, Lieutenant (j.g.) Egidio Di Batista, dives after the Zero pilot who shot down his section leader and soon the Zero spurts flame and wings over into a fatal plunge.

Harris manages to avoid the diving enemy fighters. He sees an F6F smash into the ground below, quickly followed by a Zero. He can't tell where the Hellcat came from. Ahead is Zeimer's wingman, Di Batista, and on Harris' right and slightly behind, his own wingman, Burley. He must protect Di Batista and get the three together, but before he can pull abreast, he sees a dot, above, plunging downward. The dot, growing larger and larger, is the unmistakable silhouette of a Zero. It's at ten o'clock, diving on Di Batista at twelve o'clock. Harris presses the mike button:

"Zero diving on you from above and behind!" Up above, the Hellcats flying top cover have seen the Zero and yell another warning. Harris goes to full throttle to close in behind for the Zero. Di Batista is at 1,500 feet. The enemy fighter is leveling out for a firing pass from astern. The American can't get out of the line of fire. The Zero is closing at six o'clock. At the same time, Harris is bringing the enemy into his sight, closing faster. The three fighters, strung out in line, roar over the rolling green hills at full throttle.

Harris opens fire first. His aim is true—luckily for Di Batista. But the enemy's 20mm fire also strikes "Debat," as fellow pilots have nicknamed him. Harris' guns take a heavier toll. The Zero is pierced by too many .50-caliber shells in fuselage and wing and curves out of the line of fire, in a steady decline, trailing smoke. Harris, withholding fire, watches as the Zero heads straight for the trees, but also clears his rear and looks above. The enemy pilot goes straight in and a burst of flame spreads through the trees—victory number three.

Once again, however, even before Harris can regain altitude, the radio—Di Batista is badly hurt. The Zero had scored heavily. Harris radios Di Batista instructions to turn left and head for *Intrepid*. He and his wingman will escort him. Di Batista's damage report is pessimistic; he considers ditching on the beach. Harris urges him to try to reach *Intrepid*. "We'll keep you covered," he promises. Di Batista reports his engine rough, hydraulic system damaged, controls not functioning properly. Harris insists he must try. Murphy, high above, sees the three Hellcats set course for *Intrepid*; he calls and says he'll join in the escort with his eight F6Fs.

Closing in on Di Batista, Harris gets a shock when he spots a formation of Zeros above. Can Murphy get to them in time? The Hellcats at altitude above wing over in a dive. They have seen the enemy. But several Zeros, lower, now dive on the three Hellcats. Harris banks into position directly behind Di Batista to defend his rear. The coast is crossed, the three Hellcats slowly climb southeast. The Zeros come on.

An enemy fighter closes from behind, above, and others follow. The nearest behind, with altitude advantage, is now in position to dive on Di Batista; Harris can't turn into the Zero for a head-on pass. That would leave Di Batista even more unprotected and expose his two comrades to heavy odds, for more than 20 Zeros are now in sight behind. He'll play possum, maintain position, and let the enemy begin a firing pass, as if he's undetected.

He'll stay with Di Batista until the last second, delaying his 180-degree turn. The tactic will require split-second timing; if he allows the now-diving Zero to approach too closely, he'll become a victim. The Zero is also so much more maneuverable that he might not be able to shake him off.

Harris takes the chance. The enemy comes on, closer and closer. Harris checks Burley, to the right . . . in position. The Zero behind is gaining. Now he's but a few thousand feet behind and above. Harris flies straight and level.

The Zero pilot now begins his pass, increasing his speed. Other Zeroes are preparing to follow their leader, now rapidly approaching from the rear.

The enemy behind is about down to his level. Harris has seconds. True to his expectations, the enemy fighter pulls directly in behind him, not DeBat. The Zero is almost within range. Now Harris slams his stick left, with hard left rudder. The Hellcat shudders into a violent, vertical left turn. Harris, Burley following, apparently leaves the crippled DeBat alone, flying straight ahead. They are at 900 feet.

As soon as he rolls out of the left turn, Harris glances back. Has the enemy pilot followed him? The Zero is closing on the stricken Hellcat! Harris slams the stick right and hits right rudder. The Hellcat drains blood from his head again as he banks just as violently back right. At full throttle, he streaks for the Zero, now at three o'clock.

DeBat and the Zero are down to 500 feet. The enemy pilot now senses what's happening. Two Hellcats are moving in on him from the left. They hadn't run away. The Zero, not very high and not yet close enough to open fire on DeBat, streaks for the deck to escape.

The two Hellcats, separated by 200 feet, begin to lessen the distance. DeBat, momentarily relieved, continues southeast at low altitude. The lone Zero and two pursuing Hellcats, only a few hundred feet high, roar toward the coast at maximum power.

The Hellcats close and Harris' eyes focus on the sight ring at the enemy silhouette on the gunsight glass. The wingspan widens. It stretches past the inner circle and approaches the sides of the outer circle. The enemy pilot is back over the coast on top of the trees, at full throttle, but the Hellcats still gain. Now the Zero is squarely in Harris's sight and his right forefinger pulls the stick trigger for the fourth time this morning. The Hellcat's guns send a salvo of shells—a hundred a second—into the enemy. Holes appear in the Zero and before the pilot can take effective evasive action, a stream of black smoke streaks backward.

Harris is almost at point-blank range. The left wing goes up and the green enemy fighter seems to slide downward, right. Harris watches the enemy fighter hit the trees only a few feet below. A wing tears loose as the Zero hits. The two Hellcats rocket over a splash of fire at the fatal spot. Burley yells: "You got another one!"

Harris looks appreciatively at "Chink" Burley to his right, and is thankful he has a wingman who stuck with him all the way and protected him from surprise attack. The enemy respects a section of two, not a lone fighter.

Harris rejoins Di Batista on course for *Intrepid*, both glancing backward to see if other Zeros are following. The quick work he made of the leading zero and the sighting of Murphy's fighters above apparently discourage the other enemy fighters. They remain a respectful distance behind.

Harris scans the sky behind and above, and makes out a group of fighters. He recognizes the silhouettes . . . Hellcats! The Zeros, below at a disadvantage, now become the hunted and turn away. Now over the radio he can hear Murphy, calling *Intrepid*. The rest of the squadron follows them home. DeBat reports difficulty with his controls, though he's managing to hold course. Every few minutes brings them closer to the carrier, but can DeBat safely land his crippled fighter on the deck?

Ahead, Harris sees the outer screen of Carrier Group 2. As the Hellcats come closer and closer, many shapes on the sea become ships. The whole fleet soon spreads out on the horizon. It's a majestic sight, and one welcome to every pilot who has ever flown alone over the ocean.

In minutes the three Hellcats and the squadron above are bearing down on *Intrepid*. She turns into the wind to prepare to take them aboard. DeBat will get landing preference. Can he sufficiently control his shot-up fighter? The big ship is steaming directly into the wind. But over the radio DeBat reports that each time he slackens speed, he loses control. He can't land at cruising speed.

He reports the critical control damage to the air officer aboard *Intrepid*. The danger involves not only DeBat but the carrier, for an out-of-control Hellcat and high-octane gasoline are a menace to the ship and other aircraft, and to more than 2000 men aboard.

The air office orders DeBat to bail out. Other Hellcat pilots watch as he climbs. Destroyers around *Intrepid* are alerted. DeBat must slip out of his parachute quickly once in the water and inflate his Mae West, if he can manage to successfully jump from his hard-to-control fighter.

The crippled F6F climbs and approaches the big carrier from the rear off the port quarter. DeBat slides the canopy back and attempts a clean jump. The damaged Hellcat, however, doesn't behave. The tail assembly of the erratic fighter strikes him. In spite of this, DeBat remains conscious and pulls the ripcord. A parachute billows open as the F6F plunges into the sea.

All eyes in the squadron follow the descending parachute and injured pilot, who plunges into the water under the big white chute behind *Intrepid*. He manages to get out from under his chute and inflates his jacket. A destroyer approaches, pilots relaying directions.

Harris and others now turn toward *Intrepid* and in minutes are touching down, one by one, hooks trailing from fuselages and engaging the big cables stretched across *Intrepid's* rear deck, which jerk them to a quick halt.

As soon as Harris shuts off his throttle, crewmen ask about his combat (having heard radio traffic during the mission.) Harris tells them he bagged two bombers and two fighters. Oil covers his wing and canopy (from the second bomber destroyed), but there's not a nick or hole!

In the ready room below, he reports that his division shot down four twin-engined enemy bombers and three Zeros.

Di Batista is picked up successfully by a destroyer—with a broken leg.

Interrogation officers listened to Harris's story with admiration, but Harris wasn't impressed with his efforts. In fact, in a few hours he was taking off again from *Intrepid*, escorting bombers on another Formosa raid. His commanding officer, however, realized the flying skill he had witnessed. He recommended Harris for the Silver Star and the recommendation was approved. The citation accompanying it read in part:

"For conspicuous gallantry and intrepidity as a Fighter Pilot in Fighting Squadron 18 . . . on Northern Formosa, October 12, 1944 . . . he braved intense enemy aircraft fire . . . to execute an attack upon an important airfield installation and, during the same flight, valiantly engaged in an aerial dogfight with numerically superior aircraft . . . succeeding in shooting down four of the hostile craft . . . on two instances saved two of his teammates during the action . . . . "

That day Task Force 38 sent three strikes against Formosa. U.S. aircraft losses were heavy—48 aircraft. But enemy losses were over three times that number. The late Samuel E. Morison reports in *Leyte* (one of his admirable volumes on U.S. naval operations in World War II) that the Japanese admiral commanding the defense of Formosa, watching the destruction of his fighters by Navy pilots above the island, was thoroughly dismayed, describing his defending planes as "so many eggs" thrown at a strong wall of enemy aircraft.

Shortly after Harris shot down his third "foursome," *Intrepid* was struck by two kamikazes. Harris had just taken off and circled the stricken ship. For hours he watched the burning carrier fight for her life. He managed one consolation: Enemy aircraft approached again and Harris turned in behind a Zero that might have been a kamikaze and shot down his 24th victim of the war!

With the battering of *Intrepid*, Fighting Squadron 18, which had achieved one of the best combat records of U.S. Navy fighter squadrons in World War II, was temporarily withdrawn from combat.

Back in the United States, Harris reinformed the squadron and prepared for further combat. Its pilots had received the new F8F Bearcat fighter and were preparing to return to the Pacific when, on August 14, Japan surrendered. Had not Japanese kamikazes hit *Intrepid*, removing its famed fighter squadron from combat, there seems little doubt that the volunteer from South Dakota would have added to his victory total.

Chapter 12

Night Torpedo Attack: Norway

The war was almost over (and lost by Germany) when a young Irish pilot, Lt. John Godley, was summoned to appear before his commanding officer on January 13th, 1945, at the Royal Navy's airfield on the northern Irish coast near Londonderry. Godley had been flying the slow Stringbag (which Percy Gick had flown against *Bismarck* four years earlier) throughout the war. For the last two years he had been flying anti-submarine patrols (convoy escort) from MACs (merchant aircraft carriers) crossing the Atlantic. He had become thoroughly familiar with this kind of work, and accepted his role as part of the merchant navy, in a sense. He knew, like others who had watched the war's progress over the years, the end was near. That was why he had been astonished to be informed he had been promoted to the acting rank of Lt. Commander, and appointed commanding officer of 835 Swordfish Squadron. The future Lord Kilbracken was surprised even more by his squadron's assignment: convoy escort to Murmansk aboard Royal Navy escort carrier *Nairana*—the Murmansk run, in winter! Few pilots would cherish that assignment. And what his C.O. now told him seemed to confirm the grim picture. The present commanding officer of 835 was in need of rest. Morale in the squadron was low. Godley was to take over at once—day after tomorrow!

For a 24-year-old classics major (Balliol College, Oxford) of the reserve (the Wavy Navy—sleeve stripes were wavy, not straight), who had never before served on a regular RN warship, the new command was a considerable challenge. It meant that Godley now became one of the two or three youngest Lt. Commanders in the Navy, and would command 20 aircraft (fighters and torpedo bombers) and 200 men. It meant he would have to leave his nearby wife and 12-day-old son, fly to Scotland, and begin to operate regularly off the *Nairana* in the foulest kind of arctic weather for weeks on end. Already somewhat war-weary but not willing to admit it, Godley was nevertheless determined to rise to the challenge and to succeed in the new assignment.

When he reached his new Scottish base at Machrihanish on the 15th—in awful weather—and had his first talk with members of 835, it became apparent how low morale actually was. Pilots were discouraged and intimidated by having to fly incessantly in the worst kind of weather—and blamed this on *Nairana's* captain, who, of course, was a non-flying officer. Several pilots who had been on operations too long had the twitch (nerves); new pilots were due in next day to replace them. Godley had but one week to work up his squadron, get to know the pilots, and mix in new arrivals with the old. They were flying Swordfish IIIs, which had a great bulge in the fuselage where the newest radar set was located. In fact, it was of such size and value that it replaced one member of the crew—the III carried only a pilot and observer but no gunner, as earlier models always had. The III also carried two rockets, one beneath each wing—not for use against the enemy, but to assist in takeoff. Known as RATOG, these were fired as the takeoff aircraft reached the island amidships, and boosted speed considerably to facilitate a quicker and safer takeoff. An advanced Pegasus XXX engine was the best ever in the decade-old Stringbag, destined to remain operational until the end of the war—only four months away.

Godley worked hard over the next few days to improve morale and train his pilots, to make 835 Squadron an effective torpedo bomber squadron in the shortest period of time. He could sense that morale was rising but knew his pilots needed some kind of success to build the pride in the squadron he wanted to see. And shortly, they got that opportunity.

Called into the captain's office aboard *Nairana* soon after he had landed his squadron aboard the escort carrier, he was informed *Nairana* and a a small strike force would sail from Scapa Flow on the 27th for a strike against shipping off the Norwegian coast. They would begin convoy duty after that.

There was a full moon on the 28th and visibility was expected to be very good. Godley explained the unexpected mission to his pilots and asked them to personally check their aircraft the next day. There would be night landing practice. Excitement increased. There were no complaints about no shore leave. Godley was pleased that morale was definitely better. And he told his newly arrived young pilots that he would be flying night practice landings with them. To himself, he had serious doubts about the decision to employ these old biplanes on such a mission. Yet he set about to do his best to make it a success and he explained the purpose of a night strike at ships off the Norwegian coast, with torpedoes and bombs, to his pilots without revealing his doubts. He recalls:

"The hard-pressed enemy was bringing large supplies of vital war material from northern Norway at this time, especially iron ore, shipped in convoy or independent vessels close inshore. These ships had been attacked by the RAF in daylight using Mosquitoes and had taken to night sailings after suffering heavy losses. It seemed there was nothing, though to us it appeared incredible, that the RAF—whose job it should have been—could send against them at night for a low-level attack, the only way of making certain of results. So the Stringbag had once again been called upon. With her absurdly low speed and extremely tight turning circle, she was still, apparently, even in 1945, the only kite for the job.

"But the operation ahead of us seems in retrospect so foolhardy, so unnecessary. Our target area was well within range of RAF bases, from which hundreds of modern bombers were being sent out every night. How could it be that none of these was available for the job in conditions of brilliant moonlight? And to bring two squadrons of obsolete biplanes—835 on board *Nairana*, 813 on board *Campania*—to within range of the shipping lane, no fewer than nine warships would sail to within 60 miles of the enemy-occupied coast in waters where U-boats might be lurking, within easy range of shore-based bombers, even fighters. A cruiser (*Berwick*), two destroyers (*Algonquin* and *Cavendish*), and four smaller warships besides the two carriers—all at risk, very probably for nothing, as four weeks earlier. To fly just one operation against a possibly absent enemy. And in any case no target of real importance expected. Then scuttling back to Scapa.

"But ours not to reason why. We sailed at 1900, *Nairana* under the command of Captain V.N. Surtees, on January 27th and would take 25 hours to reach our takeoff position, 140 miles northwest of Bergen and less than half that distance from the coast. The weather was perfect, not much swell, maximum visibility. From the small hours of the 28th, we and *Campania* between us kept at least one Stringbag airborne to sweep the sea ahead of us for U-boats. During the few daylight hours—our most northerly latitude would be 62 degrees—we also had a pair of Wildcats ranged permanently on the flight deck in case a shadower should find us, but they were never needed. One of my Stringbags and two of *Campania's* were unfortunately damaged on landing, which reduced our combined striking force to 25.

"Briefing at 1830 by Lt. Cdr. John Ball, in overall charge of air operations but not flying, known as Wings. Already within 100 miles of Norway. Captain Surtees also attends, in the small ops room. We are to fly off in two waves. The first strike to scramble at 2000, seven Stringbags from *Nairana* and six from *Campania*. Each of these flights to act independently, with its own specified search area. We in 835 to head for the entrance to Rovde Fjord. This isn't a fjord in the usual sense, but an open-ended channel—the route followed by all shipping—between the mainland and a group of offshore islands, a mile or two wide, with mountains rising precipitously up to 3000 feet on either side. We were to follow it for 40 miles and attack any targets seen. *Campania's* six aircraft had a similar search area some 40 miles to northward.

"Lt. Cdr. Ball tells me I can best establish my position by heading first for Riste, a small island several miles from the coast, easily picked up by ASV. Inhabited, he assures me, by nothing more hostile than some farmers and their cows. Unexplained why, after coming all this way, we will be covering only 40 miles of the enemy shipping lane, which will take only half-an-hour. Allowing for 90 minutes to get there and back from the ship. We could have spent at least two hours on patrol, covering four or five times that distance—even more if on reaching Riste we split up into subflights, two or three aircraft in each, each with its own search area, whistling up the others if a target is sighted.

"The second strike, six Stringbags from each carrier, to scramble at 2040. Would orbit safely offshore, in their respective back-up positions, awaiting orders from their leaders who would then be completing their patrols.

"I give orders that one aircraft in each strike is to be armed with six bombs, the rest with eight armour-piercing rockets. By 19:15, in the most brilliant moonlight, the seven white Stringbags (with green and brown camouflage paint on wingtops) of the first strike have been ranged on the flight deck. My own, A for Able, waits in front, facing fore-and-aft amidships, the others, wings already spread, angled inwards in pairs astern of it. Dressed in a fur-lined brown leather flying jacket and silk scarf over my uniform, and in flying boots with my Mae West, helmet and goggles, I climb into the cockpit at 19:40 and check equipment. Two crewmen on the port side begin to crank the inertia starter just behind the engine. After it begins to whine fast enough, they call Contact! I pull the toggle on my left. The Pegasus roars to life. Props begin turning on all aircraft. At 19:55 the nine ships turn together into wind. Both flights are to scramble simultaneously. George Strong, my observer, sits silently behind me. *Campania* is close on our starboard beam. Now we are ready and I glance from my crewmen, ready to pull the chocks, to the bridge. In a moment the green light flashes from *Nairana's* bridge. With a wave back and forth across my face, I signal that chocks are to be removed from in front of the wheels. In the wind and considerable noise, my crewmen dash underneath and pull away the chocks. I press on the brakes and open up full throttle. In a few seconds I release them and begin to roll. After going 80 yards, I press the button to fire my takeoff-assist rockets (RATOG) and am propelled at once skywards into the brilliance of the clear winter night, the freezing slipstream blowing in my face. I ease off on the throttle and keep my airspeed below 70, making a long sweeping turn to port so that the others can quickly come up with me. (The CO of 813, to avoid any risk of collision, is doing the same to starboard.) In less than five minutes we are in extended echelon formation. I set a northeast course of 042, climbing slowly at 80 knots over the dark, sparkling waters of the North Sea, headed for the Norwegian Coast and Riste, 65 miles east and 45 minutes away.

"I feel perfectly calm and confident—no therapy to compare with commanding an operational squadron! The silvered full moon in a sky without a cloud, so bright that it's nearly like daytime. We have reached cruising altitude of 1200 feet and can soon see the great snow-covered mountains of the enemy coast at a range of 30 miles. And Riste is now clearly visible ahead, not many minutes after George has located it by radar and given me a new course to bring us directly overhead, where the first excitement awaits us. For reasons I've now forgotten if I ever knew them, my orders are to overfly the little island at cherubs twelve (1200 feet), then use my own discretion—instead of safely at sea level, remaining so much longer undetected by enemy radar. So I'm leading seven aircraft in formation, straight and level at 80 knots, between it and the moon at this most vulnerable altitude. Now two batteries of

Bofors guns change all our previous notions of farmers and cows! Streams of multicolored tracer come streaking up towards us—at first so slowly, as always, then with lethal acceleration.

"We should have been dead ducks—George and I anyway, for most of the flak was aimed at our leading aircraft, and we presented the simplest possible target. But once again our slow speed saved us. Accustomed to Mosquitoes at least four times as fast, the gunners simply couldn't believe we were stooging in at 80 knots. For a couple of seconds the tracer comes streaming up some 50 yards ahead of us. That was their chance. Before they can correct aim, I've put A for Able into a steep diving turn to port, the rest of the pilots following without delay behind me. In a series of twisting turns to sea level, alternating port and starboard, which the gunners cannot follow, to the safety of the wavetops beyond siting range.

"But this firing will have alerted gun positions ashore. Already before diving I had seen the entrance to our fjord. Now, though still several miles distant, I see streams of tracer crisscrossing it from batteries on the mainland and the nearest offshore island. What did they think they were firing at? I must lead my Stringbags through this deadly curtain. No way I can escape this. My thoughts at this moment fly to son Christopher, four weeks old. Surely not now of all times.

"To make matters worse, I see that one of my junior pilots, in the excitement of the moment, has accidentally switched on his navigation lights. He's lit up like a Christmas tree. George calls him on the radio: "Hopscotch X-Ray, for Christ's sake dowse your lights." Message not even acknowledged. "Hopscotch X-Ray, this is Hopscotch Able. Now do you hear me?" Still no response. We pride ourselves on our radio techniques, but at this critical moment his isn't working! We send the message by Aldis lamp. The penny drops as we approach the mainland and his lights go off, but our presence is now certainly known to every gun position.

"Perhaps I'm wrong but I think he'd done us a favor. To the well-guarded fjord entrance. Prepared for a hot welcome. In very open formation, flying as low as we dare to avoid being silhouetted. But the antiaircraft gunners never open up. And I believe they must have reached the conclusion, accustomed as they were to ultramodern aircraft, that this little clutch of single-engined biplanes, dawdling past at under 100 knots, with wheels lowered (of course we couldn't raise them, but how were they to know this?) and lights so boldly flashing, just couldn't be the enemy. Whatever else they might be, perhaps trainees who had lost their way. How else to account for the absence of opposition from these known batteries, which minutes earlier had been firing away at nothing?

"Now flying at zero feet up the narrow waters of the Norwegian fjord. Lights coming on ahead of us in homesteads on both shores as we are heard approaching and men come to their doors, seeming to show us the way. The whole country deep in snow, the white mountains bathed in moonlight rising high above us on either side. Till at last we sight a target. A merchantman sailing towards us on her own. I lead the flight over her, hesitate, decide to fly the last 10 miles of our patrol in search of a larger vessel. But the rest of the fjord is empty. Turning back, climbing to 1500 feet, the perfect height for rockets.

"I can hardly believe it now, but I had no thoughts whatever for the men sailing in this coaster, which we were now about to sink. It was nothing compared with the nightly devastation caused by the air forces on both sides. And it was a specific target of strategic importance, not a city where those who suffered most were the civilians. But it amazes me that I never thought for a moment, as I still clearly remember, of the men on board that ship. It was wholly impersonal. I now turned the switch to fuse the rockets.

"My aim, as I banked to dive, absolutely calm, at the correct angle of 20 degrees towards this doomed vessel, was to strike her with my rockets below the water level. Flak may have been coming up, but I simply wasn't aware of it. I was concentrating solely on my aim. I'd had so much practice and the conditions were so perfect that I expected to be accurate within a very few feet. And I was. In the descent, I pressed the button on the throttle four times, firing my eight rockets in a ripple of four pairs at two second intervals, at a range closing from 1000 to 600 feet. They swished away with smoke and fire. I saw them all striking the water as planned, a yard or two short of the merchantman amidships.

"A steep turn to starboard to watch the others. The next two pilots, Roffey and Payne, also score several hits. My own rockets alone would have probably been enough. Now I knew the 1500-ton coaster has no chance of surviving. She is stopped and on fire. I call on the four others to break off the attack, to seek targets ashore. Two of them, Gough and Supple, choose the flak positions at the entrance to the fjord and must have silenced them. In any event, they never fired again.

"The aircraft in my flight are soon heading independently back to the ship. I return at low altitude to where the stricken vessel is now low in the water, lifeboats being lowered. And I decide to make one more sweep of the search area. After only a few minutes, flying low over the water, I see two more merchantmen on the point of entering Rovde Fjord—from a smaller fjord running steeply inland to southward. At once I radio my second flight, which has arrived recently offshore, led by my Senior Pilot, Geoffrey Summers. Three to attack each ship. After a short time, they approach and I lead them to their two targets, another 1500-ton ship and a slighter larger one, perhaps 2000 tons. They steer slowly into the Fjord, now doomed.

"All around me the silent mountains. I can clearly see each cottage on the rock-strewn mainland shore. The steady hum of my Peggy. Quite a contrast to what is about to happen below! Summers, Paine, and Cridland now dive to attack one ship. They score hits with at least six rockets. Two of my most junior pilots are badly off aim as they swoop down on the larger vessel. But Provis with his bombs scores a direct hit and two near misses. The first target is on fire but the crew manage to beach her before she can sink. The second is now settling rapidly. Three ships sighted, all successfully attacked! But I can't stay to observe her. I've been airborne over three hours. Our normal maximum endurance is 4 1/4 hours with a war-load and we still have to locate *Nairana* and land on. We set course westward for the 45-minute flight back. Soon the Norwegian Coast fades from view. In another half hour, *Nairana* comes in view to the west.

"We approach her soon before midnight. I check on my petrol, find I still have nearly 40 gallons, enough for over an hour. Well, there's a damn good engine for you. The six other aircraft of the first strike have been back for over an hour. Now some of the pilots in the second strike, who think they've been hit by flak or developed engine trouble, are requesting emergency landings. I assure Wings by radio that I've plenty of gas though airborne 40 minutes before them, so they are allowed to pancake ahead of me. In the end I'm almost the last to get the signal to land, at 0017, after four hours and 18 minutes. My Stringbag carries only dim navigational lights. On the *Nairana*, plowing through the smooth North Sea below at 20 knots, I see the long line of very dim white lights on the flight deck. 'Come On Ahead,' signals the batsman with his lighted bats in each hand. My airspeed is 65. I close the throttle slightly, ease back on the stick to lose five knots. The batsman now changes his signal—'A Wee Bit Lower.' I slightly close the throttle and come forward a bit with the stick. He tells me to come as I am. A last-moment 'Come Lower' and I throttle back, then cross the stern at 15 feet. He gives me the mandatory crossed-bats signal, a command to cut the engine. I do so and sink gently to a three-pointer, and catch the first arresting wire. After over four hours, I begin to relax. Ground crews race toward me from the safety nets to disengage the hook. Then I taxi ahead of the barrier and switch the engine off. Half a dozen crewmen now rush up to maneuver the aircraft into its place. I climb slowly out of the cockpit as does Strong, and go off to report to Ball and Captain Surtees, both pleased at our success.

"We are already heading home—and quite expecting a counterattack. We had been using radio and the position of warships that included at least one carrier must have been well known to the enemy. But none develops. After a long debriefing, I go below to the hangar to see what damage done. Not a single scratch. And the Stringbag damaged the previous day has been repaired so that all my aircraft are again serviceable.

"A couple of hours' sleep. At first light we range the Wildcats in case an attack by bombers, a couple of Stringbags for defensive patrols if ordered. Their services are not needed.

"Back to the hangar to check the aircraft, speak to the men. All spirits high. Great show last night, sir. A piece of cake. But my air fitter looks down to me from working on the engine with something less than a grin.

" 'Do you know how much petrol you had when you landed, sir?'

" 'Yes, Titchmarsh. That's one hell of a good kite. Over 30 gallons after 4 1/4 hours.'

" 'Well sir, I don't know whether to tell you. But I didn't see how it was possible. So I took a reading with a dipstick. Sir, your fuel gauge was unserviceable. You had so little gas it didn't register on the dipstick. Three or four gallons at most.'

"Three or four gallons! Enough for five or six minutes. A moment or two of silence, then gales of laughter.

" 'Well, Titchmarsh, for heaven's sake, fix that fuel gauge.'

" 'Sir, I've already done so.'

" 'Well, for heaven's sake, keep it fixed.'

"*Campania's* 12 aircraft had flown an inconclusive mission. Apparently they'd carried out an attack but without known results 'in the absence of a flare-dropping aircraft.' It seems strange, it was nearly bright as day, but that's what they reported.

"We dropped our hook in Scapa Flow a few minutes after 2000.

Everyone in high spirits.

"By luck, we'd had that one success to set the squadron up—just when we most needed it."

For gallantry and leadership, flying the ancient Swordfish from 1940 to 1946, Godley was awarded the Distinguished Service Cross. I became acquainted with this fellow author-pilot only long after the war, in the preparation of this book, and Godley recalled (and has written) that by the summer of 1945 his nerves were worn thin by the constant danger of flying. Flying in all kinds of weather far out over the ominous sea and watching over the years comrades become victims of accidents, engine failures, or enemy action, had taken a toll. What brought on the final degree of fatigue was Russian convoy duty, following the successful strike off the Norwegian coast just related.

Escort duty was both demanding and nerve-wracking. The slow convoys to Murmansk and return in the bleakest weather were shadowed almost constantly by JU 88 bombers and often attacked. Though these were the last weeks of the Luftwaffe's assault against Russian convoys, none of the pilots flying off escort carrier decks in that bitter winter, with only limited hours of daylight, could know this. Godley managed to keep going, and to fly the toughest missions himself. But all the aircrew on the escort carriers were under considerable strain. In addition to the Luftwaffe, U-boats were often detected and ships were sunk and aircraft downed in seas where recovery—because of the bitter cold—was practically impossible.

Godley recalls one of the flights made during this convoy escort duty when the convoy was on an easterly heading far to the north—about 1,000 miles east of Greenland, in icy waters. It was, he says, about the most unpleasant flight he ever made. The temperature was below zero Fahrenheit, the wind was gusting at over 50 knots, and in his open cockpit, exposed to this weather, he was flying in a pitchblack night, almost totally by instruments. The ceiling was below 1,000 feet. He and observer George Strong were searching for a U-boat, which they never found. Both knew that if their single engine faltered or stopped in such weather, their chances were zero. The convoy commander could not have spared an escort vessel to search for them and, in this cold, they would probably have lasted only a few minutes. Godley completed the mission and finally found *Nairana* again and managed a landing on her pitching deck in the heavy seas. He estimates groundspeed at touchdown that night at less than 10 knots because of the strong wind. *Nairana* that night traveled only 60 miles in 12 hours into the gale. Godley was called on to fly another mission before sunrise!

The strain of such duty began to tell. By the end of the war, Godley knew his nerves were shattered, and that he should ground himself or tell his superiors. But he waited and waited. In the very last days of the European war he was appointed commanding officer of 714 Squadron, equipped with Barracudas. He dreaded soloing in them, but with much apprehension carried on and soloed successfully. V-E day came on May 8th, but the war with Japan continued and it was time—on May 18th—for Godley to report to his new station to take over a new command, at Aberdeen. He began to have an ominous presentiment he was going to crash. It didn't help when he watched another pilot, who had also flown Swordfish for many years, stall in the landing pattern and crash to his death in the suspect Barracuda.

Increasing the strain on pilots was a fault in the Barracuda's hydraulic system, which sometimes leaked ether into cockpit, putting pilots to sleep, who then crashed to their death. The cause was unknown at the time of these first crashes. On June 28th Godley made his last flight as a pilot. On it, ether leaked into his cockpit as he was preparing to land. He almost passed out before touching down, but with a desperate effort managed to stay awake until on the grass, then slipped into unconsciousness. The Barracuda rolled to a stop on its own and the ambulance crew removed him and managed to revive him. When he came to, he knew he had made his last flight. But still he refused to reveal the true state of his nerves and expected to be posted to the Far East when he had completed training 714, which he continued to do—without flying.

Somehow, everyone understood. No questions were asked. Then the Americans dropped the world's first A-bombs and the war soon ended. Only after that did he finally report to the Surgeon-Commander to reveal the state of his nerves. He was, of course, grounded promptly. His years of operational flying, which had included crashing into the Atlantic during convoy duty there, added up to too much strain.

And Godley was never to experience a joy in flight again. In the first five years after the war he never flew, even as a passenger. And in the postwar years, he says, he also realized that the war effort was, in a sense, all for nothing, since violence is futile and foes turn to allies and allies turn to foes.

After studying philosophy, politics, and economics for two years at the end of the war, Godley began to travel the world, which he did for 20 years, writing and reporting from various parts of the globe. Gradually he overcame his fear of flying and eventually returned to Ireland, where he became the third baron of Killegar, in Cavan, and a member of the House of Lords. He now lives on his estate there and is a stockbreeder and writer, with many successful books to his credit, including *Bring Back My Stringbag*, published in 1980. In it he describes his long flying career in Swordfish, including the Atlantic convoy runs and the dangerous Murmansk runs of the last winter—and this chapter's attack on shipping off the coast of Norway in January 1945.

Today, in his late sixties, Lord Kilbracken flies frequently. He long ago lost all fear, from necessity. He has switched from the Liberal to the Labor party, taken up ornithology and beekeeping, and continues to write, which he did well even in 1937, having won the school prize for English verse at Eton that year.

Just prior to the war, he was studying at Balliol College, Oxford, reading the greats—the classics. World War II changed all that. Afterwards, Plato and Virgil seemed less relevant. Neither, after all, had ever flown a Stringbag over the cold northern seas, at night, in hurricane winds, in an open cockpit, year after year after year.

Index